PRINCIPLES OF INSTRUCTIONAL DESIGN

PRINCIPLES OF INSTRUCTIONAL DESIGN

Robert M. Gagné
Leslie J. Briggs
Florida State University

HOLT, RINEHART AND WINSTON, INC.
New York   Chicago   San Francisco   Atlanta
Dallas   Montreal   Toronto   London   Sydney

Library of Congress Cataloging in Publication Data

Gagné, Robert Mills, 1916–
  Principles of instructional design.

  Includes bibliographies.
  1. Learning, Psychology of.   2. Lesson planning.
I. Briggs, Leslie J., joint author.   II. Title.
LB1051.G196   371.3   73–14708

ISBN: 0–03–008171–8

PREFACE

In writing this book, we have had in mind the need we perceive for knowledge of how instruction may be systematically designed, on the part of teachers, curriculum developers, instructional leaders and managers, and those in related educational professions. We have adopted the purpose of conveying principles of design and development of plans and procedures for instruction. Our intention has been to describe an intellectually consistent basis for practical procedures of instructional design.

The book describes both the derivation and application of methods which can be used to design topics, courses, and lessons of instruction, in a variety of subjects, based upon principles of human learning and performance analysis. These methods are also related to the design and evaluation of instructional systems.

An introductory chapter contains a background of learning principles on which the design of instruction will be based, and includes a brief overview of the contents of succeeding parts. Chapter 2 defines and illustrates the major classes of learning outcomes for programs of instruction, including intellectual skills, information, attitudes, motor skills, and cognitive strategies. Chapters 3 and 4 describe the conditions of learning applicable to the acquisition of these capabilities.

Beginning Part Two, which describes methods of designing instruction, Chapter 5 deals with procedures for defining learning outcomes. The following chapter, 6, provides an account of procedures for determining sequences of instruction applicable to courses and to curricula. Chapter 7 introduces some general principles for the design of instructional events at the level of the lesson, and Chapter 8 deals with practical procedures for the arrangement of effective learning conditions in the design of single lessons. The topic of assessing student performance is taken up in Chapter 9.

In Part Three, Chapter 10 describes the larger framework of instructional design in terms of a complete system such as might be adopted by a school system. The employment of procedures for individualized instruction in such a system is detailed in Chapter 11. A final chapter, 12, deals with procedures for the evaluation of programs of instruction.

The book is intended for use in the education of teachers and other educational specialists having responsibility for the planning and operation of instructional programs. Its educational effects are directed at the function of designing curriculum and instructional sequences, and also at the function of skillful development of individual lesson plans and procedures for assessment of teaching outcomes.

Specifically, it is expected that the book will fill a need in teacher training courses, at both the undergraduate and graduate levels. Instructors of courses in teaching methods, instructional planning, curriculum theory, and classroom techniques should find the book useful. In graduate-level education, uses for the text may be found in these same areas, as well as in courses on learning and educational psychology.

Tallahassee, Florida   R.M.G.
September 1973   L.J.B.

CONTENTS

PRINCIPLES OF INSTRUCTIONAL DESIGN

ONE

BASIC PROCESSES IN LEARNING AND INSTRUCTION

1
INTRODUCTION

Instructing is done to help people learn. It can be done well or badly. Sometimes it is even difficult to tell which of these ways has been chosen. Most people would say, though, that it should be done responsibly.

Human beings are highly adaptable in their learning. Consequently, it is not surprising that one kind of plan for instruction may seem to be about as good as another, and differences between the effects of such plans may be difficult to demonstrate. People are engaged in learning a great deal of the time. When one undertakes to instruct, he is not assuming responsibility for all of the learning which will take place. Instead, instruction which is deliberately planned will affect only a part, perhaps a small part, of what each person learns.

If it is true that the effects of planned and systematic instruction are somewhat limited, what may be the purpose of such planning? What is the function of schools, so far as learning is concerned? The answers are to be sought by examining the adult individuals who make up our society. Is everyone reasonably well adjusted to the demands of modern life? To what extent is each one a truly responsible citizen? Is each engaged in lifetime work which absorbs his interest? Is each person enjoying himself?

To the extent that these questions can be answered positively, it may be said that previous learning, whether planned or unplanned, has been successful for each individual person. To the extent that these ideals are not achieved for every person, the learning that has already taken place must somehow have been inadequate. For some reason, the learning which has been part of each person's experience has failed to permit the individual to "live life to the full." Of course, this is an ideal, and no one expects it to be achieved completely. Nevertheless, the ideal of optimal use of one's mind and body in living a full life is also a standard. It is the standard of excellence (Gardner, 1961), and a standard against which the need for planned instruction must be assessed.

Learning must be planned, rather than haphazard, so that each person will come closer to the goals of optimal use of his talents, enjoyment of life, and integration with his physical and social environment. Naturally, this does not mean that the planning of instruction will have the effect of making different individuals more alike. To the contrary, diversity among individuals will be enhanced. Planned instruction has the purpose of helping each person to develop as fully as possible, in his own individual directions.

Basic Assumptions
about Instructional Design

How is such instruction to be designed? How can one approach such a task, and how begin it? There must surely be alternative ways. In this book we describe one way which we believe to be both feasible and worthwhile. This way of planning and designing instruction has certain characteristics that need to be mentioned at the outset.

First, we adopt the assumption that instructional planning must be *for the individual*. We are not here concerned with "mass" changes in opinions or capabilities, or with education in the sense of "diffusion" of information or attitudes within and among societies. Instead, the instruction we describe is oriented toward the human individual in his development from child to adult, as well as throughout his life.

Second, instructional design has phases that are *both immediate and long-range*. Design in the immediate sense is what the teacher does in preparing a "lesson plan" some hours before the instruction is given. The longer-range aspects of instructional design are more complex and varied. They are more likely to be concerned with a set of lessons organized into "topics," a set of topics to constitute a course or course sequence, or perhaps with an entire instructional system. Such design is sometimes undertaken by individual teachers, and also by groups or teams of teachers, by committees of school people, by groups and organizations of curriculum planners, by textbook writers, and by groups of scholars representing academic disciplines.

The immediate and long-range phases of instructional planning can best be done as separate tasks, and not mixed together. The job of the teacher in carrying out instruction is a highly demanding one in terms of time, effort, and intellectual challenge. The teacher has a great deal to do in planning instruction on an immediate, day-to-day or hour-to-hour basis. Such a task can be greatly facilitated when the products of careful long-range instructional design are made available in the form of textbooks, audio-visual aids, and other materials. Trying to accomplish both immediate and long-range instructional design, while at the same time teaching twenty or thirty students, is simply too big a job for one person, and can readily lead to neglect of essential teaching functions. This is not to suggest, however, that teachers cannot or should not undertake long-range instructional design, either on their own or as part of a larger team. Teachers have essential contributions to make to long-range instructional design, and such contributions are best made during periods when teaching itself is not being done.

A third assumption to be made in this work is that *systematically designed instruction can greatly affect individual human development*. There are hints in some educational writings (e.g., Friedenberg, 1965; Silberman, 1970) of a belief that education would perhaps be best if it were designed simply to provide a nurturing environment in which the child and youth were allowed to grow up in his own way, without the imposition of any plan for the direction of his learning. We consider this line of thinking to be mistaken. Unplanned and undirected learning, we believe, is almost certain to lead to the development of individuals who are in one way or another incompetent to derive personal satisfaction from living in our society of today and tomorrow. A fundamental reason for instructional design is to insure that no one is "educationally disadvantaged", that everyone has an equal opportunity to use his individual talents to the fullest degree.

A fourth and final point to be mentioned will be expanded upon in the next section, and also throughout the book. It is that *designing instruction must be based upon knowledge of how human beings learn*. In considering how an individual's abilities are to be developed, it is not enough to state what they should be; one must examine closely the question of how they can come to be acquired. Materials for instruction need to reflect not simply what their author knows, but also how the student is intended to learn such knowledge. Accordingly, instructional design must take fully into account *learning conditions* that need to be established in order for the desired effects to occur.

SOME LEARNING PRINCIPLES

At this point, it seems appropriate to expand upon the idea of basing instructional design on knowledge of the conditions of human learning. What sort of knowledge of learning is needed in order to design instruction?

The process of learning has been investigated by the methods of science (mainly by psychologists) for many years. As a scientist, the learning investigator is basically interested in explaining how learning takes place. In pursuing this interest, he usually constructs *theories* about structures and events (generally conceived as occurring in the central nervous system) that could operate to bring about the remarkable behavior that can be directly observed as "an act of learning." From these theories, he deduces certain consequences which he can test out by a set of controlled observations.

In the course of this entire scientific process of theory-building and experimentation, much knowledge is accumulated. The effects of particular events on learning may be, and usually are, checked again and again under a great variety of conditions. In this way there grows up a body of "facts" about learning, and a body of "principles" which hold true under a broad variety of conditions. As an example, a rather well-known principle of learning is the following: When a fact such as the name of a person is learned, and is immediately followed by the learning of names of other persons, forgetting of the first-learned name is likely to occur. It is interesting to note that even such a well-known principle has to be stated with careful denoting of conditions. To attempt to simplify by stating something like, "whatever is learned is forgotten over time" would be quite incorrect.

Some of the facts and principles of human learning which have been accumulated in this manner are highly relevant to the design of instruction, while others are less so. For example, it has been found that lists of nonsense syllables with unfamiliar letter combinations, like ZEQ, XYR, etc., are more difficult to learn than those with familiar letter combinations, such as BOJ, REK, etc. While such a finding has some importance to theory-making, it is of little direct relevance to the design of instruction, because the latter is hardly ever concerned with this kind of nonsensical learning task. A contrasting example is provided by the finding that a list of words like MAN AND BOY WENT FAR AWAY is easier to learn and remember than the sequence

FAR BOY AWAY MAN AND WENT (Miller and Selfridge, 1950). In this case, the principle *has* some relevance, because instruction sometimes does concern itself with the learning of words, classes of words, and word sequences. There are many examples of this sort in the scientific literature on human learning (Deese and Hulse, 1967).

Similar comments may be made about learning theories themselves— some of their ideas are highly relevant to instruction, while some are not. For example, a theory of learning might propose that a single event of learning produces a particular change in the chemical composition of the activated nerve cells. This may be exciting theory; but by itself it cannot be expected to be relevant to the task of designing instruction. A different theory might hold that the presentation of an "alerting" signal just prior to presentation of the stimulus for learning, activates some particular neural circuits in such a way as to facilitate learning. Were such a theoretical idea to be verified, it would probably be considered of importance for the design of instruction. Those aspects of learning theory which are important for instruction are those which relate to *controllable events and conditions*. If one is concerned to design instruction so that learning will occur efficiently, he must look for those elements of learning theory that pertain to the events that an instructor can do something about.

Some Time-Tested Learning Principles

What are some of the principles derived from learning theory and learning research, which may be expected to be relevant to instructional design? First, we shall mention some principles that have been with us for many years. In some basic sense, they are still valid principles. But they may need some new interpretations in the light of modern theory.

Contiguity This principle states that the stimulus situation to which one wants the learner to respond must be presented *contiguously in time* with the desired response. One has to think hard to provide an example of a violation of the principle of contiguity. Suppose, for example, one wants a young child to learn to print an E. An unskilled teacher might be tempted to do it as follows: First, give the verbal instruction, "Show me how you print an E." Following this, show the child a printed E on a page, in order to illustrate what it looks like. Leave the page open on the child's table. The child then draws an E. Now, has the child learned to print an E? Referring to the principle of contiguity, one would have to say, probably not yet. What has been made contiguous in this situation is:

Stimulus situation: a printed E
Child's response: printing E

whereas what is intended as an objective of the lesson is:

Stimulus situation: "Show me how you print an E."
Child's response: printing E.

Somehow, in order that the principle of contiguity will exert its expected effect, the first set of events must be replaced by the second, by a staged removal of the intervening stimulus (the printed E). In the first case, the verbal instructions are *remote from* the expected response, rather than contiguous with it.

Repetition   This principle states that the stimulus situation and its response need to be repeated, or practiced, in order for learning to be improved and retention more certain. There are some situations where the need for repetition is very apparent. For example, if one is learning to pronounce a new French word like *variété*, repeated trials certainly lead one closer and closer to an acceptable pronunciation. Modern learning theory, however, casts much doubt on the idea that repetition works by "strengthening learned connections." Furthermore, there are many situations in which repetition of newly learned ideas does not improve either learning or retention (cf. Ausubel, 1968; Gagné, 1970). It is perhaps best to think of repetition, not as a fundamental condition of learning, but merely as a practical procedure ("practice") which may be necessary in order to make sure that other conditions for learning are present.

Reinforcement   Historically, this principle was stated in the following form (Thorndike, 1913): learning of a new act is strengthened when the occurrence of that act is followed by a satisfying state of affairs (that is, a "reward"). Such a view of reinforcement is still a lively theoretical issue, and there is a good deal of evidence for it. For instructional purposes, however, one is inclined to depend on another conception of reinforcement, which may be stated in this form: A new act (A) is most readily learned when it is immediately followed by an "old" act (B) which the individual performs readily, in such a way that doing B is made contingent on doing A (Premack, 1965). Suppose a young child is fond of looking at pictures of animals, and it is desired that he learn how to make drawings of animals. The new capability of animal drawing, according to this principle, will be most readily learned if one "attaches" it to looking at additional animal pictures. In other words, the opportunity to look at animal pictures is made *contingent* upon drawing one or more animals. In this form, the principle of reinforcement is a most powerful one.

Some Newer Learning Principles

As the study of human learning has proceeded, it has gradually become apparent that theories must be increasingly sophisticated. Contiguity, repetition, and reinforcement are all good principles, and one of their outstanding characteristics is that they refer to controllable instructional events. The designer of instruction, as well as the teacher, can readily devise situations which include these principles. Nevertheless, when all these things are done, an efficient learning situation is not guaranteed. Something seems to be missing.

The missing conditions are to be sought *within* the individual, rather than in his external environment. They are states of mind that the learner brings with him to the learning task; in other words, they are *previously learned capabilities* of the learner himself. These capabilities appear to be a highly important set of factors in insuring effective learning.

Internal Processes in Learning

An act of learning requires the presence of some varieties of internal states that have been previously learned. For example, a student who is learning about the mechanical advantage of levers, expressed in the equation $Fd = F'd'$, must have readily accessible the information that F is a symbol for force, which may be expressed in pounds; that d stands for distance from the fulcrum, stated in feet; and similar *information* of this sort. Second, he must have available some *intellectual skills*, such as that of substituting specific values of variables in proper places, solving simple equations, and others. And third, his learning will be facilitated to the extent that he has the kind of "self-management" *strategies* that govern his own behavior in attending, in storing and retrieving information, and in organizing problem solution. Each of these kinds of internal states depends, to a greater or lesser extent, upon *prior learning*.

Other kinds of internal events important for learning are *motivation* and an *attitude of confidence* in learning (sometimes included in the idea of "self-concept"). These internal states are essential for successful learning. It should be noted that we do not deal with them directly in our discussion of learning processes. They are, instead, assumed to be present as preconditions for the instruction to be designed. Initial stages of instruction, preceding those we shall describe, are often concerned with the establishment and channeling of motivation.

Factual information must be brought to bear upon an act of learning. Actually, this can occur in three different ways. First, and most obviously, it may simply be communicated to the learner in a form that remains accessible to him. For example, printed "directions" may remain available for reference throughout an act of learning. Second, it may have been just previously learned. For instance, the student who is presented with a problem in mechanical advantage may have been told on a previous page that "*d* is a symbol for distance, and is usually expressed in feet." He may then keep this in his working memory, while learning to solve problems in mechanical advantage. Third, factual information may need to be retrieved from his memory, because it has been learned and stored months or years ago. In this case, he must search his memory for the information.

Intellectual skills needed for learning must be recalled, in order for learning to occur. The learner has to have ways of doing things, particularly with language and other symbols, in order to learn new things. He may be stimulated to recall these intellectual skills by means of some verbal "cues." For example, the student faced with the learning of a rule about mechanical advantage may be told, "You remember how to find the value of a variable in an equation," or something similar. It is important to note that an intellectual skill can typically not be conveyed by "directions." It must have been previously learned, in order to be available for recall at the proper moment. Can it not be learned just immediately prior to the new learning, or perhaps almost simultaneously? Yes, it can, but this procedure may make the learning more difficult.

A learning event requires the activation of strategies for learning and remembering. The individual may bring into play *strategies* of attending to complex stimulation; of selecting and coding parts of it; of solving problems; and of retrieving what has previously been learned. Much learning, except that of the youngest children, is aided by these capabilities of "self-management" of the learning process. In contrast to intellectual skills, strategies are highly general in their applicability to a variety of situations. Self-management strategies may show improvement over a period of many years. For any particular learning event, the strategies brought into play may be simply the best the learner has available at the moment. They may be expected to improve with continued practice. In most cases of being instructed, learning is supported by stimulation provided by the teacher. As the learner gains experience in learning, he comes to depend increasingly upon internalized strategies. In other words, he becomes more and more of a "self-learner."

Figure 1 depicts the two categories of factors involved in a learning event. Older learning theories gave greatest weight to *external* factors, and the model of what was required internally consisted almost entirely of "connections to be strengthened." The newer model places greater emphasis on the importance of factors which originate from the *internal* source of the

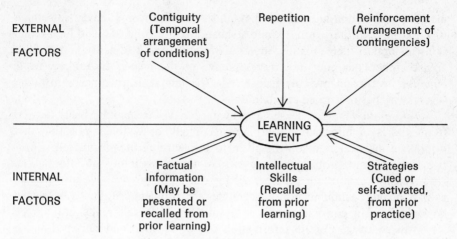

FIGURE 1   External and internal factors affecting the learning event.

individual's memory. The influences of these factors occur through memories of what has previously been learned. Thus the design of instruction must take into account not only the immediate external situation stimulating the learner, but also those capabilities which the learner brings with him. Instructional planning must also provide for the prior learning of these latter capabilities.

Learning Emphases in Instruction

There are several varieties of learned capabilities that instruction aims to establish. For purposes of illustration, we have already mentioned three —*information, intellectual skills, cognitive strategies*—and the next chapter will complete the list with *motor skills* and *attitudes*. Any of these may represent a category of what is to be learned. Any or all of them may need to be recalled as a previously learned capability at the time of new learning. Which of these should be the primary aim of instruction? Is it possible to assign priorities to them, on theoretical or practical grounds?

Concentrating instruction on any one type of capability alone, or any two in combination, is insufficient. Factual information, in and of itself, would represent a highly inadequate instructional goal. Learning intellectual skills leads to practical competence. Yet these too are insufficient for new learning, because such learning makes use of information as well. Furthermore, the learning of intellectual skills does not by itself equip the learner with the strategies of learning and remembering which he needs to become an independent self-learner. Turning to cognitive strategies themselves, it is apparent that these cannot be learned or progressively improved without the involvement of information and skills—they must, in other words, have "something to work on." Attitudes, too, require a substrate of information and intellectual skills to support them. Finally, motor skills constitute a somewhat specialized area of school learning, not representative of the whole. In sum, *multiple aims* for instruction must be recognized. The human learner needs to attain several varieties of learned capabilities.

Information   Since learning principles have frequently been derived from studies of information learning, one might draw the implication that priority in instruction should be given to the learning of information. Effective learning and problem solving require the accessibility of information. However, information for problem solving *can* be made available to a student as part of the communication which states the problem. Alternatively, it can be looked up in convenient reference sources; it doesn't really have to be stored in all cases. Certain information can be recalled and retrieved at the time of a learning event; other information can be communicated as part of the problem description; still other things can be looked up and stored in memory for the duration of the learning event. Because all of these alternatives are feasible, the design of instruction around factual information seems a highly inadequate course of action.

Cognitive Strategies   Some educational theorists appear to award priority consideration to cognitive strategies as an instructional aim. These are emphasized, for example, in the writings of Bruner (1960, 1971). In some respects, this emphasis is reasonable and desirable. It is based upon the idea that an ultimate goal of instruction is to insure that the student becomes an efficient self-learner. The learning of strategies, however, cannot be critically affected by instruction on a minute-to-minute basis. Such capabilities are improved in quality and effectiveness over relatively long periods of time—months and years. For example, over a period of years a person who continues to read will become a more efficient reader, a more insightful reader, a reader with greater virtuosity. Entire sequences of instruction may be planned so that learners will improve their cognitive strategies of attending, of coding verbal information, of storing and retrieving what they have learned, of attacking and solving problems. Plans for attainment of such strategies appear to require arrangements for a variety of practice situations, extending over a period of many months.

Intellectual Skills as Building Blocks for Instruction.   For purposes of planning instruction in scope ranging from entire systems to individual lessons, intellectual skills have a number of desirable characteristics as components of a design framework (Gagné, 1970). An intellectual skill cannot be learned by being simply looked up, or provided to the learner by a verbal communication. It must be learned, recalled, and put into use at the proper time. As an example, consider the intellectual skill of spelling words containing a "long a" sound. When the learner possesses this skill, he is able to perform such spelling rapidly and without the necessity of looking up a set of rules. His performance shows that he is able to recall such rules and put them immediately into effect. At the same time, learning the necessary rules for spelling words with "long a" is not something that takes a period of many months to accomplish (as seems to be true of cognitive strategies). Essentially flawless performance calling upon such an intellectual skill can be expected to be established in a short space of time.

There are other advantages to intellectual skills as a major framework for instruction and instructional design. Such skills come to be highly interrelated to each other, and to build elaborate internal intellectual structures of a cumulative sort (Gagné, 1970). The learning of one skill aids the learning of other "higher-order" skills. Suppose an individual has learned the skill of substituting specific numerical values for letters in a symbolic expression like the following:

$$\sigma^2 = E(X - m)^2.$$

Such a skill will aid the learning of many kinds of advanced skills, not simply in mathematics, but in many areas of science and social studies. Intellectual skills are rich in transfer effects, which bring about the building of increasingly complex structures of intellectual competence.

Another advantage of intellectual skills as a primary component in instruction is the relative ease with which they can be reliably observed. When a learner has attained an intellectual skill, as, for example, "representing quantitative increases graphically," it is not difficult to see what must be done to show that he has indeed learned the skill. One would provide him with numerical values of any increasing variable, and ask him to construct a graph to show the changes in that variable. An intellectual skill can always be defined in operational terms; that is, it can always be related to a class of human performances—to something the successful learner *is able to do*.

The choice of intellectual skills as a primary point of reference in the design of instruction, then, is based mainly upon practical considerations. In contrast to factual information, skills cannot be simply looked up or made available by "telling," but must be learned. In contrast to cognitive strategies, intellectual skills are typically learned over relatively short time periods, and do not have to be refined and sharpened by months or years of practice. Intellectual skills build upon each other in a cumulative fashion to form increasingly elaborate intellectual structures. Through the mechanism of transfer of learning, they make possible an ever-broadening intellectual competence in each individual. And finally, such skills can be readily observed, so that it is easy to tell that they have been learned.

THE RATIONALE FOR
INSTRUCTIONAL DESIGN

The design of instruction must be undertaken with suitable attention to the conditions under which learning occurs. With reference to the learner, learning conditions are both external and internal. These conditions are in turn dependent upon *what* is being learned.

How can these basic ideas be used to design instruction? How can they be applied to the design of single lessons, of courses, and of entire systems of instruction? These are the questions we shall try to answer in this book. To do this, we must first consider the parts in order to build the whole.

The Derivation of Instruction

The rational steps in the derivation of procedures for instruction may be outlined briefly as follows:

1. The lasting effects of learning are conceived to be the acquisition by the learner of various *capabilities*. We need at the outset to consider what kinds of capabilities may be learned. We shall describe the varieties of human *performance* made possible to the learner by each kind of learned capability —intellectual skills, cognitive strategies, information, attitudes, and motor skills.

2. As outcomes of instruction and learning, human capabilities are usually specified in terms of the classes of human performance which they make possible. Such statements are sometimes referred to as "behavioral objectives" or *performance objectives*, and we shall use the latter term. They are "objectives" in that they identify the expected or planned outcomes of the events of learning. They refer to classes of human performance which can be reliably observed.

3. The identification of performance objectives makes possible the classification of capabilities into useful categories. Without these categories, we should only be able to deal with learning principles on a very general basis. With them, it becomes possible to infer what *kinds* of learned capabilities are being acquired. As a further step, it is possible to describe what *conditions*, internal and external, will be needed to bring about learning with greatest efficiency. When performance objectives are known, it becomes possible to infer, first, what *kind* of learned capability is being acquired; and as a second step, what conditions (internal as well as external) will be needed to bring about the learning with greatest efficiency.

4. The inference of conditions for learning makes possible the planning of *sequences of instruction*. This is so because the information and skills which need to be recalled for any given learning event must themselves have been previously learned. As a simple example from language study, learning the intellectual skill of using a pronoun in the objective case when the object of a preposition, requires the recall of other "subordinate" skills of identifying prepositions, pronouns, the cases of pronouns, and the concept "object of." Thus by tracing backwards from the outcome of learning for a particular topic, one can identify the sequence of intermediate (or "prerequisite") objectives that must be met to make possible the desired learning. In this way, instructional sequences may be specified that are applicable to topics, to courses, or even to entire curricula. The sequences thus derived are like *terrain maps* of intellectual development to be visited when students progress from one level of capability to another.

5. Once a course has been designed in terms of a sequence of performance objectives, and a means is at hand for assessing these objectives, one can proceed to the detailed planning of instruction in terms of the *individual lesson*. Here again the first reference for such planning is the performance objective which represents the outcome of the lesson. Attention centers on the arrangement of *external conditions* which will be most effective in bringing about the desired learning. What are the events that must be arranged by the teacher, or by the instructional designer, which will insure learning on the part of the student? It is these events, together with their arrangement and sequencing, that comprise *instruction*. The determination of the conditions for instruction also involves the choice of appropriate media and combinations of media that may be employed to promote learning.

6. The additional element that is required for completion of instructional design is a set of procedures for *assessment* of what has been learned by students. In conception, this component follows naturally from the definitions of instructional objectives. The latter statements describe domains from which are selected "items." These in turn may be teacher observations, or may be assembled as tests. Assessment procedures are designed to provide *criterion-referenced* measurement of learning outcomes (Popham, 1971). They are intended as direct measures of what students have learned as a result of instruction.

7. The design of lessons and courses with their accompanying techniques of assessing learning outcomes makes possible the planning of entire *systems*. Instructional systems aim to achieve comprehensive goals in schools and school systems. Means must be found to fit the various components together by way of a management system, sometimes called an "instructional delivery system." Naturally, teachers play key roles in the operation of such a

system. A particular class of instructional systems is concerned with *individualized instruction*, involving a set of procedures to insure optimal development of the individual student.

Finally, attention must be paid to *evaluation* of whatever instructional entity has been designed. Procedures for evaluation are first applied to the design effort itself. Evidence is sought for needed revisions aimed at the improvement and refinement of the instruction ("formative evaluation"). At a later stage, "summative evaluation" is undertaken to seek evidence of the learning effectiveness of what has been designed.

WHAT THE BOOK IS ABOUT

The rationale for the design of instruction is embodied in chapters of this book, as follows:

Part 1—Basic Processes of Learning and Instruction

Chapter 1, the Introduction, gives a brief account of principles of human learning, and outlines how these are to be taken into account in the design of instruction.

Chapter 2 introduces the reader to the five major categories of human capabilities which are learned as a result of instruction. The varieties of human performance which these capabilities make possible are described and distinguished.

Chapter 3 enters into an intensive description of the characteristics and conditions of learning for two of these categories of learned capabilities —intellectual skills and cognitive strategies.

Chapter 4 extends this description of learned capabilities to the three additional categories of information, attitudes, and motor skills.

Part 2—Designing Instruction

Chapter 5 deals with the derivation and description of instructional objectives (performance objectives). These are related on the one hand to general educational goals, and on the other to the learned capabilities which are the focus of interest in instruction.

Chapter 6 discusses principles applicable to the sequencing of instruction, beginning with courses, and continuing with smaller instructional entities such as topics and lessons within topics. Particular emphasis is given to the use of learning hierarchies in the identification of prerequisite intellectual skills.

Chapter 7 gives an account of the events of instruction that are typically used to form the structure of a lesson.

Chapter 8 describes procedures for designing individual lessons, including the placement of parts of lessons in sequence, the arrangement of effective conditions for learning appropriate to different types of lesson objectives, and the use of media.

Chapter 9 deals with methods of assessing student performances as outcomes of instruction.

Part 3—Instructional Systems

Chapter 10 provides an account of how the various components which have been designed can be combined into systematic procedures for individualized instruction.

Chapter 11 considers factors in the design of total instructional systems, such as might be done for a school or school system, making use of the various components that have previously been discussed.

Chapter 12 contains an account of the logic of evaluation studies. Evaluation utilizes evidence of the feasibility and effectiveness of instruction, from lessons to systems.

SUMMARY

Instruction is planned for the purpose of supporting learning. In this book, we describe methods involved in the design of instruction aimed at the individual learner. We assume that planned instruction has both short-range and long-range purposes in its effects on human development.

Instructional design must take into account some principles of human learning, specifically, the conditions under which learning occurs. Theories of learning have identified a number of conditions for learning, and some of these are controllable by the procedures of instruction. Older theories emphasize particularly the external conditions for learning, embodied in the principles of contiguity, repetition, and reinforcement. Modern theories add to these some internal conditions, those that arise within the learner. These internal states are made possible by the recall of previously learned material from the learner's memory.

An act of learning is greatly affected by these internally generated processes. In particular, new learning is influenced by the recall of previously learned information, intellectual skills, and cognitive strategies. These and other human capabilities, established by learning, will be described in the chapters to follow. These varieties of learned capabilities, and the conditions for their learning, constitute the basis for instructional planning. Derived from these principles is the rationale for a set of practical procedures for the design of effective instruction.

The student who uses the book will find it possible to follow up the ideas derived from research on human learning with further exploration and study of the references at the end of each chapter. The student who is interested in becoming skillful in designing instruction will need to undertake practice exercises that exemplify the procedures described. Because of the anticipated variety of particular courses and educational settings in which the book might be used, it has been our general expectation that these would be supplied by a course instructor. Examples and exercises of particular relevance for such a purpose are provided in two previously published volumes by Briggs (1970, 1972).

REFERENCES

Ausubel, D. P. *Educational Psychology: A Cognitive View*. New York: Holt, Rinehart and Winston, 1968.

Briggs, L. J. *Handbook of Procedures for the Design of Instruction*. Pittsburgh, Pa.: American Institutes for Research, 1970.

Briggs, L. J. *Student's Guide to Handbook of Procedures for the Design of Instruction*. Pittsburgh, Pa.: American Institutes for Research, 1972.

Bruner, J. S. *The Process of Education*. Cambridge, Mass.: Harvard University Press, 1960.

Bruner, J. S. *The Relevance of Education*. New York: Norton, 1971.

Deese, J., and Hulse, S. H. *The Psychology of Learning*. New York: McGraw-Hill, 1967.

Friedenberg, E. Z. *Coming of Age in America: Growth and Acquiescence*. New York: Random House, 1965.

Gagné, R. M. *The Conditions of Learning*. 2d Ed. New York: Holt, Rinehart and Winston, 1970.

Gardner, J. W. *Excellence*. New York: Harper & Row, 1961.

Miller, G. A., and Selfridge, J. A. Verbal context and the recall of meaningful material. *American Journal of Psychology*, 1950, *63*, 176–185.

Popham, W. J. (Ed.). *Criterion-Referenced Measurement*. Englewood Cliffs, N.J.: Educational Technology Publications, 1971.

Premack, D. Reinforcement Theory. In D. Levine (Ed.), *Nebraska Symposium on Motivation*. Lincoln: University of Nebraska Press, 1965.

Silberman, C. E. *Crisis in the Classroom*. New York: Random House, 1970.

Thorndike, E. L. *The Psychology of Learning: Educational Psychology*, Vol. 2. New York: Teachers College, Columbia University, 1913.

2

THE OUTCOMES OF INSTRUCTION

The best way to design instruction is to work backwards from the outcomes it is expected to have. Some ways of working backwards, and their implications for the content of instruction, are described in this chapter. These procedures begin with the identification of human capabilities to be established by instruction. These instructional outcomes, introduced and defined here in terms of five broad categories, run throughout the book as a framework on which the design of instruction is based.

INSTRUCTION AND EDUCATIONAL GOALS

The basic reason for designing instruction is to make possible the attainment of a set of educational goals. The society in which we live has certain functions to perform in serving the needs of its people. Many of these functions—in fact, most of them—require human activities which must be learned. Accordingly, one of the functions of a society is to insure that such learning takes place. Every society, in one way or another, makes provision for the education of people in order that the variety of functions necessary for its survival can be carried out. *Educational goals* are those human activities which contribute to the functioning of a society (including the functioning of an individual *in* the society), and which can be acquired through learning.

Naturally, in societies whose organization is simple—often called "primitive" societies—the goals of education and the means used to reach them are fairly easy to describe and understand. In a primitive society whose economy revolves around hunting animals, for example, the most prominent educational goals center upon the activities of hunting. The son of a hunter is educated in these activities by his father, or perhaps by other hunters of the village to which he belongs. Fundamentally, educational goals have the same kind of origin in a modern complex society. Obviously, though, as societies become more complex, so must educational goals.

Every so often in our own society, we hold conferences, appoint committees, or establish commissions to make studies of educational goals. One of the most famous of these bodies formulated a set of goals called the "Cardinal Principles of Secondary Education" (1918). The key statement of this document was as follows (p. 9):

> Education in a democracy, both within and without the school, should develop in each individual the knowledge, interests, ideals, habits, and powers whereby he will find his place and use that place to shape both himself and society toward ever nobler ends.

The composition of the "knowledge, interests, ideals, habits, and powers" was considered by this commission to fall into the seven areas of (1) health, (2) command of basic skills, (3) worthy home-membership, (4) pursuing a vocation, (5) citizenship, (6) worthy use of leisure, and (7) ethical character.

It might be supposed that more specific objectives for education could be derived from broad statements such as these. This sort of analysis, however, becomes a stupendous task, so great that it has never really been attempted for our society. Instead, we depend upon a number of kinds of simplifications to accomplish the purpose of specifying educational goals in detail. These simplifying approaches condense information in several stages, and thus lose some information along the way.

Thus it has come about that we tend to structure education in terms of "subject matters" that are actually gross simplifications of educational goals, rather than activities reflecting the actual functions of human beings in society. It is as though the activity of shooting a bear in a primitive society were to be transformed into a "subject" called "marksmanship." We represent an educational goal with the subject-matter name of "English" rather than with the many different human activities which are performed with language. One of the best known of recent efforts on a national scale has been the formulation of educational goals within various subject-matter fields by the National Assessment of Educational Progress program (Womer, 1970).

Goals as Educational Outcomes

The reflection of societal needs in educational goals typically finds expression in statements describing categories of *human activity*. A goal is preferably stated, not as "health," but as "performing those activities which will maintain health." The goal, or goals, are most inadequately conveyed by the topic of "citizenship"; they are more adequately reflected in a statement such as "carries out the activities of a citizen in a democratic society."

What would be desirable for educational scholars to accomplish, but which has not as yet been accomplished, is the derivation of an array of human *capabilities* which would make possible the kinds of activities expressed in educational goals. It is these capabilities which represent the proximate goals of instruction. In order to carry out the activities required for maintaining health, the individual must possess certain kinds of capabilities (knowledge, skills, attitudes). In most cases he has learned these through deliberately planned instruction. Similarly, in order to perform the various activities appropriate to being a citizen, the individual must have learned a variety of capabilities through instruction.

Educational goals are statements of the outcomes of education. They refer particularly to those activities made possible by learning, which in turn is often brought about by deliberately planned instruction. The rationale is not different in our society from that of a primitive society. In the latter, for example, the educational goal of "hunting activity" is achieved by a customary regime of instruction in the various component human capabilities (locating prey, stalking, shooting, etc.) that make possible the total activity of "hunting." The difference, however, is an important one. In the more complex society, the *capabilities* required for one activity may be shared by a number of others. Thus, the human capability of "performing arithmetic operations" serves not a single educational goal, such as making a family budget, but several others as well, including changing money and making scientific measurements.

In order to design instruction, one must seek a means of identifying the *human capabilities* that lead to the outcomes called educational goals. If these goals were uncomplicated, as in a primitive society, defining these human capabilities might be equally simple. But such is not the case in a highly differentiated and specialized society. Instruction cannot be adequately planned separately for each educational goal necessary for a modern society. One must seek, instead, to identify the human capabilities that contribute to a number of different goals. A capability like "reading comprehension," for example, obviously serves several purposes. The present chapter is intended to serve as an introduction to the concept of human capabilities.

Courses and Their Objectives

The planning of instruction is often carried out for a single *course*, rather than for larger units of a total curriculum. There is no necessary fixed length to a course, or no fixed specification of "what is to be covered." A number of factors may influence the choice of duration or amount of content. Often the length of time available in a semester or year is the primary determining factor. In any case, a course is usually defined rather arbitrarily by the designation of some topics which are understood within the local environment of the school. A course may take on a general title like "American History," "Beginning French," "English 1," and so on.

The ambiguity in meaning of courses with such titles is evident. Is "American History" in grade 6 the same as or different from the course of the same title in grade 12? Is "English 1" concerned with composition, literature, or both? These are by no means idle questions, because they represent sources of difficulty for many students in many places, particularly when they are planning programs of study. It is not entirely uncommon, for example, for a student to choose a course like "First-year French," only to find that he should have elected "Beginning French."

Ambiguity in the meaning of courses with title or topic designations can readily be avoided when courses are described in terms of their *objectives* (Mager, 1962; Popham & Baker, 1970). Examples of objectives in many subject areas are described in a volume by Bloom, Hastings, & Madaus (1971). Thus, if "English 1" has an objective "the student will be able to compose a unified composition on any assigned single topic, in acceptable printed English, within an hour" it is perfectly clear to everyone what a portion of the course is all about. It will not help the student, in any direct fashion, to "identify imagery in modern poetry," nor to "analyze the conflicts in works of fiction." It will, however, if successful, teach him the basic craft of writing a composition. Similarly, if an objective of "Beginning French" is that the student will be able to "conjugate irregular verbs," this is obviously fairly clear. It will not readily be confused with an objective that makes it possible for the student to "write French sentences from dictation."

As usually planned, courses often have several objectives, and not just one. A course in social studies may have the intention of providing the student with several capabilities: "describing the context of (specified) historical events," "evaluating the sources of written history," and "showing a positive liking for the study of history." A course in science may wish to establish in the student the ability to "formulate and test hypotheses," to "engage in scientific problem solving," and also to "value the activities of scientists." Each of these kinds of objectives within a single course may be considered equally worthwhile. They may also be differentially valued by different teachers. The main point to be noted about them at this juncture, however, is that they are different. The most important difference among them is that each requires a different plan for its achievement. Instruction must be differentially designed, in order to insure that each objective is attainable by students within the context of a course.

Are there a great many specific objectives for which individual instructional planning must be done, or can this task be reduced in some manner? The task of instructional planning can be vastly simplified by assigning objectives to *five major categories of human capabilities*. Such categories can be formed because each leads to a different class of human performance, and each requires a different set of instructional conditions for effective learning. Within each category, regardless of the subject matter of instruction, the same conditions apply. Of course, there may be subcategories within each of the five categories. In fact, there *are* subcategories which are useful for instructional planning, as later chapters of this book will show. But for the moment, in taking a fairly general look at instructional planning from the standpoint of courses, five categories provide the comprehensive view.

FIVE CATEGORIES OF LEARNING OUTCOMES

What are the categories of objectives, expected as learning outcomes resulting from instruction? A brief description of each is given in the following sections. This is later followed by a fuller description of their usefulness as human capabilities. Conditions necessary for learning these capabilities are to be described in following chapters.

Intellectual Skills Intellectual skills are the capabilities that make the human individual *competent* (Gagné, 1970). They enable him to respond to conceptualizations of his environment. They make up the most basic, and at the same time the most pervasive, structure of formal education. They range from elementary language skills like composing a sentence to the advanced technical skills of science, engineering, and other disciplines. Examples of intellectual skills of the latter sort are finding the stresses in a bridge, or predicting the effects of a currency devaluation. Their learning begins in the early grades with the three R's, and progresses to whatever level is compatible with the individual's interests, or as may be limited by his intellectual capacity.

Cognitive Strategies   These are a special kind of skill, and a very important kind. They are the capabilities that govern the individual's own learning, remembering, and thinking behavior. For example, they control his behavior when he is attending in the process of reading with the intent to learn; and the internal ways he uses to "get to the heart of a problem." The phrase "cognitive strategy" is usually attributed to Bruner (Bruner, Goodnow, & Austin, 1956); Rothkopf (1968) has named them "mathemagenic behaviors"; Skinner (1968) "self-management behaviors." One expects that such skills will improve over a relatively long period of time as the individual engages in more and more studying, learning, and thinking. It has long been a goal of education to develop in students capabilities of creative problem solving. If this is indeed a learnable and generalizable trait, or possibly a collection of traits, it deserves to be included with many simpler learning skills under the heading of cognitive strategy.

Verbal Information   All of us have learned a great deal of verbal information, or verbal knowledge. We have readily available in our memories many commonly used items of information such as the names of months, days of the week, letters, numerals, towns, cities, states, countries, and so on. We also have a great store of more highly organized information, such as many events of American history, the forms of government, the major achievements of science and technology, the components of the economy. The verbal information we learn in school is in part "for the course only," and in part the kind of knowledge we are expected to be able to recall readily as adults.

Motor Skills   Another kind of capability we expect human beings to learn is a motor skill (Fitts & Posner, 1967). The individual learns to skate, to ride a bicycle, to steer an automobile, to use a can-opener, to jump rope. There are also motor skills to be learned as part of formal school instruction, like printing letters, drawing a straight line, aligning a pointer on a dial face. Despite the fact that school instruction is so largely concerned with intellectual functions, we do not expect a well-educated adult to be lacking in certain motor skills, some of which (like writing) he may use every day.

Attitudes   Passing now to what is often called the "affective domain" (Krathwohl et al., 1964), we can identify a class of learned capabilities called attitudes. All of us possess attitudes of many sorts towards different things, persons, and situations. The effect of an attitude is to amplify an individual's positive or negative reactions toward some person, or thing, or situation. The strength of a person's attitude toward some item may be indicated by the frequency with which he *chooses* that item in a variety of circumstances. Thus, an individual with a strong attitude toward helping other people will offer his help in many situations; whereas a person with a weaker attitude of this sort will tend to restrict his offers of help to fewer situations. The schools are often expected to establish socially approved attitudes such as respect for other people, cooperativeness, personal responsibility, as well as positive attitudes toward knowledge and learning, and an attitude of self-esteem.

Capabilities and Human Performance

Each of the five categories of learning outcome is an acquired capability of the person who has learned, as the previous examples have illustrated. Once learned, these capabilities can be observed again and again in a variety of human performances. They are called *capabilities* because they make possible the prediction of many particular instances of performance on the part of the learner. If he has acquired the capability (motor skill) of figure-skating, we infer that he carries this capability around with him. He may exhibit it on any specific occasion when he is on ice and wearing skates. The same holds true for the other kinds of capabilities, intellectual skills, cognitive strategies, verbal information, and attitudes. Of course, some of these may be forgotten more easily than others, but that is another story. Learned capabilities, until they have been forgotten, are exhibited as specific human performances. They are not the same as these performances; instead, they may be said to *mediate* the performances that are observed.

These categories of learned capabilities are distinguished from each other because they make possible distinctive categories of human performance. As we shall see in the following chapters, they also require different arrangements of conditions in order for the learning of each to occur. At this point, though, it will be worthwhile to summarize the distinguishing features of each class of learned human capability, including the category of performance that each makes possible. This information is given in Table 1.

The first column of Table 1 contains the five kinds of capability which may result from learning. The second column contains an example of each capability. Next, column three describes the inferences one may make about the function served by each kind of capability. Current understanding of

TABLE 1   *Five Kinds of Learned Capabilities*

Kind of Capability	Example	Function	Performance Category
Intellectual Skill	Using a metaphor to describe an object	Component of further learning and thinking	Showing how an intellectual operation is carried out in specific application
Cognitive Strategy	Induction of the concept "magnetic field"	Controls learner's behavior in learning and thinking	Solving a variety of practical problems by efficient means
Verbal Information	"Boiling point of water is 100° C"	(1) Provides directions for learning; (2) aids transfer of learning	Stating or otherwise communicating information
Motor Skill	Printing letters	Mediates motor performance	Carrying out the motor activity in a variety of contexts
Attitude	Preference for listening to music as a leisure activity	Modifies individual's choices of action	Choosing a course of action toward a class of objects, persons, or events

these functions seems likely to be incomplete at the present time, and additional clarification may be expected from research sources. Finally, the table contains a column which describes the category of human performance made possible by each of the capabilities.

Intellectual Skill A student of the English language learns at some point in his studies what a metaphor is. More specifically, if his instruction is adequate, he learns to *use* a metaphor. (In the next chapter, we identify this particular subcategory of intellectual skill as a *rule*. In other words, it may be said that the student has learned to use a rule to show what a metaphor is; or that he has learned to apply a rule.) This skill then has the function of becoming a component of further learning. That is to say, the skill of using a metaphor now may contribute to the learning of more complex intellectual skills, such as writing illustrative sentences, describing scenes and events, composing essays.

If one wishes to know whether the student has learned this intellectual skill, one must observe a category of *performance*. Usually this is done by asking the student to "show what a metaphor is" in one or more specific instances. In other words, observations might be made as to whether the student performed adequately when asked to use a metaphor to describe (1) a cat's movements, (2) a cloudy day, and perhaps (3) the moon's surface. As the fourth column of the table indicates, he is showing how this intellectual skill may be applied in specific instances.

Cognitive Strategy Internally organized strategies that govern the learner's behavior come in several varieties. At present, it is not possible to identify them singly with any degree of confidence, much less name them. Nevertheless, their effects in determining human performance appear quite evident. The example given in the table is the process of *inference*, or *induction*. Suppose that a student has become acquainted with magnetic attraction in a bar magnet—he has noted that a force is exerted by each pole of the magnet on certain kinds of metal objects. Now he is given some iron filings which he sprinkles on a piece of paper placed over the magnet. When the paper is tapped, the filings exhibit "lines of force" around each pole of the magnet. The student proceeds to verify his observation in other situations, perhaps using other magnets and other kinds of metal objects. These observations, together with other knowledge, may lead him to induce the idea of a magnetic field of force surrounding each pole of the magnet. It is important to note, in this example, that the student has not been told of the magnetic field beforehand, nor has he been given instruction in "how to induce." But he does carry out this kind of mental operation.

Learning a cognitive strategy like induction, however, does not appear to be done on a single occasion. Instead, this kind of capability develops over fairly long periods of time. Presumably, the learner must have a number of experiences with induction, in widely different situations, in order for the strategy to become dependably useful.

When a learner becomes capable of induction, he may obviously use it as a strategy in a great variety of other situations. Provided other requisite intellectual skills and information have been learned, he may use an induction strategy to arrive at an explanation of what makes smoke rise in the air, or of why pebbles in a stream are rounded and smooth, or of what intention a writer has had in composing an editorial essay. In other words, the cognitive strategy of induction may be put to use in a great many situations of thinking and learning—situations which are enormously varied in their describable properties. In fact, the performances that the learner is able to exhibit in these situations may be seen to resemble each other only in the respect that they involve induction. And this, of course, is the basic reason for believing that such a cognitive strategy exists—it is by an act of induction that one arrives at the presence of the cognitive strategy of induction in other people.

The performance that a cognitive strategy like induction makes possible, as indicated in the final column of the table, is solving a variety of practical problems efficiently. Variety of problems is necessary, because one cannot infer the capability of this cognitive strategy from one or even two problem solutions. Such instances may result from the simpler process of rule application, as would be observed if a student showed he could "solve" five algebraic equations of the same type one after another. However, if one can observe a student using induction to solve problems in mechanics, in plant growth, in governmental affairs, and in literature, one then feels relatively confident that the student has acquired and is employing this cognitive strategy.

Verbal Information   The student of science learns much verbal information, just as he does in other fields of study. He learns the properties of materials, objects, and living things, for example. A large number of "science facts" may not constitute a defensible primary goal of science instruction. Nevertheless, the learning of such "facts" is an essential part of the learning of science. Without information, learning in any subject could have no continuity, no "substance."

The example shown in Table 1 supposes that a student has learned the item of information "the boiling point of water is 100° C." One major function such information serves is to provide the learner with directions for how to proceed in further learning. Thus, in learning about the change of state of materials from liquid to gaseous form, the learner may be acquiring an intellectual skill (that is, a rule) which relates atmospheric pressure to vaporization. In working with this relationship, he may be asked to apply the rule to a situation which describes the temperature of boiling water at an altitude of nine thousand feet. At this juncture he must recall the *information* given in the example in order to proceed with the application of the rule. One may be inclined to say this information is not particularly important—rather, the learning of the intellectual skill is the important thing. There is no disagreement about this point. However, the *information is essential* to these events. The learner must have such information available to him, in order to learn.

Information may also be of importance for the transfer of learning from one situation to another. For example, the student of government may hit upon the idea that the persistence of a bureaucracy bears some resemblance to the growth of an abscess in the human body. If he has some information about abscesses, such an analogy may make it possible for him to think of causal relationships pertaining to bureaucracies which would not otherwise be possible. A variety of cognitive strategies and intellectual skills may now be brought to bear on this problem by the student, and new knowledge thereby generated. The initial transfer in such an instance is made possible by an "association of ideas," in other words, by the possession and use of certain classes of information.

Finding out whether the student has learned some particular facts, or some particular organized items of information, is a matter of observing whether he can communicate them. The simplest way to do this, of course, is to ask him to state the information, either orally or in writing. This is the basic method commonly employed by a teacher to assess what information has been learned. In the early grades, assessing the communications children can make may require the use of simple questions, orally given. Pictures and objects that the child can point to and manipulate may also be employed.

Motor Skill   A motor skill is one of the most obvious kinds of human capabilities to observe. The child learns a motor skill for each printed letter he makes with a pencil on paper. The function of the skill, as a capability, is simply to make possible the motor performance. Of course, these motor performances may themselves enter into the further learning of the student. For example, he employs the skill of printing letters when he is learning to make (and print) words and sentences. The acquisition of a motor skill can be reasonably inferred when the student can perform the act in a variety of contexts. Thus, if a youngster has acquired the *skill* of printing the letter E he should be able to perform this motor act with a pen, a pencil, a crayon, on any flat surface, constructing letters with a range of sizes. Obviously one would not want to conclude that the skill has been learned from a single instance of an E printed with pencil on a particular piece of paper. But several E's, in several different contexts, observably distinct from F's or H's, provide convincing evidence that this kind of capability has been learned.

Attitude   A student learns to have preferences for various kinds of activities; he prefers certain people to others; he shows an interest in certain events rather than others. One infers from a set of such observations that the student has *attitudes* toward objects, persons, or events which influence his choice of courses of action towards them. Naturally, there are many such attitudes that are acquired outside of the school, and many that schools cannot appropriately consider relevant to their instructional function. As one possibility, though, school instruction might have the objective of establishing positive attitudes toward subjects being studied (cf. Mager, 1968). Often, too, school learning is successful in modifying attitudes toward activities that provide esthetic enjoyment. The example of Table 1 is a positive attitude toward listening to music.

Considered as a human capability, an attitude is a persisting state that modifies the individual's choices of action. A positive attitude toward listening to music makes the student *tend* to choose such activity over others, when such choices are possible. Of course, this does not mean he will always be listening to music, under all circumstances. Rather, it means that when he has a chance and an opportunity for leisure (as opposed to other pressing concerns) the probability of his choosing to listen to music is noticeably high. If one were able to observe the student over a reasonable period of time, one would be able to note that the choice of this activity was relatively frequent. From such a set of observations, it could be concluded that the student had a positive attitude toward listening to music.

In practice, of course, making such a set of observations about a single student, not to mention a class of students, would be an exceedingly time-consuming and therefore expensive undertaking. As a result, inferences about the possession of attitudes are usually made on the basis of "self-reports." These may be obtained by means of questionnaires which ask students what choices of action they would make (or in some cases, *did* make) in a variety of situations. There are of course technical problems in the use of such self-reports for attitude assessment. Since their intentions are rather obvious, students can readily make self-reports of choices which do not reflect reality. However, when proper precautions are taken, such reports make possible the inference that a particular attitude has been learned, or modified in a particular direction.

Thus, the performance that is affected by an attitude is the *choice of a course of personal action*. The tendency to make such a choice, towards a particular class of objects, persons, or events, may be stronger in one student than in another. A change in an attitude would be revealed as a change in the probability of choosing a particular course of action on the part of the student. Over a period of time, or as a result of instruction, the probability of choosing the activity "listening to music" may be altered, to follow the example given here. The observation of such change would give rise to the inference that the students' attitude toward listening to music had changed, that is, had become "stronger" in the positive direction.

Human Capabilities as Course Goals

A single course of instruction usually has objectives that fit into several categories of human capability. The major categories, which cut across the "content" of courses, are the five we have described. From the standpoint of the expected outcomes of instruction, the major reason for distinguishing these five categories is that they *make possible different kinds of human performance*.

For example, a course in elementary science may foresee as general objectives such learning outcomes as these: (1) solving problems of velocity, time, and acceleration; (2) designing an experiment to provide a scientific test of a stated hypothesis; and (3) valuing the activities of science. Number one obviously names *intellectual skills* and therefore implies some performances involving intellectual operations which the student can show he can do.

Number two pertains to the use of *cognitive strategies*, since it implies that the student will need to exhibit this complex performance in a novel situation, where little guidance is provided in the selection and use of rules and concepts he has previously learned. Number three has to do with an *attitude*, or possibly with a set of attitudes, which ·will be exhibited in behavior as choices of actions directed toward science activities.

The human capabilities distinguished in these five categories also differ from each other in another highly important way. They each require *a different set of learning conditions* for their efficient learning. The conditions necessary for learning these capabilities efficiently, and the distinctions among these conditions, constitute the subjects of the next two chapters. There, an account is given of the conditions of learning which apply to the acquisition of each of these kinds of human capability, beginning with intellectual skills and cognitive strategies, and following with the remaining three categories.

DESIGNING INSTRUCTION
USING HUMAN CAPABILITIES

The point of view presented in this chapter is that instruction should always be designed to meet accepted educational goals. When goals are matched with societal needs, the ideal condition exists for the planning of a total program of education. Were such an undertaking to be attempted, the result would be, as a first step, a list of human activities, each of which would have associated with it an estimate of its importance in meeting the needs of the society.

When human activities derived from societal needs are in turn analyzed, they yield a set of *human capabilities*. These are descriptions of what human adults in a particular society ought to *know*, and particularly what they ought to *know how to do*. Such a set of capabilities would probably not bear a close resemblance to the traditional "subject-matter" categories of the school curriculum. There would, of course, be a relationship between human capabilities and the "subjects" of the curriculum, but it would probably not be a simple correspondence.

Most instructional design, as currently carried out, centers upon *course* planning and design. Such a framework is therefore accepted for the account to be given in this book. However, we shall continue to maintain an orientation toward the *goals* of instruction. Learning outcomes cannot always be well identified, it appears, by the topical titles of courses. They *can* be identified as the varieties of learned human capabilities which make possible different types of human performances. Accordingly, the present chapter has provided an introduction to the five major categories of capabilities, which will carry throughout the book as the basic framework of instructional design.

If the instructional designer says to himself, "These five categories are all well and good, but all that I'm *really* interested in is producing creative thinkers," he is engaging in a game of fooling himself. With the exception of motor skills, *all* of these categories are likely to be involved in the planning of any course. One cannot have a course without information, and one cannot have a course that doesn't affect attitudes to some degree. And most important of all, one cannot have a course without intellectual skills.

There are a couple of reasons why intellectual skills play a central role in designing the structure of a course of study. First, they are the kinds of capabilities which determine what the student can *do*, and thus are intimately bound up with the description of a course in terms of its learning outcomes. A second reason is that intellectual skills have a *cumulative* nature—they build upon each other in a predictable manner. Accordingly, they provide the most useful model for the sequencing of course structure. In the next chapter, we begin to look more closely at intellectual skills—what kinds are there, how can they be learned, and how does one know when they are learned?

SUMMARY

This chapter has shown that the defining of goals for education is a complex problem. In part this is because so much is expected of education. Some persons would wish that education emphasize the importance of understanding the past history of mankind; some would wish it to perpetuate the present culture or present academic disciplines; some would stress the need to help children and young adults adjust to a rapidly changing society; and others would hope that education can prepare students to become change agents to improve themselves and the society in which they live.

One source of complexity in defining educational goals arises from the need to translate goals from very general ones to increasingly specific ones. Many "layers" of such goals would be needed to be sure that each topic in the curriculum actually moves the learner a step toward a more distant goal. Probably this mapping has never been done completely for any curriculum. Thus there tend to be large gaps from general goals to the specific objectives for "courses" in the curriculum. A major problem then remains—the need to define "course objectives" in the absence of an entire network of connections between the most general goals and the specific course objectives.

Despite the involved nature of this problem, means are available for classifying course objectives into categories, which then make it possible to examine the scope of types of *human capabilities* the course is intended to develop. One purpose of such taxonomies (sets of performance categories) is to evaluate the objectives themselves in their entirety. The taxonomy presented in this chapter contains the following categories of learned capabilities:

1. Intellectual skills
2. Cognitive strategies
3. Verbal information
4. Motor skills
5. Attitudes

The usefulness of learning each of these types of capabilities has been discussed, and will be treated in greater detail in later chapters.

Uses of such a taxonomy, in addition to the evaluation of the variety of capabilities a course is intended to produce in the learner, include the following:

1. The taxonomy can help to group specific objectives of a similar nature together, and thus reduce the work needed to design a total instructional strategy.
2. The groupings of objectives can aid in determining sequence of segments of a course of study.
3. The grouping of objectives into types of capabilities can then be utilized to plan the internal and external conditions of learning estimated to be required for successful learning.

Each performance objective of a course defines a unique performance expected as an outcome of the instruction. By grouping objectives into the five categories of capabilities which have been described, one also can assess the adequacy of coverage in each category, while capitalizing upon the fact the conditions of learning are the same for each objective within that category. Identification of the conditions of learning for each type of human capability is the main topic of the next two chapters.

REFERENCES

Bloom, B. S., Hastings, J. T., & Madaus, G. F. *Handbook on Formative and Summative Evaluation of Student Learning.* New York: McGraw-Hill, 1971.

Bruner, J. S., Goodnow, J. J., & Austin, G. A. *A Study of Thinking.* New York: Wiley, 1956.

Commission on the Reorganization of Secondary Education, *Cardinal Principles of Secondary Education.* Washington, D.C.: Department of the Interior, Bureau of Education, 1918. (Bulletin No. 35).

Fitts, P. M., & Posner, M. I. *Human Performance.* Belmont, Calif.: Brooks/Cole, 1967.

Gagné, R. M. *The Conditions of Learning,* 2d Ed. New York: Holt, Rinehart and Winston, 1970.

Krathwohl, D. R., Bloom, B. S., & Masia, B. B. *Taxonomy of Educational Objectives. Handbook II: Affective Domain.* New York: McKay, 1964.

Mager, R. F. *Preparing Objectives for Instruction.* Belmont, Calif.: Fearon, 1962.

Mager, R. F. *Developing Attitude Toward Learning.* Belmont, Calif.: Fearon, 1968.

Popham, W. J. & Baker, E. L. *Establishing Instructional Goals.* Englewood Cliffs, N. J.: Prentice-Hall, 1970.

Rothkopf, E. Z. Two scientific approaches to the management of instruction. In R. M. Gagné and W. R. Gephart (Eds.), *Learning Research and School Subjects.* Itasca, Ill.: Peacock, 1968.

Skinner, B. F. *The Technology of Teaching.* New York: Appleton-Century-Crofts, 1968.

Womer, F. B. *What Is National Assessment?* Denver: Education Commission of the States, 1970.

3

VARIETIES OF LEARNING:
Intellectual Skills and Strategies

When one begins to think about the application of learning principles to instruction, he finds no better guide than to face the question, *what* is to be learned? We have seen that the answer to this question may in any given instance fall into one of the general classes (1) intellectual skills, (2) cognitive strategies, (3) information, (4) motor skills, or (5) attitudes. In this chapter, we intend to consider the conditions affecting the learning of *intellectual skills*, which are of central importance to school learning, and which in addition provide the best structural model for instructional design. It is a reasonable step to proceed then to a consideration of *cognitive strategies*, which are a special kind of intellectual skill deserving of a separate categorization. In the following chapter, consideration will be given to learning requirements for the remaining three classes of human capabilities.

An intellectual skill makes it possible for an individual to respond to his environment through symbols. Language, numbers, and other kinds of symbols represent the actual objects of the person's environment. Words "stand for" objects. They also represent relations among objects, such as "above," "behind," "within." Numbers represent the quantity of things in the environment, and various symbols are used to represent relations among these quantities ($+$, $=$, etc.). Other kinds of symbols are commonly used to represent spatial relations, like lines, arrows, and circles. The human individual communicates aspects of his experience to others by using such symbols. Symbol-using is one of the major ways the person remembers and thinks about the world in which he lives. We need to provide here an expanded description of these intellectual skills. What kinds of intellectual skills may be learned, and how are they learned?

TYPES OF INTELLECTUAL SKILLS

The intellectual skills learned by the individual during his school years are many, surely numbering in the thousands. One can appreciate this fact by thinking of a single domain—language skills. Even topics of instruction like oral reading, expressive reading, sentence composition, paragraph construction, conversing, persuasive speaking, all contain within themselves scores of specific intellectual skills which must be learned. This is also true of skills of number and quantification within the various fields of mathematics. Many skills of spatial and temporal patterning form a part of such subjects as geometry and science. In dealing with intellectual skills, one must be prepared to look at the "fine-grain" structure of human intellectual functioning.

In whatever domain of subject matter they occur, intellectual skills can be categorized on a dimension of *complexity*. By this is meant the intricacy of the mental process that may be inferred to account for the human performance. For example, suppose that a learner is shown two novel and distinctive-looking objects, and told to learn how to tell them apart when they are brought back at a later time. The kind of mental processing required is not very complex. One can infer that what he has learned in this situation, and recalled when asked to, is a "discrimination."

Quite a different level of complexity is indicated by the following example: The learner is able, following instruction, to comprehend adjectives in the German language which he has never before encountered, constructed by adding the suffix "lich" (as with Gemüt—gemütlich). This kind of performance is often referred to as *rule-governed*, because the kind of mental processing it requires is "applying a rule." It is not necessary for the learner to state the rule, or even for him to be able to state it. He is, however, performing in a way that implies he must have learned an internal capability that makes his behavior regular, or rule-governed. What he has learned is called a *rule*. Obviously, such a process is more complex than the discrimination referred to in the previous paragraph.

Different levels of complexity of mental processing, then, provide a possibility for classification of intellectual skills. Such categories cut across, and are independent of, types of subject matter (cf. Gagné, 1964). How many levels of complexity of intellectual processing can be distinguished, or need to be? The answer to this question proposed by Gagné (1970) is shown in Figure 2.

It should be borne in mind in examining this figure, that Gagné has attempted to include the entire range of learned capabilities possible to the human individual. The lower levels of complexity identified here are very simple indeed, and do not normally play a substantial role in school learning.

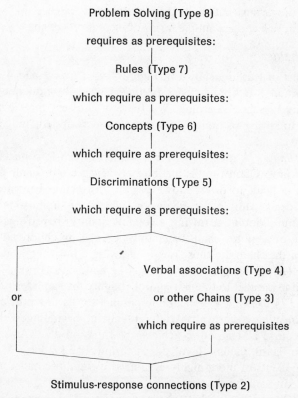

FIGURE 2   Levels of complexity in intellectual skills. (From R. M. Gagné, *The Conditions of Learning*, 2d Ed. Holt, Rinehart and Winston, 1970, p. 66.)

So far as intellectual development of the individual is concerned, the more complex kinds of intellectual processing are based upon these simpler varieties. In order to acquire the capability called a *concept*, for example, the learner must previously have learned some intellectual capabilities called *discriminations*; and in order to acquire discriminations, he must previously have learned *chains*, or at an even simpler level, *S-R connections*. The child who is learning to identify the printed "E" (a concept) must have previously learned to discriminate three horizontal lines (≡≡≡) from two (══), and he must also have learned some response chains which enable him to show that he can identify an "E" (like saying its name, or pointing to it). Obviously, though, the teacher who is concerned with instruction designed to get the child to identify E may wish to assume that he already knows two lines from three, and also that he knows how to say "ee." In school learning, the simpler capabilities are often assumed to have been learned previously. Usually, this assumption is quite correct. If it is not, one may have to design instruction so that the learner "catches up" with specific capabilities that reflect these simple forms of mental processing.

Response Chains

The forms of learning shown in Figure 1 as Types 3 and 4 are actually *chains* of learned S-R connections. In themselves, they do not occur with high frequency in school learning. We therefore review their characteristics briefly in the following sections. More complete descriptions may be found in Gagné (1970).

Motor Chains A motor chain is a sequence of S-R connections that is acquired as a unit. Often the distinction between a motor chain and a single connection is difficult to draw. However, the distinction becomes quite evident as one deals with longer chains in which the unitary responses are themselves quite different. Drawing a roughly square-shaped figure on paper is an example of a motor chain commonly learned by children. The simpler connections in the chain are those of (1) drawing a horizontal line, (2) making a corner, (3) drawing a vertical line, (4) making a corner, (5) drawing a horizontal line parallel to the first and of roughly the same length, (6) making a corner, (7) drawing a vertical line parallel to the one previously drawn, and (8) connecting a corner. A different chain, beginning with a vertical line, may of course be learned to achieve the same product. An older student may need to learn chains involved in using hand tools. Motor chains become components of more highly organized capabilities called *motor skills*, as we shall see in the next chapter.

Verbal Chains A verbal chain consists of a sequence of verbal responses acquired as a unit. There are likely to be many of these in a person's repertoire. Little attention is usually paid to teaching them deliberately. As "verbal associations," short verbal chains may be the basic components of informational memory. Examples of such chains are boy-girl, table-chair, summer-winter, red-green, light-bulb. Longer verbal chains often become parts of sentences in conversation and writing, such as "inevitable consequences," "raving mad," "stark naked," "just between you and me," "with fear and trembling." Many such phrases come originally from the Bible or from classical literature. A variety of verbal chain of special importance is the *name* or *label* used to identify things, places, or people.

Discriminations

A discrimination is a capability of making different responses to stimuli that differ from each other along one or more physical dimensions. Examples of discrimination occur frequently in instruction for the kindergarten and first grade. Here children are asked to distinguish two "pictures," one having vertical lines and another horizontal lines; or, one having a circle and the other a square. Matching to a sample is another variant form of the discrimination task; the child may be asked to match a red-colored block with one that is the same color in a group of blocks of various colors. In beginning music instruction, the child may be asked to learn to discriminate which of two tones is louder, or which of two tone-pairs contains tones that are "the same" or "different" in pitch.

A discrimination is a very basic kind of intellectual skill. Mainly, discrimination learning is encountered most frequently in young children, and also in mental retardates. Otherwise, discriminations are usually assumed to have been previously learned early in life, so far as most school learning is concerned. Every once in a while, however, one is surprised to realize that these elementary discriminations may not have been learned, and cannot be assumed. Does the learner of the French uvular and frontal "r" actually hear this distinction (that is, has he learned it as a discrimination)? Has the student microscopist actually seen the distinction (i.e., discriminated) between a bright and dark boundary which he will later learn to identify as a cell wall?

In describing the characteristics of a discrimination, as well as of other types of intellectual skills to follow, we need to account for three components of the learning situation. These are:

1. The *performance* which is acquired, or to be acquired. What is it that the learner will be able to do after learning that he was not able to do before?
2. The *internal conditions* which must be present in order for the learning to

occur. These consist of capabilities which are recalled from the learner's memory, and which then become integrated into the newly acquired capability.
3. The *external conditions* which provide stimulation to the learner. These may be visually present objects, symbols, pictures, sounds, or meaningful verbal communications.

For discrimination learning, these characteristics are described in the following paragraphs.

Performance   A simple response (or response chain) which indicates that the learner can distinguish stimuli which differ along one or more physical dimensions.

Internal Conditions   Individual S-R connections must be recalled in order for the individual to indicate the distinction which has been learned. In some instances, such response connections may be as simple as pointing; or, they may take the form of simple motor chains, such as making a check mark or drawing a circle around a pictured object.

External Conditions   Some of the most general principles of learning (Chapter 1) are applicable here. Contiguity is necessary in that the response must follow the stimulus within a short time span. Reinforcement is of particular importance to discrimination learning, and is made to occur *differentially* for right and wrong responses. A response indicating a correct distinction between "same" or "different" stimuli is followed by a pleasant familiar activity (for example, circling *other* figures of the same sort), whereas a response which is incorrect is not followed by such activity. When reinforcement occurs in this manner, the discrimination will soon be learned. Repetition also plays a particular role. The situation may need to be repeated several times, in order that the correct stimulus difference is selected. Sometimes this may happen in one trial, but often a few repetitions may be necessary in order to permit reinforcement to take its effect. Additional repetitions become necessary when *multiple* discriminations are being learned, as for example when several different object-shapes must be distinguished at one time.

Concrete Concepts

A concept is a capability that makes it possible for an individual to identify a stimulus as a member of a class having some characteristic in common, even though such stimuli may otherwise differ from each other markedly. The basic meaning of concrete concept is that of identifying an *object property* or object attribute (color, shape, etc.). Such concepts are called "concrete" because the human performance they require is one of pointing to an instance of a concrete object.

Examples of object properties are round, square, blue, three, smooth, curved, flat, and so on. One can tell whether a concrete concept has been learned by asking the individual to identify, by "pointing to," two or more numbers belonging to the same object-property class; for example, by pointing to a penny, an automobile tire, and the full moon as round. The operation of pointing may be carried out practically in many different ways; often, it is a matter of choosing, checking, circling, or grasping. Frequently, the operation of pointing is carried out by naming (labeling). Thus, the particular *response* made by the individual is of no consequence, so long as it can be assumed that he knows how to do it.

An important variety of concrete concept is *object position*. This can be conceived as an object property, since it can be identified by "pointing." It is clear, however, that the position of an object must be in relation to that of another object. Examples of object positions are above, below, beside, surrounding, right, left, middle, on, in front of. Obviously, one can ask that such positional characteristics be "pointed to" in some manner or other. Thus, object positions qualify as concrete concepts.

The distinction between a discrimination and a concept is easy to see. A young child may have learned to tell the difference between a triangle and a rectangle drawn on a piece of paper. That is, he may show that he sees these as different objects, by choosing, pointing, or by responding to their names. Such a performance permits only the conclusion that the child can *discriminate* between these particular objects. To test whether he has the concept "triangle," however, one would need to ask him to identify several objects exhibiting this property—objects which otherwise differ widely in their other qualities such as size, color, border thickness, and so on. One must determine, in other words, that the individual is capable of identifying the *class* of object properties, in order to conclude that he has acquired a concrete concept.

The capability of identifying concrete concepts is of fundamental importance for more complex learning. Many investigators have emphasized the importance of "concrete learning" as a prerequisite to "the learning of abstract ideas." Piaget (1950) makes this distinction a key idea in his theory of intellectual development. The acquisition of *concepts by definition* (to be described next) requires that the learner be able to identify the referents of the words used in such definitions. Thus, to acquire the concept *rim* by way of the definition "the edge of a round thing," the learner must have as prerequisites the concrete concepts "edge" and "round." If he is not able to identify these concepts concretely, it will not be possible for him in any true or complete sense to "know the meaning" of *rim*.

Performance   Identifying a class of object properties, including object positions, by "pointing to" two or more members of the class. The "pointing" may be done in any of a number of ways (checking, circling, etc.) equivalent only in the sense that identification occurs.

Internal Conditions   In acquiring a concrete concept, discriminations must be recalled. Thus, an individual who is learning the concept *two* must be able to discriminate a variation in object quality like this: | || from one like this: | ▮ . The variation between o and O must have been previously discriminated from o and ⊖, in order for the concept "o" to be learned.

External Conditions   Instances of the class are presented, varying as widely as possible in their nonrelevant characteristics, and the individual is asked to identify each by pointing or naming. For example, a concept like *two* may be identified by objects as vastly different in other characteristics as two dots on a page, two children, two buildings, two baseballs. Negative instances are often of value as well. It may be that their function is primarily that of stimulating the recall of the necessary discriminations, as when // ("two") is distinguished from /// ("not two").

Defined Concepts

An individual is said to have learned a defined concept when he can demonstrate the "meaning" of some particular class of objects, events, or relations. For example, consider the concept "brother." An individual who has learned such a concept will be able to demonstrate that a brother is a male offspring of his parents. The demonstration may take the form of giving the definition, and this is an adequate demonstration when one assumes he knows the meaning of the words "male," "offspring," and "parents." If such knowledge cannot be assumed, it may be necessary to ask for the demonstration in other terms, perhaps involving pointing to pictures or to people. *Demonstration* of the meaning is emphasized in order to establish a distinction between this kind of mental processing and that involved in the memorized verbal information "A brother is the male offspring of my parents."

A simple example of a defined concept is *sidewalk*, the definition of which may be stated as "a walkway beside a street." Again, the defined concept must be demonstrated, in order for an external observer to know that it has been learned. Such a demonstration by the learner would consist, essentially, of (1) identifying a *walkway* (which might be done in this instance by a "pointing" operation, using a picture); (2) identifying a *street* (again possibly by pointing); and (3) demonstrating *beside* (by placing or drawing the two identified objects, walkway and street, in the correct spatial position).

Why doesn't one just ask the question, what does *sidewalk* mean? Why describe this elaborate procedure? The reason has been mentioned previously

—only by insuring that the individual is capable of operations identifying the *referents* of the words can one be confident that the meaning of a defined concept has been learned. In practice, of course, the procedure of obtaining verbal answers to verbal questions is often used. But such a procedure is always subject to the ambiguity that the learner may be repeating a verbal chain, and that he doesn't know the meaning of the concept after all. It is for this reason that we use the phrase *demonstrate a concept* rather than a simpler phrase like *state a definition* or *define*. We want to imply that the learner has a "real understanding" of a defined concept, rather than the superficial acquaintance indicated by his reeling off a string of words.

Performance Demonstrating the concept by identifying instances of concepts which are components of the definition, and showing an instance of their relation to one another.

Internal Conditions In order to acquire a concept by definition, the learner must recall all of the component concepts included in the definition, including the concepts which represent relations among them. (In the example of the sidewalk, *beside* is the relational concept.)

External Conditions A defined concept may be learned by having the learner watch a demonstration. Most frequently, though, the concept is "demonstrated" by means of a verbally stated definition. Thus, the concept *scum* may be communicated by the statement "a filmy covering floating on a liquid." Provided the internal conditions are met, such a statement is sufficient to induce learning of the concept. What must be recalled are the concepts "filmy," "covering," "liquid," and "floating on"; not just the words.

Rules

A rule has been learned when it is possible to say with confidence that the learner's performance has a kind of "regularity" over a variety of specific situations. In other words, the learner shows that he is able to respond with a *class* of relationships among *classes* of objects and events. When a learner shows that he can sort cards marked X into a bin marked A, and cards marked Y into a bin marked B, this is insufficient evidence that his behavior is "rule-governed." (He may simply be exhibiting learning of the concrete concepts X and Y.) But suppose he has learned to put each X card into any bin two positions away from his last choice, and each Y card one position away from his last choice. In that case, he has learned a rule. He is responding to classes of objects (X and Y cards) with classes of relationships (one position away, two positions away). His behavior cannot be described in terms of a *particular* relation between the stimulus (the card) and his sorting response to a bin.

There are many common examples of rule-governed behavior. In fact, most behavior of human beings falls into this category. When a child orally makes a sentence using a given word such as *boy*, as in "The boy rode a bicycle," he is using a number of rules. For example, he begins the sentence with "The," not with "boy," employing a rule for use of the definite article. He follows the subject of the sentence with a predicate, placing a verb next in order—that is, he says "The boy rode," and not "Rode the boy." The verb in turn is followed by the object "bicycle," which, according to one rule is placed in a particular order, and according to another is preceded (in this case) by the indefinite article "a." Finally, he completed the sentence by bringing it to a close, which in written form involves a rule for the use of a period. If the child has acquired each of these rules, he will be able to construct *any* sentence of the same structure, with *any* given word as its subject.

Obviously, possessing the capability called a *rule* does not mean being able to state it verbally. The child performs the behavior of constructing sentences long before he has heard of grammatical rules. The observer of learning behavior may have to "state the rule" being learned in order to explain what he is talking about. The learner, however, may be quite unable to state the rule, even though his performance indicates that he "knows" it.

Now that we have indicated what a rule is, we can admit that a defined concept, as previously described, is actually not formally different from a rule, and is learned in much the same way. In other words, a defined concept is a particular category or rule whose purpose is to classify objects and events; it is a *classifying rule*. Rules, however, include many other categories besides classifying. They deal with such relationships as equal to, similar to, greater than, less than, before, after, and many, many others.

Performance   Demonstrating the rule by showing one or more instances of the relation of the component concepts to one another. (The rule for pronunciation of vowels in words with consonants followed by final "e" would be exhibited by the performance of correct pronunciation of words such as *made, code, bite, node*, etc.)

Internal Conditions   In learning a rule, the learner must recall each of the component concepts of the rule, including the concepts that represent relations. It is assumed that these concepts have been previously learned, and can be recalled. (In the example given, the learner must be able to recall "sounds of long vowels," "consonants," and the relation "followed by e at end.")

External Conditions   Usually, the external conditions for learning rules involve the use of verbal communications. The rule may be stated, although not necessarily in a formally correct manner. The purpose of such verbal communication is to *cue* the arrangement of concepts in a correct order by the learner. It does not have the purpose of teaching the learner a formal proposition which represents the rule. Thus, a teacher may say, "Notice that the letter a has a long sound when followed by a consonant, in a word that ends in e. This is true in words that you know like *made, pale, fate*. When the word does not end in e, the letter *a* has a short sound, as in *mad, pal, fat*. Now tell me how to pronounce these words which you may not have seen before: *dade, pate, kale*."

The basic reasons for the verbal communication are two: (1) to remind the learner of component concepts to be recalled (such as "long vowel sounds," "consonants"); and (2) to get the learner to arrange component concepts in the proper order, that is, "consonant followed by final e," not "vowel followed by final consonant," nor "vowel followed by final e," nor "consonant followed by final vowel," nor any other incorrect ordering.

It is evident that the verbal communication used in rule learning may be more or less lengthy. Accordingly, it may leave up to the learner more or less of the task of actually constructing the rule. Another way to say this is that the external conditions for instruction in a rule may provide different amounts of *learning guidance*. When minimal amounts of learning guidance are provided, instruction is said to emphasize *discovery* on the part of the learner (Bruner, 1961; Shulman and Keislar, 1966). Conversely, discovery is de-emphasized when the amount of learning guidance provided is large, as tends to be true in more detailed verbal communications. Studies of "discovery learning" suggest that small amounts of learning guidance have advantages for retention and transfer of the rules which are learned (cf. Worthen, 1968). Often, techniques of bringing about learning by discovery incorporate the use of pointed questioning of the learner. These questions lead him to discover the proper ordering of component concepts by himself.

Higher-Order Rules—Problem Solving

Sometimes, the rules which human beings learn are complex combinations of simpler rules. Moreover, it is often the case that these more complex, or "higher-order" rules are *invented* for the purpose of solving a practical problem or class of problems. The capability of problem solving is, naturally, a major aim of the educational process—most educators agree that the school should give priority to teaching the student "how to think clearly." When a student works out the solution to a problem which represents real events, he is engaging in the behavior of thinking. There are, of course, many kinds of problems, and an even greater number of possible solutions to them. In attaining a workable solution to a problem, the student also achieves a new capability. He learns something which can be generalized to other problems having similar formal characteristics. This means he has acquired a new rule, or perhaps a new set of rules.

Suppose that a small car has been parked near a low brick fence, and is discovered to have a flat tire on one of its front wheels. No jack is available, but there is a ten-foot two-by-four, and a piece of sturdy rope. Can the front of the car be raised? In this situation, a possible solution might be found by using the two-by-four as a lever, the wall as a fulcrum, and the rope to secure the end of the lever when the car is in a raised position. This solution is invented to meet a particular problem situation. It is evident that the solution represents a "putting together" of certain rules which may not have been previously applied to similar situations in the past history of the individual who is solving the problem. One rule pertains to the application of force on an end of the car to achieve a lifting of that end. Another rule pertains to the use of the wall as a fulcrum on which an estimated weight will bear. And still another, of course, is the rule regarding use of the two-by-four as a lever. All of these rules, in order to be used in an act of problem solving, must be recalled by the individual, which means they must have been previously learned. (Note once again that the rules we refer to cannot necessarily be verbalized by the problem solver; nor have they necessarily been learned in a physics course.) These previously acquired rules are then brought together by the individual to achieve the solution to his problem. And when he has solved it, he has learned a new rule, more complex than those he has used in combination. The newly learned rule will be stored in his memory and used again to solve other problems.

The invention of a complex rule can be illustrated with a problem in mathematics. Suppose a student has learned to add monomials such as $2X$ and $5X$, $3X^2$ and $4X^2$, $2X^3$ and $6X^3$. Now he is shown a set of polynomials, such as:

$$2X + 3X^2 + 1$$
$$2 + 3X + 4X^2.$$

The student is asked, "What do you suppose is the sum of these two expressions?" With this question, he is being asked to solve a new problem, which (we assume) he has not previously encountered. Possibly, he may make some false starts, which could be corrected. The chances are, however, that he has already learned the subordinate rules which will permit him to think out the solution to this problem. For example, he probably has acquired the rule that a variable a added to the variable a^2 results in the sum $a + a^2$. He also has the rule for adding monomials, such as $2a^2 + 3a^2 = 5a^2$. It is probably not a difficult problem for him, therefore, to devise the complex rule: Add variables with the same exponents; express the sum as a set of terms connected by the $+$ sign. Again in this example, the problem solver has "combined" simpler rules, which he recalls, into a more complex rule which is the solution to the problem.

The essential condition that makes this sort of learning a problem-solving event is the *absence* of any learning guidance, whether in the form of a verbal communication or in some other form. The solution has been "discovered," or invented. The learning guidance is provided by the problem-solver himself, not by a teacher or other external source. One may guess that he is probably bringing to bear some problem-solving *strategies* which he may have learned in quite different situations. But in any case, he has recalled relevant rules and combined them to form a new "higher-order" rule.

Performance Inventing and using a complex rule to achieve the solution of a problem which is novel to the individual. When the higher-order rule has been acquired, it should also be possible for the learner to demonstrate its use in other physically different, but formally similar, situations. In other words, the new complex rule which has been acquired exhibits transfer of learning.

Internal Conditions In solving a problem, the learner must recall relevant subordinate rules and also relevant information. It is assumed that these capabilities have been previously learned.

External Conditions The learner is confronted with an actual, or a represented, problem situation which he has not previously encountered. Cues in the form of verbal communications are at a minimum, or may be absent entirely. The learner engages in "discovery learning"; he invents a solution.

COGNITIVE STRATEGIES

A very special kind of intellectual skill, which is in addition a type of particular importance in problem solving, is called a *cognitive strategy*. This variety of capability is given a different name because, although it may be categorized as an intellectual skill, it has some highly distinctive characteristics (cf. Gagné, 1970, pp. 229–233). Most important of these is that a cognitive strategy is an *internally organized* skill which governs the learner's own behavior. Several of Bruner's writings (1966, 1971) describe the operation and the importance of cognitive strategies.

The term cognitive strategies applies rather generally to various skills that are used by the learner to *manage* the processes of attending, learning, remembering, and thinking. In this chapter, however, we intend to deal only with the last-mentioned variety, those that are called into play when the learner defines and thinks out the solution to a highly novel problem. It should also be pointed out that one can relate cognitive strategies of thinking to the theory of Piaget (1950) concerning intellectual development (cf. Flavell, 1963). Piaget's basic view is that the intellect of the child develops in identifiable stages, each of which represents the capability of using an increasingly complex form of logical operations. Thus, to Piaget, the capabilities which are here called cognitive strategies set limits to the kinds of problem solving children of various ages can successfully perform.

Within the framework of Piaget's theory, one can readily accommodate the learning of more specific intellectual skills such as are described in previous sections. One can alternatively espouse a different theory, which is to the effect that cognitive strategies, rather than simply maturing as the child grows, develop *out of* these more specifically learned intellectual skills by a process of generalization (Gagné, 1970, pp. 289–301). The latter theoretical view is what leads us here to treat cognitive strategies as the crowning accomplishment of a great deal of specific learning, and accordingly to deal with them as a special variety of intellectual skill.

Learning Cognitive Strategies

A cognitive strategy is an internally organized skill that selects and guides the internal processes involved in defining and solving novel problems. In other words, it is a skill by means of which the learner manages his own thinking behavior. Notice that it is the *object* of the skill which differentiates cognitive strategies from other intellectual skills. The latter are oriented toward environmental objects and events, such as sentences, graphs, or mathematical equations. In contrast, cognitive strategies have as their objects the *learner's own thought processes*. Undoubtedly, the efficacy of an individual's cognitive strategies exerts a crucial effect upon the quality of his thought. They may determine, for example, how creatively he thinks, how fluently he thinks, and how critically he thinks.

Statements of educational goals often give highest priority to cognitive strategies. Many statements of goals for school learning give a prominent place to "teaching students how to think." While it would be difficult to find disagreement with the importance of such a goal, it seems wise to temper one's enthusiasm for it with a couple of facts pertaining to the feasibility of reaching it. First, one should realize that genetic factors, not amenable to the influence of education, are likely to play at least a large part in the determination of creative thought (cf. Tyler, 1965; Ausubel, 1968, Chapter 16). In other words, there are bound to be enormous differences among people in intellectual capacity, which can never be completely overcome by environmental influences such as education. Second, the internally organized nature of cognitive strategies means that the conditions of instruction can have only an indirect effect upon their acquisition and improvement. In the case of other types of intellectual skills, one can plan a sequence of learning events external to the learner which will insure the learning of those skills. But cognitive strategies require a more indirect control; one has to organize external events so as to increase the probability of certain internal events; and these in turn determine the learning of the cognitive strategy. Accordingly, the design of instruction for cognitive strategies has to be done in terms of "favorable conditions," and cannot be accomplished by specifying the "sufficient conditions." Generally, the favorable conditions are those which *provide opportunities for development and use* of cognitive strategies. In other words, in order to "learn to think," the student needs to be given opportunities to think.

Performance   Originating novel solutions to problem situations, in which neither the class of solution nor the specific manner of solution are specified for the learner.

Internal Conditions   The learner needs to have available a variety of cognitive strategies of problem solution from which he can make a selection. Obviously, too, if he is to arrive at a specific solution following such a selection, the intellectual skills involved in this solution must be available.

External Conditions   Novel problems need to be presented for which the class of solution required is not specified. If a learner is asked "What kinds of things would a man be able to do if he had two thumbs on each hand?" it is evident that he must search his repertoire of cognitive strategies to attack the problem. Will he first think of the most unusual things two thumbs could do? Or will he carefully categorize the kinds of things thumbs can perform? Ultimately, he must probably use both these approaches. The particular way he attacks the problem is what is meant by his cognitive strategy. Externally, what can be done is to insure that the problem presented is novel, and therefore that it represents a "favorable condition" for thought.

VARIETIES OF INTELLECTUAL SKILLS
IN SCHOOL SUBJECTS

The range of human capabilities called intellectual skills includes the varieties of discriminations, concrete concepts, defined concepts, rules, and the higher-order rules often acquired in problem solving. An additional category of internally organized skills is cognitive strategies, which govern the learner's behavior in learning and thinking, and thus determine its quality and efficiency. These varieties of learning are distinguishable (a) by the class of *performance* they make possible; (b) by the internal and external *conditions* necessary for their occurrence; and (c) by the *complexity* of the internal process which they establish in the individual's memory.

Any school subject may at one time or another involve any of these types of learned capabilities. However, the frequency with which they are encountered in various school subjects varies widely. Examples of discriminations can be found in such elementary subjects as printing letters and reading music. In contrast, there are few examples of this type, and many more of defined concepts, in a course in history. However, quite a few examples of discriminations also occur in the beginning study of a foreign language, which may be undertaken in the ninth grade. In the same grade, the writing of compositions very frequently involves defined concepts and rules, but seems not to require the learning of discriminations or concrete concepts. In this case, the necessary learnings of these varieties have been accomplished years ago.

Any school subject *can* be analyzed to reveal the relevance of *all* of these kinds of learning. But this is not always a practical course of action, because the subject as presented in a particular grade may begin with the assumption that simpler kinds of learning have already been accomplished. Thus, discrimination of ·· from · is certainly relevant to the study of algebra. But one doesn't begin the study of algebra with the learning of discriminations, because it is possible to assume these discriminations have been previously learned. In science, however, certain discriminations, such as those involved in using a microscope or spectrophotometer, may have to be newly acquired. Such simple skills must be learned before the student can progress to the concepts, rules, and problem solving which may represent the major aims of the course.

It should be evident that learning of the various types of capability is not related to age of the learner in any one-to-one sense. The human individual does not learn all of his motor chains at age four, all of his discriminations at age five, and so on. Reasonable tasks of rule-learning and problem solving are quite appropriate for four- and five-year-old children. Any learning tasks are "reasonable" ones when the particular skills that are prerequisite to them have been previously learned. It is true that, in the first grade, learning of discriminations is likely to occur with greater frequency than is the case in the sixth grade. In the tenth grade, one expects the learning of defined concepts and rules to occur with greater frequency than it does in the fourth grade. The general principle is that the kind of learning that may be required can be predicted, not from age, but only from the nature of the performance being sought as the objective of learning.

Is there, then, a *structure* of intellectual skills which represents the "path of greatest learning efficiency" for every subject in the curriculum? In theory, there is. Do we know what this structure is? Only vaguely, as yet. After all, teachers, curriculum specialists, and textbook writers *try* to represent structure in their lesson and curriculum plans, and have been trying for many years. Nevertheless, their efforts must on the whole be characterized as partial and inadequate. The purpose of this book is to describe a systematic method of approaching the problem, as free of culs-de-sac as possible. Such a method will also be subject to empirical verification, and to revision and refinement. The application of the method to be described can lead to descriptions of the "learning structure" of any subject taught in the school. This structure may be represented as a kind of *map* of the terrain to be covered in progressing from one point in human development to any other point.

The mapping of learning structures does not lead to "routinization" or "mechanization" of the process of learning. A map indicates starting points, destinations, and alternative routes in between; it does not tell how to make the journey. Making the "learning journey" requires a different set of internal events for each and every individual. In a fundamental sense, there are as many learning "styles" as there are individuals. Describing the learning structures for a progression of objectives within any school subject does not lead to prescribing how the individual student must learn. On the contrary, learning structures are simply descriptions of the accepted goals, or *outcomes* of learning, together with subordinate stops along the way.

SUMMARY

Starting with the need to identify goals as the desired outcomes of the educational system, Chapter 2 proposed that in attempting to design specific courses, topics, and lessons there is a need to classify performance objectives into broad categories: intellectual skills, cognitive strategies, verbal information, motor skills, and attitudes. Doing so, it was shown, facilitates (a) review of the adequacy of the objectives; (b) determination of the sequencing of instruction; and (c) planning for the conditions of learning needed for successful instruction.

The present chapter has begun the account of the *nature* of the performance capabilities implied by each of the five categories of learned capabilities, beginning with intellectual skills and cognitive strategies. For each of these two domains, this chapter has (a) presented examples of learned performances in terms of different school subjects; (b) identified the kinds of internal conditions of learning needed to reach the new capability; and (c) identified the external conditions affecting its learning.

For intellectual skills, several subcategories were identified: discriminations, concrete and defined concepts, rules, and the higher-order rules often learned by problem solving. Each represents a different class of performance, and each is supported by different sets of internal and external conditions of learning. Cognitive strategies were not broken down into subcategories, as was the case for intellectual skills. Research may in the future suggest that this can and should be done.

The next chapter gives a corresponding kind of treatment to the remaining kinds of learned capabilities: information, attitudes, and motor skills. The purpose of Chapters 3 and 4 is to move one more step toward specification of an orderly series of steps to be used in the actual design of instruction for a lesson, a unit, a course, or an entire instructional system. Specifically, these chapters identify the appropriate internal and external conditions of learning for each kind of learned capability. They lead to suggestions of how to proceed with two aspects of instructional design: (a) how to take account of the *prior* learning that is assumed to be necessary for the learner before he can undertake the new learning to be attempted next; and (b) how to plan for the *new* learning in terms of the appropriate *external conditions* needed for the attainment of each type of learning outcome. In later chapters, these conditions will be translated into guidelines for instructional planning.

REFERENCES

Ausubel, D. P. *Educational Psychology: A Cognitive View.* New York: Holt, Rinehart and Winston, 1968.

Bruner, J. S. The art of discovery. *Harvard Educational Review*, 1961, *31*, 21–32.

Bruner, J. S. *Toward a Theory of Instruction.* Cambridge, Mass.: Harvard University Press, 1966.

Bruner, J. S. *The Relevance of Education.* New York: Norton, 1971.

Flavell, J. H. *The Developmental Psychology of Jean Piaget.* Princeton, N.J.: Van Nostrand, 1963.

Gagné, R. M. Problem solving. In A. W. Melton (Ed.), *Categories of Human Learning.* New York: Academic Press, 1964.

Gagné, R. M. *The Conditions of Learning*, 2d Ed. New York: Holt, Rinehart and Winston, 1970.

Piaget, J. *The Psychology of Intelligence.* New York: Harcourt Brace Jovanovich, 1950.

Shulman, L. S., and Keislar, E. R. *Learning by Discovery: A Critical Appraisal.* Chicago: Rand-McNally, 1966.

Tyler, L. E. *The Psychology of Human Differences*, 3d Ed. New York: Appleton-Century-Crofts, 1965.

Worthen, B. R. Discovery and expository task presentation in elementary mathematics. *Journal of Educational Psychology, Monograph Supplement*, 1968, *59*, No. 1, Part 2.

VARIETIES OF LEARNING:
Information, Attitudes, Motor Skills

In this chapter, we need to continue our description of the varieties of human capabilities which may be learned. The courses and lessons that are designed for instruction are of course not always aimed at developing intellectual skills or cognitive strategies as discussed in the previous chapter. Furthermore, a topic or course of study, and even an individual lesson, may have more than one class of objective as a learning outcome. Instruction is typically designed to encompass several objectives in any given unit of instruction, and to achieve a suitable balance among them.

We shall be describing here the conditions applicable to the learning of three additional classes of learning outcomes: the learning of *information*, the establishment or changing of *attitudes*, and the acquisition of *motor skills.* As in the previous chapter, we need to consider three aspects of the learning situation, for each of these varieties:

1. The *performance* to be acquired as a result of learning
2. The *internal conditions* that need to be present for learning to occur
3. The *external conditions* which are established to bring essential stimulation to bear upon the learner.

INFORMATION AND KNOWLEDGE

A great deal of information is learned and stored in memory as a result of instruction in the school. Of course, an enormous amount is acquired outside of school as well, from the reading of books, magazines, newspapers, and by way of radio and television programs. From this very fact, it is apparent that special means of "instruction" do not have to be provided in order for a large amount of learning to occur. The communications provided by the various media are able to bring about learning in many people, provided of course that those who hear or see or read these communications possess the basic intellectual skills for interpreting them.

In school learning, however, there are many circumstances in which one desires greater certainty of learning than can ordinarily be expected from various extra-school communications. The literate individual may gain much information from a radio lecture on modern developments in chemistry. The amount of information learned by this means may vary greatly among different individuals, depending on their interests and previous experience. A formally planned course in chemistry, in contrast, may have the aim of teaching all students certain information deemed essential for further study of the subject, such as the names of elements, the states exhibited by compounds, and so on. Similarly, a course in American Government may have the aim of teaching all students the content of the articles of the United States Constitution. Planned instruction in school subjects is undertaken because of this need for certainty of learning particular bodies of information.

Two primary reasons exist for desiring a high degree of certainty in the learning of information. The first of these reasons has already been mentioned: Particular information may be needed in order for a learner to continue his learning of a topic or subject. Of course, some of the detailed information he needs may be looked up in a book or other source. A great deal of it, however, may need to be recalled and used again and again in pursuing study within a subject. Thus there is typically a body of information which is "basic" in the sense that future learning will be more efficiently conducted if it is acquired and retained.

A second reason for learning information is that much of its content may be continually useful to the individual throughout his life. Everyone needs to know the names of letters, numerals, common objects, and a host of facts about himself and his environment in order to receive and give communications. A great deal of such factual information is acquired informally without any particular plan being made for it. In addition, an individual may acquire unusual quantities of factual information in one or more areas of particular interest to him, as when he learns a mass of facts about flowers, or automobiles, or the game of baseball. The problem faced in designing school curricula is one of distinguishing between information in any area that is more or less essential. Some may be used by the individual for communication purposes throughout his lifetime. Other information may be interesting to him as a person, but not essential. The former category is one for which the standard of certainty of learning becomes the concern of formal education. As for that information a person wishes to learn because of his particular interests or desire for further learning, there would appear to be no reason to set limits upon it.

When information is organized into bodies of meaningfully interconnected facts and generalizations, it is usually referred to as knowledge. Obviously, the information possessed by an individual within his own particular field of work or study is usually organized as a "body of knowledge." Thus we expect a chemist, for example, to have learned and stored a specialized body of knowledge about chemistry; and similarly, we expect a cabinetmaker to possess a body of knowledge about woods and joints and tools. Besides these masses of specialized knowledge, one must face the question of whether there is a value to acquiring knowledge that may be called *general*. It may be noted that most human societies, if not all, have answered this question affirmatively. In one way or another, means have been found to pass on the knowledge accumulated by the society from one generation to the next. Information about the origins of the society, tribe, or nation, its development through time, its goals and values, its place in the world, is usually considered a body of knowledge desirable to include in the education of each individual.

Within our own society, there was in earlier years a body of general knowledge, fairly well agreed upon, that was considered to be desirable for the "educated class" (those who went to college) to learn. It was composed of historical information about Western culture extending back to the early Greek civilization, along with related information from literature and the arts. Over a period of years, as mass education has progressively replaced class education, there has been an accompanying reduction in the amount of general cultural knowledge considered desirable for all students to learn. In recent years, there has been a growing emphasis upon an informal type of instruction involving student choices of what to learn. This development would seem to make it virtually impossible to identify a consistent body of knowledge that may be said to constitute general education. At most, such common cultural knowledge appears to be increasingly confined to the few courses in American history and government required by law in many states. The desirability of this trend away from the learning of general cultural information appears open to serious question from the standpoint of societal stability.

What function does general knowledge of the cultural sort serve in the life of the individual? Evidently, such knowledge serves the purpose of communication, particularly in those aspects of life pertaining to citizenship. Knowing the facts about his community, his state, and his nation, as well as the responsibilities he owes to them and the services they provide, enables the individual to engage in the communications necessary for the citizen's role. Cultural and historical knowledge may also contribute to the achievement and maintenance of the individual's "identity," or sense of himself—he is aware of his own origins in relation to those of the society of which he is a member.

A much more critical function of general knowledge can be conceived and speculated about, although evidence concerning it is incomplete. This is the notion that knowledge is the *vehicle* for thought and problem solving. We have seen in the previous chapter that thinking in the sense of problem solving requires certain prerequisite intellectual skills, as well as cognitive strategies. These are the tools the individual possesses that enable him to think clearly and precisely. How does he think "broadly"? How can a scientist, say, think about the social problem of the isolation of aged people? Or how can a poet capture in words the essential conflict of youthful rebellion and alienation? It is not unlikely that problem solution in both instances depends upon the possession by these individuals of bodies of knowledge which are not special to their fields, but which are shared by many other people. The thinking that takes place is "carried" by the associations, metaphors, and analogies of language within these bodies of knowledge. The importance of a "knowledge background" for creative thought has been discussed by many writers, and in recent years by Polanyi (1958).

In summary, it is evident that a number of important reasons can be identified for the learning of information, whether this is conceived as facts, generalizations, or as organized bodies of meaningful knowledge. Factual information is needed in learning the increasingly complex intellectual skills of a subject or discipline. Such information may in part be looked up, but is often more conveniently stored in memory. Certain types and categories of factual information must be learned because it is necessary for communication pertaining to the affairs of everyday living. Information is often learned and remembered as organized bodies of knowledge. Specialized knowledge of this sort may be accumulated by the individual learner within a field of study or work he is pursuing. General knowledge, particularly of the sort which reflects the cultural heritage, is often considered desirable or even essential in making possible the communications necessary for functioning as a citizen of a community or nation. In addition, however, it seems likely that such bodies of general knowledge become the carriers of thought for the human being engaged in reflective thinking and problem solving.

THE LEARNING OF INFORMATION

Information may be presented to the learner in various ways. It may be delivered to his ears in the form of oral communications, or to his eyes, mainly in the form of printed words, with or without accompanying pictures. There are many interesting questions for research relating to the effectiveness of communication media (Bretz, 1971), and some of the implications these have for instructional design will be discussed in the next chapter. At this point, however, we wish to attend to a different set of dimensions, which cut across those of the communication media. Information that is presented for learning may vary in amount and in the way it is organized. Some variations along these dimensions appear to be more important for the design of school instruction than are others. From this point of view, it seems desirable to distinguish three kinds of learning situations. The first concerns the learning of *labels*, or *names*. A second pertains to the learning of isolated or *single facts*, which may or may not be parts of larger meaningful communications. The third kind of situation to be discussed is the learning of *organized information*, or knowledge.

Learning Labels

To learn a label simply means to acquire the capabliity of making a consistent verbal response to an object or object class in such a way that it is "named." The verbal response itself may be of almost any variety, "X-1," "petunia," "pocket dictionary," or "spectrophotometer." Information in this form is simply a short *verbal chain*, the characteristics of which were briefly described in the previous chapter. Reference to the substantial body of research on the learning of verbal "paired-associates" may be found in many texts (e.g., Deese & Hulse, 1967; Jung, 1968).

Learning the name of an object in the sense of a label is quite distinct from learning the *meaning* of that name. The latter phrase implies the acquisition of a *concept*, which has also been described previously. Teachers are well acquainted with the distinction between "knowing the name of something" versus "knowing what the name means." The performance of knowing a label is exhibited by the student when he can simply supply the name of a specific object. To know that object as a concept (that is, know its meaning) he must be able to identify examples and nonexamples that serve to define and delimit the class.

In practice, the learning of a name for a concept is often carried out at the same time the concept is learned, or just prior to that time. Although easy to accomplish for one or two objects at a time, the task of name-learning increases rapidly in difficulty when six different names for six objects must be learned at once, or ten names, or twelve. Such a situation arises in school learning when children are asked to acquire the names of a set of trees, or a set of leaves, or a set of some other natural objects. Children engaged in such tasks may properly be said to be "memorizing" the names, but there is scarcely a harm in that, and children often enjoy doing it. In any case, label-learning is a highly useful activity, which establishes the basis for communication between the learner and the teacher, or between the learner and a text.

Learning Facts

A fact is a verbal statement which expresses a relation between two or more named objects or events. An example is, "That book has a blue cover." In normal communication, the relation expressed by the fact is assumed to exist in the natural world. Thus, the words which make up the fact have *referents* in the environment of the learner. The words refer to these objects and to the relation between them. In the example given, the objects are "book" and "blue cover" and the relation is "has." It is of some importance to emphasize that a fact, as employed here, is defined as the *verbal statement* and not the referent or referents to which it refers. (Alternative meanings of a common word like "fact" may readily be found in other contexts.)

Students learn a host of facts in connection with their studies in school. Some of these are isolated in the sense of being unrelated to other facts or bodies of information. Others form a part of a connected set, related to each other in various ways. For example, children may learn the fact that "the town siren is sounded at noontime," and this may be a fairly isolated fact which is well remembered, even though not directly related to other information. Isolated facts may be learned and remembered for no apparent reason; in studying history, a student may learn and remember that Charles G. Dawes served as vice president in the administration of Calvin Coolidge, and at the same time learn the names of other vice presidents. More frequently, though, a specific learned fact is related to others in a total set, or to a larger body of information. For example, a student may learn a number of facts about Mexico, which are related to each other in the sense that they pertain to aspects of Mexico's geography, or its economy, or its culture. Such facts may also be related to a larger body of information including facts about the culture, economy, and geography of other countries, including the student's native country.

Whether isolated or connected with a larger set, learned facts are of obvious value to the student, for two major reasons. The first is that they may be essential to his everyday living. Examples are the fact that many stores and banks are closed on Sunday, or the fact that molasses is sticky, or the fact that his birthday is the tenth of February. The second reason for the importance of learned facts, even more obvious to the student, is that they are used by him in further learning. In order to learn to find the circumference of a circle, for example, he needs to know the value of pi. In order to complete a chemical equation, he may need to know the valence of the element sodium.

With regard to the function of facts as elements in the learning of skills or additional information, it is evident that such facts *can* be looked up in convenient reference books or tables, at the time this further learning is about to take place. There are many instances in which "looking up" may be a proper and desirable procedure. The alternative is for the student to learn the facts, and store them in his memory, so that he may then retrieve them whenever he needs them. This alternative is often chosen as a matter of convenience and efficiency. Facts that are likely to be used again and again might as well be stored in memory—the student would likely find the constant looking-up a nuisance. The designer of instruction, however, has the obligation of deciding which of a great many facts in a given course are (1) of such infrequent usage that they had better be looked up; (2) of such relatively frequent reference that learning them would be an efficient strategy; or (3) of such fundamental importance that they ought to be remembered for a lifetime.

Performance The performance that indicates a fact has been learned consists in stating a relation between two or more named objects or events. The statement may be made either orally or in writing.

Internal Conditions For acquisition and storage, an organized context of information needs to be recalled, to which the newly acquired fact must be related. For example, to learn and remember that Mount Whitney is the highest peak in the continental United States, a larger meaningful context of information (which may differ for each individual learner) needs to be recalled, such as classification of mountain peaks and ranges or a set of categories of mountains in the United States. A visual image of the range of mountains that includes Mount Whitney may also be an integral component of this information (cf. Rohwer, 1970). The new fact is associated by the learner with this larger information context.

External Conditions   Externally, a verbal communication, picture, or other cue is presented for the purpose of stimulating the recall of the larger body of meaningful information. The new fact is then presented, usually by means of a verbal statement. The external communication may also suggest the association to be acquired, as in conveying the idea that Mount Whitney "sticks up highest" in the Sierra Nevada range. Time needs to be allowed for the rehearsal of the new fact or repetition of it in the form of a spaced review.

Learning Bodies of Knowledge

Larger bodies of interconnected facts, such as those pertaining to periods of history or to categories of art, science, or literature, may also be learned and remembered. Essentially the same conditions apply to such learning as to that of single facts. Larger bodies of knowledge are organized from smaller units so that they form meaningful wholes. A new factual unit is apparently learned by being related to or incorporated into another set of factual information, which then becomes stored in memory in a newly combined form.

The key to remembering bodies of information appears to be one of having them *organized* in such a way that they can be readily retrieved (Ausubel, 1968; Mandler, 1967). The periodic table of chemical elements, for example, besides having a theoretical rationale, also helps students of chemistry to remember the names and properties of a large number of elements. Similarly, students of American history may have acquired a framework of historical "periods" into which many individual facts can be fitted for learning and remembering. The more highly organized is this previously acquired information, the easier it is for a student to acquire and retain any given new fact which can be related to this organized structure.

Repetition has long been known to have a marked effect on the remembering of information, and this is true whether one is dealing with isolated facts or with larger bodies of information. The effective employment of repetition, however, is in providing *spaced* occasions for the learner to *recall* the information he has learned. The processes put into effect when information is retrieved from memory are apparently the most important factors in the remembering of such information.

LEARNING ATTITUDES

It would be difficult to overemphasize the importance of attitudes in school learning. In the first place, as is so evident to the teacher, the student's attitudes toward attending school, toward cooperating with his teacher and his classmates, toward giving attention to the communications presented to him, and toward the act of learning itself, are all of great significance in determining how readily he learns.

A second large class of attitudes are those that the school aims to establish or change as a result of school learning. Attitudes of tolerance and civility towards other individuals are often mentioned as goals of education in the schools. Positive attitudes towards the seeking and learning of new skills and knowledge are usually stated as educational goals of far-reaching importance for the individual. More specific likings for the various subjects of the school curriculum, such as science, or literature, or music, are often conceived as objectives of high value within each subject area. And finally, there are the attitudes of broad generality, usually called *values*, to which schools may be expected to contribute and to influence. These are attitudes pertaining to such social behaviors as are implied by the words fairness, honesty, charitableness, and a number of others.

Regardless of the great variety exhibited by the content of these types of attitudes, one must expect that they all resemble each other in their formal properties. That is to say, whatever the particular content of an attitude, it functions to affect "approaching" or "avoiding." In so doing, an attitude influences a large set of specific behaviors of the individual. It is reasonable to suppose, then, that there are some general principles of learning that apply to the acquisition and changing of attitudes.

Definition of Attitude

Attitudes are complex states of the human organism which affect his behavior towards people, things, and events. Many investigators have studied, and emphasized in their writings, the conception of an attitude as a system of beliefs (Fishbein, 1965), or as a state arising from a conflict or disparity in beliefs (Festinger, 1957). These views serve to point out the *cognitive* aspects of attitudes. Other writers deal with their *affective* components, the feelings they give rise to or which accompany them, as in liking and disliking. Learning outcomes in the "affective domain" are described by Krathwohl, Bloom & Masia (1964).

For a number of reasons, including practical ones, it seems desirable in the present context to give emphasis to the aspect of attitudes relating to *action*. Acknowledging that an attitude may arise from some complex of beliefs, and that it may be accompanied and invigorated by emotion, the important question would appear to be, what action does it support? The general answer to this question is that an attitude influences *a choice of action* on the part of the individual. A definition of attitude, then, is *an internal state which affects an individual's choice of action toward some object, person, or event.*

Portions of this definition require some comments. An attitude is an *internal state*, inferred from observations (or often, from reports) of the individual's behavior; it is not the behavior itself. If one observes an individual depositing a gum wrapper in a waste basket, he cannot infer from that single instance alone that the individual has a positive attitude towards disposing of personal trash, or a negative attitude towards pollution, and certainly not his attitude towards gum wrappers. A number of instances of behavior of this general class, however, may occur in a number of different situations. Such instances make possible the inference that this person has a positive attitude toward the disposal of personal trash, or a negative attitude toward littering. The inference is that some internal state affects a whole class of specific instances, in each of which the individual is making a *choice*.

The choice the individual makes and which is inferred to be affected by the attitude is of a *personal action*. Thus he may choose to throw away a gum wrapper or to hold it until a trash basket is handy. He may choose to vote for a presidential candidate or to vote against him—the choice indicates his attitude. A student may choose to speak in a friendly manner to a classmate of another race or not to speak to him—again, an indicator which may (along with other instances) reveal his attitude. In following this definition, one does not ask the question, what is this person's attitude toward black Americans, because that is altogether too general a question to be answered sensibly. Instead, one asks, what is this person's attitude toward *working with* black people, or *living near* black people or *sitting beside* a black person? It is the choice of a personal action in each case that is affected by an attitude. In connection with school learning, one may be interested in a student's attitude toward *reading* books, toward *doing* scientific experiments, toward *writing* stories, or toward *constructing* an art object.

This definition implies that attitudes should be measured in terms of the choices of personal action taken by the individual. In some instances, such measurement can be done by observation over a period of time. For example, a teacher may record her observations of an elementary pupil over a weekly period, recording the number of times he helps his classmates as opposed to interfering with their activities. (cf. Mager, 1968). A proportion of this sort, recorded over several such periods, can serve well as a measure of "attitude toward helping others." Of course, such direct indicators of choice cannot always be obtained. The teacher, for example, would be hard pressed to obtain behavioral measures of "attitude towards listening to classical music," or "attitude towards reading novels," because many of these choices are made outside of the school environment. Attitude measures are therefore frequently based upon "self-reports" of choices in situations described in questionnaires. Typical questions, for example, may ask the student to check the probability of his choice on a ten-point scale, when asked a variety of questions such as: "When choosing a book from the public library to read on a summer afternoon, how likely are you to pick a novel about adventure on the seas?" This method of attitude measurement, emphasizing choices of action, has been described in the work of Triandis (1964).

Attitude Learning

The learning of attitudes and the means of bringing about changes in attitudes are rather complex matters, concerning which much is yet to be discovered. Certainly the methods of instruction to be employed in establishing desired attitudes differ considerably from those applicable to the learning of intellectual skills and information (cf. Gagné, 1972).

How does the individual acquire or modify an internal state that influences his choices in a particular area of action? One way that this is *not* done, according to a great deal of evidence, is solely by the use of persuasive communication (McGuire, 1969). Perhaps most adults would recognize the ineffectiveness of repeated use of such maxims as "Be kind to others," or "Learn to appreciate good music," or "Drive carefully." Even more elaborate communications, however, often have equally poor effects, such as those which make emotional appeals or those which are developed by a careful chain of reasoning. Apparently, one must seek more sophisticated means than these of changing attitudes, and more elaborately specified conditions for attitude learning.

Direct Methods   There are direct methods of establishing and changing attitudes, which sometimes occur naturally and without prior plan. On occasion, such direct methods can also be employed deliberately. At least, it is worthwhile to understand how attitude change can come about by these means.

A conditioned response of the classical sort (cf. Gagné, 1970, pp. 94–100) may establish an attitude of approach or avoidance toward some particular class of objects, events, or persons. Many years ago, Watson and Rayner (1920) demonstrated that a child could be conditioned to "fear" (that is, to run away from) a rabbit he previously had accepted and petted. The unconditioned stimulus used to bring about this marked change in the child's behavior was a sudden sharp sound made behind the child's head, when the rabbit (the conditioned stimulus) was present. While this finding may not have specific pedagogical usefulness, it is important to realize that attitudes can be established in this way, and that some attitudes which a student brings to school with him may be dependent upon an earlier conditioning experience. A tendency to avoid birds, or spiders, or snakes, for example, may be instances of attitudes having their origin in a prior event of conditioning. In theory, almost any attitude might be established in this way.

Another direct method of attitude learning having more usefulness for school situations is based upon the idea of arranging *contingencies of reinforcement* (Skinner, 1968). If a new skill or element of knowledge to be learned is followed by some preferred or rewarding activity, in such a way that the latter is contingent upon achieving the former, this general situation describes the basic prototype of learning, according to Skinner. In addition, the student who begins with a "liking" for the second activity (called a "reinforcer") will in the course of this act of learning acquire a liking for the first task. Following this principle, one might make a preferred activity for an elementary pupil, such as examining a collection of pictures, contingent upon his asking to see the pictures by means of a whole complete sentence ("May I look at the pictures?") as opposed to asking by blurting out a single word ("Pictures?"). Continuation of this practice in a consistent way and in a variety of situations will likely result in the child's using complete sentences when he makes a request. He will also come to enjoy the newly learned way of asking for things, because he has experienced success in doing so. In other words, his attitude toward "using complete sentences" will take a positive turn.

Generalizing somewhat from this specific learning principle of reinforcement contingencies, it may be said that *success* in some learning accomplishment is likely to lead to a positive attitude toward that activity. The child or young person acquires a definitely positive attitude toward ice skating when he achieves some success at it. The student develops a positive attitude toward listening to classical music when he realizes he is able to recognize the musical forms or themes it contains.

An Important Indirect Method   A method of establishing or changing attitudes of great importance and widespread utility for school learning is called *human modeling* (Bandura, 1969). This method is here referred to as indirect because the chain of events that constitute the procedure for learning is longer than that required for "direct" methods. Furthermore, as its name implies, this method operates through the agency of another human being, real or imagined.

A student can observe and learn attitudes from many sorts of human models. In his younger years particularly, one or both parents serve as models for such actions as may be classified as instances of fairness, sympathy, kindness, honesty, and many others. Other members of the family such as older siblings may play this role. When he attends school, one or more teachers may become models for behavior, and this possibility remains true from kindergarten through graduate school. But the varieties of human modeling do not stop at the school. Public figures may become models, or prominent sports people, or famous scientists or artists. It is not essential that people who function as human models be seen or known personally—they can be seen on television or in movies. In fact, they can even be read about in books. This latter fact serves to emphasize the enormous potential that literature has for the determination of attitudes and values.

The human model must, of course, be someone whom the learner *respects*; or as some writers would have it, someone with whom he can *identify*. The model must be observed (or read about) performing the desired kind of behavior. He may be exhibiting kindness, rejecting drugs, or cleaning up trash. A teacher "model" may be dispensing praise consistently and impartially. Having perceived the action, whatever it may be, the learner also must see that such action leads to satisfaction or pleasure on the part of the model. This step in the process is called *vicarious reinforcement* by Bandura (1969). A sports figure may receive an award or display his pleasure in breaking a record; a scientist may exhibit his satisfaction in discovering something new, or even in getting closer to such a discovery. The teacher may show that she is glad to have helped a slow-learning child to acquire a new skill.

The essential conditions for learning attitudes by human modeling are summarized in the following paragraphs.

Performance   An attitude is indicated by the choice of a class of personal actions. These actions can be categorized as showing positive-to-negative tendencies towards some objects, events, or persons.

Internal Conditions   An attitude of respect for or identification with the human model must preferably be already present in the learner. If it is not, it needs to be established as a first step in the process. Intellectual skills and knowledge related to the behavior exhibited by the model must have been previously acquired, in order for this behavior to be imitated. (For example, one could not expect a learner to acquire a positive attitude towards solving differential equations unless he at least has learned what differential equations are!)

External Conditions   These may be described as a sequence of steps, as follows:

1. Presentation (or continued presence) of the respected human model.
2. Demonstration by the model, or description by the model, of the desirable behavior.
3. Demonstration by the model of pleasure or satisfaction with some outcome of his behavior. This is the step which is expected to lead to vicarious reinforcement on the part of the learner.

Of course, modifications of these steps are possible when the human model is not directly seen and when the desired performance cannot be directly observed. The essential conditions may still be present when the learner is viewing television or reading a book.

The modification of attitudes undoubtedly takes place all the time in every portion of the student's daily life. Adult models with whom the student comes in contact bear a tremendous responsibility for the determination of socially desirable attitudes in him. The teacher obviously needs to appreciate the importance of his role as a human model, if for no other reason than the large proportion of time the student spends in his presence. It is likely that those teachers the student later remembers as "good teachers" are the ones who have modeled positive attitudes.

MOTOR SKILLS

The relatively simple sequences of motor responses described as motor chains (Chapter 3) are often combined into more complex performances called *motor skills*. Sometimes these are referred to as "perceptual-motor skills," or "psychomotor skills," but these phrases appear to carry no useful added meaning. They imply, of course, that the learning and performance of motor skills involve the senses and the brain as well as the muscles; however, this fact is well known.

Characteristics of Motor Skills

Motor skills are learned capabilities that underlie performances whose outcomes are reflected in the rapidity, accuracy, force, or smoothness of bodily movement. In the school, these skills are interwoven throughout the curriculum at every age, and include such diverse activities as using a pencil, penmanship, writing with chalk, drawing pictures, painting, using a variety of measuring instruments, and of course, engaging in various physical games and sports. Basic motor skills such as printing numerals on paper are learned in early grades and assumed to be present thereafter. One does not expect a course in fifth-grade arithmetic to be concerned with motor skills learning, even though the students' performances in such a course are in fact dependent upon the basic motor skills learned earlier. In contrast, a motor skill like tying a bowline knot may not previously have been learned by a fifth-grader, and so could conceivably constitute a reasonable objective for instruction at that age or later.

Usually, motor skills can be analyzed into part-skills that compose the total performance in the sense that they occur simultaneously or in a temporal order. Swimming the crawl, for example, contains the part-skills of foot flutter and arm stroke, both of which are carried out at the same time; and also the part-skill of turning the head to breathe, which occurs in a sequence following an arm stroke. Thus the total performance of swimming is a highly organized and precisely timed activity. Learning to swim requires the integration of part-skills of various degrees of complexity, some of them as simple as motor chains. The *integration* of these parts must be learned, as well as the *component part-skills* themselves.

Learning to integrate part-skills which are already learned (to some degree, at least) has been recognized by investigators of motor skills as a highly significant aspect of the total learning required. Fitts & Posner (1967) refer to this component as an *executive sub-routine*, using a computer analogy to express its organizing function. Suppose, for example, an individual learning to drive an automobile has already mastered the part-skills of driving backwards, of turning the steering wheel to direct the motion of the car, and of driving (forwards or backwards) at minimal speed. What does such a person need yet to learn in order to turn the car around on a straight two-lane street? Evidently, he needs to learn a procedure in which these part-skills are combined in a suitable order, so that by making two or three backward and forward motions, combined with suitable turning, the car is headed in the other direction. This procedure is the executive subroutine. It is obviously an intellectual kind of process which "tells" the driver what to do next. Thus the internal process is not in itself "motor" at all.

Swimming provides an interesting comparison. It too has an executive subroutine pertaining to the timing of flutter kicks, arm movements, and head-turning to breathe. But in this case, the smooth performance of these part-skills is usually being improved by practice at the same time that the executive routine is being exercised. Many studies have been performed to find out whether practicing on the part-skills first in various motor skills has an advantage over practicing the whole skill (including the executive subroutine) from the outset (Naylor & Briggs, 1963). No clear answer has emerged from these studies, and the best one can say is that it depends on the skill; sometimes part-skill practice has the advantage, and sometimes not. It is clear, however, that *both* the executive sub-routine and the part-skills must be learned. Practice on either without the other has many times been shown to be ineffective for the learning of the total skill. A collection of studies dealing with these questions has been assembled by Singer (1972).

The relatively simple motor skill of printing the capital letter A is a school task that illustrates these principles well. Instruction may be concerned at some point with the part-skills of drawing diverging lines downward from a point, and of drawing a horizontal line segment which meets these lines without crossing them. Learning must also include the executive subroutine of which movement is executed first, which second, and which third. The total skill, comprising the three principal part-skills, is integrated by means of this executive sub-routine.

Learning Motor Skills

The learning of motor skills is best accomplished by repeated practice. There is no easy way of avoiding practice if one seeks to improve the accuracy, speed, and smoothness of motor skills. In fact, it is interesting to note that practice continues to bring about improvement in motor skills over very long periods of time (Fitts & Posner, 1967, pp. 15–19), as performers in sports, music, and gymnastics are well aware.

Performance   The performance of a motor skill is reflected in an action of bodily movement involving muscular activity. The action is observed to meet certain standards of speed, accuracy, force, or smoothness of execution.

Internal Conditions   Presumably, the prior learnings that must be recalled for the learning of part-skills are simply the individual responses or motor chains which compose them. For learning executive subroutines, concrete concepts of relevant bodily movements or subordinate part-activities must be recalled. For example, the concepts of "backing" and "turning" in an automobile must be previously acquired and recalled in order to enter into the learning of the sub-routine of "turning the car around on a street."

External Conditions   For the improvement of accuracy, speed, and quality of *part-skills*, the individual engages in practice, repeating the movements required to produce the desired outcome in each case. The provision of informative feedback to the learner, which tells him how good each try has been, is an important accompaniment to such practice. For the learning of the *executive routine*, several different kinds of communications to the learner have been successfully employed. Sometimes verbal instructions are used ("Bend your knee and put the weight on your left foot"). A "checklist" showing the sequence of movements of part-skills can be presented to the learner, with the expectation that he will memorize it as he practices. Pictures or diagrams may be used to show the sequence of movements required. Finally, the *total skill*, in which all the parts are correctly sequenced, is also improved by practice with the accompaniment of informative feedback to the learner (Merrill, 1971).

SUMMARY

The present chapter has been concerned with a description of three different kinds of learning—information, attitudes, and motor skills. While they have some features in common, their most notable characteristic is that they are in fact different. They differ, first, in the kinds of outcome performances which they make possible:

1. information—verbally stating facts or generalizations;
2. attitude—choosing a course of personal action; and
3. motor skill—executing a performance of bodily movement.

As our analysis of the conditions of learning for each of these types of capability has shown, they differ from each other markedly in the conditions necessary for their effective learning. For information, the key condition is the provision of a *larger meaningful context*. For attitude, such a context is of no great help; instead, one must provide either a directly reinforcing event, or depend upon *human modeling* to bring about vicarious reinforcement of the learner. And for the learning of motor skills, besides the provision for both part-skills and an integrating skill, the important condition is *practice* with frequent informative feedback to the learner.

The kinds of performances associated with these capabilities and the conditions of effective learning are also obviously different from those described in the previous chapter pertaining to intellectual skills. The latter have their own distinguishable learning conditions and learning outcomes. Are the types of learning dealt with in this chapter in some ways less important than intellectual skills? In most ways, they are surely not less important. The recall of information may certainly be a legitimate and desirable objective of instruction for many instances of school learning. The establishment of attitudes is widely acknowledged to be a highly significant objective of many courses of study, and some would probably accord it highest importance of all. Motor skills, although they appear often to contrast with the schools' "intellectual" orientation, individually have their own justification as fundamental components of basic skills, of art and music, of science, and of sports.

The contrasting features of these kinds of learned capabilities with those of intellectual skills, therefore, do not reside in their differing importance for school programs of instruction. The major characteristic difference to be emphasized here is the utility of intellectual skills as entities for instructional design. Intellectual skills exhibit subordinate-superordinate learning relationships with each other, as described in the previous chapter (and amplified in Chapter 6). They therefore provide a fundamental basis for determining desirable *sequences of instruction* which is lacking in the other categories. Accordingly, the system of instructional design being developed in this book is one which makes intellectual skills the central planning components. The fundamental structures of instruction are designed in terms of what the student will be able to *do* when learning has occurred, and this capability is in turn related to what he has previously learned to *do*. As will be seen, this strategy of instruction design leads to the identification of sequential relations among intellectual skills and the cognitive strategies for which they are prerequisites. To this basic structure may then be added, at appropriate points, the information, attitudes, and motor skills that must also be acquired in meeting the objectives of school learning.

Before getting to the design of instruction for specific performance objectives, two intermediate steps are necessary. These are how to define performance objectives, and how to decide upon the sequencing of instruction. Chapters 5 and 6 deal with these questions.

REFERENCES

Ausubel, D. P. *Educational Psychology: A Cognitive View.* New York: Holt, Rinehart and Winston, 1968.

Bandura, A. *Principles of Behavior Modification.* New York: Holt, Rinehart and Winston, 1969.

Bretz, R. *A Taxonomy of Communication Media.* Englewood Cliffs, N.J.: Educational Technology Publications, 1971.

Deese, J. & Hulse, S. H. *The Psychology of Learning,* 3d Ed. New York: McGraw-Hill, 1967.

Festinger, L. *A Theory of Cognitive Dissonance.* New York: Harper & Row, 1957.

Fishbein, M. A consideration of beliefs, attitudes, and their relationships. In I. D. Steiner & M. Fishbein (Eds.), *Current Studies in Social Psychology.* New York: Holt, Rinehart and Winston, 1965.

Fitts, P. M. & Posner, M. I. *Human Performance.* Belmont, Calif.: Brooks/Cole, 1967.

Gagné, R. M. *The Conditions of Learning.* 2d Ed. New York: Holt, Rinehart and Winston, 1970.

Gagné, R. M. Domains of learning. *Interchange,* 1972, *3,* 1–8.

Jung, J. *Verbal Learning.* New York: Holt, Rinehart and Winston, 1968.

Krathwohl, D. R., Bloom, B. S., & Masia, B. B. *Taxonomy of Educational Objectives. Handbook II: Affective Domain.* New York: McKay, 1964.

Mager, R. F. *Developing Attitude Toward Learning.* Belmont, Calif.: Fearon, 1968.

Mandler, G. Organization and memory. In K. W. Spence & J. T. Spence (Eds.).

The Psychology of Learning and Motivation. Vol. 1. New York: Academic Press, 1967.

McGuire, W. J. The nature of attitudes and attitude change. In G. Lindzey & E. Aronson. *Handbook of Social Psychology*, 2d Ed. Vol. III. Reading, Mass.: Addison-Wesley, 1969.

Merrill, M. D. Paradigms for psychomotor instruction. In M. D. Merrill (Ed.). *Instructional Design: Readings.* Englewood Cliffs, N. J.: Prentice-Hall, 1971.

Naylor, J. C. & Briggs, G. E. Effects of task complexity and task organization on the relative efficiency of part and whole training methods. *Journal of Experimental Psychology*, 1963, *65*, 217–224.

Polanyi, M. *Personal Knowledge.* Chicago: University of Chicago Press, 1958.

Rohwer, W. D., Jr. Images and pictures in children's learning: Research results and educational implications. *Psychological Bulletin*, 1970, *73*, 393–403.

Singer, R. N. (Ed.). *Readings in Motor Learning.* Philadelphia: Lea & Febiger, 1972.

Skinner, B. F. *The Technology of Teaching.* New York: Appleton-Century-Crofts, 1968.

Triandis, H. C. Exploratory factor analyses of the behavioral component of social attitudes. *Journal of Abnormal and Social Psychology*, 1964, *68*, 420–430.

Watson, J. B. & Rayner, R. Conditioned emotional reactions. *Journal of Experimental Psychology*, 1920, *3*, 1–14.

TWO
DESIGNING INSTRUCTION

5

DEFINING PERFORMANCE OBJECTIVES

There are, according to the previous chapters, several different kinds of human capabilities that are typically learned in the schools. Any and all of them occur within each content area such as science, social studies, mathematics, language. How does one go about sorting these out in connection with the planning of any particular course of study? How does one tell whether a topic called "mixed numerical operations" or "composition of complex sentences" includes discriminations, concepts, rules, or higher-order rules? We have seen that these *kinds* of intellectual processing make a difference in the planning of conditions of learning, and also in the determination of a sequence with which they are learned. How can one find out, then, what human capabilities are included in a topic or set of topics?

INITIAL APPROACHES TO
DEFINING OBJECTIVES

The basic action that must be taken in determining what capabilities are to be learned is one of defining objectives. This is not necessarily an easy thing to do, and it needs to be approached in several stages. Most teachers believe they know what their objectives are, or what the objectives of any given lesson are. And in a general sense, they usually do. In order to be useful for instructional planning, however, objectives need to be defined in rather precise terms. The major reason is that language can be terribly misleading—commonly used words can mean very different things to different people. Carefully defined objectives, however, should have only a single meaning, and the same meaning for all literate persons. Accordingly, they must in a sense have a *technical* meaning, conveying precise information about human performance.

Identifying Course Purposes

It seems desirable to begin the process of arriving at precisely stated objectives by attempting to identify the *purposes* of the course. At this point, one need not necessarily worry about achieving a truly communicable meaning—only one which satisfies the person himself who is trying to formulate the objectives. But even at this stage, there are some standards to be met and some pitfalls to be avoided. These are as follows:

1. The statement of the purpose of a course should be concerned with what the student will be like *after* the lesson, not what he is doing *during* the course. For example, the attempt of a novice instructional designer might read, as a statement of purpose, "to provide the student with experience in the identification of birds of the region." Now, obviously, this may be a statement of what is going to go on during the course—the student is going to "experience" birds and their identification. But the question is, what is the *purpose* of such experience? What does one expect of the student after the course? The chances are that the purpose might be expressed as "ability to identify common birds of the region." Notice the latter statement comes much closer to telling *what the student will be able to do following the instruction*.

2. The second tendency to be avoided is that of stating purposes which are too far out, too distant in terms of time. Purposes should be stated in terms of the *expected current outcomes* of instruction, not the far-distant future ones. Here is an example of this kind of pitfall: "Students will acquire a lifelong respect for the importance of conserving natural wildlife." Now, perhaps one really does believe such a lifelong respect is valuable and desirable. But this does not make such a goal a legitimate purpose for a

course. It is, in fact, quite presumptuous to think that such "lifelong respect" can be established by a single unit of instruction. If respect of this sort is going to be established, it will surely be the result of many influences. Accordingly, it is necessary to say to oneself, "That is all well and good, but in what way is the course going to contribute to that very general goal? Would the student acquire this lifelong respect just as readily *without* this course? If not, what specifically is being contributed by this course?" At this point, one is obviously brought back to the task of defining in specific terms the purpose of the individual course. Possibly it may turn out to be something like the following: "Students will be able to identify instances in which a lack of wildlife conservation has produced undesirable social consequences." Such a purpose would be quite appropriate for a course.

In summary, the initial try at defining objectives will probably be most successful if it is a statement of the *purpose* of a course. Such a statement should reflect what the student will be expected to be able to do following the course. The statement of purpose is grossly deficient if it states only some far-distant future goal (even though such a goal may itself be perfectly valid and desirable) without identifying the proximal expected outcome of the course. The purpose of instruction refers to what the student will be like *after* instruction, not what happens during instruction.

At this state of developing a precise definition, the following kinds of statements appear to be quite acceptable as course purposes:

Understands the principle of commutativity in multiplication.
Is aware of tonal differences in the sounds of violin, viola, and cello.
Comprehends the idea of nationality.
Reads with enjoyment short stories with simple plots.

ACHIEVING PRECISION IN OBJECTIVES

It may be noted that the course purposes just cited are eminently reasonable. They say what the student is expected to be like after instruction, not during it. And they say what he will be able to do more or less immediately, not in the far-distant future. These statements, therefore, are highly communicative and practical—they avoid the gross errors previously mentioned.

However, they are not models of precision. They have not managed to reduce ambiguity to the level needed for lesson planning. "Being aware" of tonal differences may well mean one thing to one teacher, and something quite different to another. "Comprehending" the idea of nationality may mean "stating a definition of nationality" to one teacher; it may mean "distinguishing nationality from birthplace" to another. It is the existence of this ambiguity which has led several writers to attempt to describe ways of overcoming it in the defining of objectives (cf. Mager, 1962; Popham & Baker, 1970).

Overcoming Ambiguity

As has often been suggested, the procedure for overcoming the ambiguity of course purpose statements and thus achieving greater precision, runs somewhat as follows: "All right, I will accept this statement as reflecting one of the purposes of the course. The question now is, *how will I know* when this purpose has been achieved?"

How will one know that the student "understands the principle of commutativity"?

How will it be known that the student "appreciates allegory in 'A Midsummer Night's Dream' "?

How can it be told that the student "comprehends spoken French"?

How will one tell that the student "reads short stories with enjoyment"?

Statements of course purposes may be quite successful in communicating general goals to fellow teachers, yet they are often not sufficiently precise for unambiguous communication of the *content* and *outcomes* of instruction. The key to their ambiguity is simply that they do not tell another person how he could *observe* what has been accomplished without being present during the lesson itself. Being able to make such an observation may be of interest to another teacher who accepts the general purpose of the course and wishes to know how to tell when it has been accomplished. It may be of interest to a parent who may not know exactly what "commutativity" means but wishes to assure himself that his son or daughter can in fact use this principle in performing arithmetic operations. It is likely to be of interest to the student, who wants to be able to tell when his own performance attains the goal that the teacher or textbook had in mind.

An objective is precisely described when it communicates to another person what he would have to do to *observe* that a stated lesson purpose has in fact been accomplished. The statement is inadequately precise if it does not enable the other person to think of how he would carry out such an observation. Consider the following instances:

1. "Realizes that most plant growth requires sunshine." Such a statement doesn't say or imply how such an outcome would be observed. Does it mean that the teacher would be satisfied with the answer to a question such as "Is the sunshine necessary for the growth of most plants?" Evidently not. How, then, would such an objective be observed?

2. "Demonstrates that sunshine affects plant growth." This statement implies that the teacher must observe instances in which the student shows that he knows the relation between sunshine and plant growth. The observation might be made in various ways (by using actual plants, pictures, or verbal statements). The main point is, it tells in a general way what sort of observation is required.

The criterion of "being able to observe" the proposed outcome of a lesson is often referred to as an *operational* criterion; and statements of objectives having this characteristic may be called *operationally defined objectives*. When defined in this precise way, definitions of objectives communicate to another person the "operations" he must carry out in order to observe the achievement of the objective.

What is observed when a second person undertakes to convince himself that an objective has been achieved? Obviously, he is observing the *performance* of a student in a situation. Accordingly, statements of objectives having this "operational" characteristic are also called *performance objectives*. In achieving precision in stating objectives, one is said to be "defining objectives in terms of human performance (or human behavior)." Basically, then, these terms "operationally defined objectives," "behaviorally defined objectives," "objectives defined in terms of performance" all mean the same thing. When objectives are so stated, they communicate to another person what he would have to do to observe the achievement of the course's purpose or purposes.

Components of Operational Descriptions of Objectives

Precisely described objectives are those which make observations of another person possible. They need to include a number of components. They must, first, describe the action that the student is taking. Obviously, too, an objective must describe the situation in which that action takes place. Something must usually be said about the limits within which the performance of the student will be expected to occur. And most important of all, the objective must indicate what kind of human performance is involved. This means they must describe what kind of human capability is to be inferred from the performance that is under observation.

Our description of the components of operational definitions of objectives is not widely different from that given by other authors (Mager, 1962; Popham & Baker, 1970; Briggs, 1970), and is not intended to differ from them in any crucial respect. There are differences in emphasis, however, resulting from our attempt to make some distinctions which other authors have not highlighted. Particularly, we distinguish verbs for *action* from verbs used to identify the *learned capability* implied by the behavior under observation.

An initial example, which will be expanded later, comes from the lesson purpose "types a letter." Such a goal might be found in a course in typing designed to establish employable skills in a typist occupation.

The incompleteness of the description "types a letter" may be indicated by the following comments:

1. *Action*. The statement is obviously most adequate with respect to this component. An observer would be able to judge that the performance had been carried out *by typing*.
2. *Object*. The object of the performance is similarly clear—the individual is expected to produce *a letter*.
3. *Situation*. What is the situation faced by the student when asked to type a letter? Is he given the components of the letter in longhand copy? Does he produce the letter from an auditory message, or from notes? Obviously, what the student actually does is highly dependent on the situation. An objective must specify the features of this situation.
4. *Tools and Other Constraints*. The main question here is *how* must the required performance be carried out. This depends on what tools are available, or what other limits are set to the performance. Does the student use an electric typewriter? Does he make a carbon? How long is the letter? Quite different limits might be set for a lesson intended for a beginning student and one for a fully trained student.
5. *Capability To Be Learned.* Here is the most important omission of all. The statement "types a letter" does not really tell the nature of the learned capability that can be inferred from the student's performance. "Types a letter" might mean "*copies* a letter," or it might mean the quite different performance, "*composes a letter*." Something must be done, therefore, to represent the *kind* of performance the student is expected to exhibit. This means one must state the inferred kind of human capability involved.

Let us see, then, what a total and precise definition of the objective "typing a letter" might be. Suppose that the task set for the typist is that of answering a piece of correspondence concerned with orders and shipping, without help from anyone as to what the contents of the letter should be. One would need to describe the total performance somewhat as follows:

> *Given a received letter*   (Situation)
> *inquiring about the*
> *shipping of an order,*

generates	(The learned capability, implying a problem-solving process)
a letter in reply	(Object)
by typing,	(Action)
using an electric typewriter, making one carbon of a one-page letter.	(Tools and other constraints)

It is difficult to pin down what may be the "important" parts of this objective statement, since each part serves a different function. Can any be left out? No, not if one wants a truly precise and complete definition, free of ambiguities. It is worth noting, however, that the *verb denoting the learned capability* is the part that brings about the major differentiation of the performance from that of a contrasting performance, that of copying a letter from longhand copy. The latter kind of activity may be described as follows:

Given a written longhand letter,	(Situation)
executes	(The learned capability, a motor skill)
a copy	(Object)
by typing,	(Action)
using an electric typewriter, making one carbon of a one-page letter.	(Tools and other constraints)

Obviously, although the implements used are the same, this is a very different kind of human activity from that given in the previous example.

The situation reacted to is different, and in particular the *learned capability* is quite a different one. "Executes" is an acceptable word for this process, implying a learned motor skill, something which is quite different from that implied by the "generates" of the other example.

Here is another example of an objective with its components, taken from elementary mathematics:

Given two "missing factor" equations, using a $\times$ sign and an $=$ sign,	(Situation)

demonstrates	(Learned capability, a rule)
supplying the missing factor in one equation from the known factor in the other equation	(Object)
by writing the missing factor,	(Action)
using the commutative property of multiplication	(Tools and other constraints)

Again it is apparent that, although all parts of the objective contribute to the description, the *learned capability* is surely one of the most important components. In this case it tells us that the individual is "demonstrating" the application of a rule (the commutative rule of multiplication).

Still another example may be given, this time pertaining to a language skill basic to beginning reading:

Given orally presented words of single syllables, beginning with consonants,	(Situation)
identifies	(Learned capability, concrete concepts)
the beginning consonant of each word,	(Object)
by printing	(Action)
in appropriate blanks	(Tools and other constraints)

This is of course a fairly simple skill, and it is therefore rather readily described. Again in this instance, it may be seen that a major contribution to precise meaning is carried by the verb "identifies," used to describe the learned capability. Notice, for example, how inappropriate a verb like "demonstrate" or "solve" would be in this case.

Choosing Action Words

The choice of verbs in the definition of an objective is a matter of critical importance. The primary reason is, of course, the avoidance of ambiguity. One wishes the statement of an objective to *communicate reliably*, in such a way that two different literate people will agree that any specific instance of an actually observed performance is or is not an example of the described objective. As a number of writers have pointed out (e.g. Mager, 1962; Popham & Baker, 1970) verbs like "knows," "understands," "appreciates," do not communicate reliably. Thus, while such verbs are appropriate for stating general purposes of a course of study, they do not by themselves yield the reliable communication necessary to an objective statement. They must usually be followed by some such line of thought as the following: "I have said 'the student will understand.' Now, how will I be able to tell that 'he understands'? What kind of performance could I point to which would convince me, and also my colleague Mr. Jones, that the student 'understands'? Well, I would be convinced he 'understands' if he could show me how to do it. Do what? Well, if he could actually supply the missing factor in an equation, for example. Let me see if I can express that action so that Mr. Jones could also agree with me, that is, so that he could identify the same performance that I have in mind. If I can do that, I shall have a defined performance objective."

Such reasoning is basic to the formulation of an objective, and leads to the choice of verbs which accomplish the primary purpose of reliable communication. There is, however, one additional distinction about the use of verbs that remains to be described. As shown by previous examples, there are two kinds of verbs in a complete definition of an objective. Likely to be thought of first is the verb denoting *Action*. While it may come second in thought, the verb which identifies the *Learned Capability* is, however, probably of even greater importance in its implications for instructional design.

Verbs for Action   Verbs denoting action are not difficult to find. Common ones are writes, draws, states orally, selects, matches, names, groups, collects, applies, employs, verifies. There are, of course, synonyms for these, and there are many others as well. Action verbs are unambiguous when they reliably communicate observable performances to another person. Beyond this criterion, no further distinctions or classifications appear feasible. After all, there are many verbs in our language; and from the total set, there are also many which communicate action rather precisely.

In the objective statement, the *action* verb normally appears in its "ing" form. (This is true in the models we are describing. It is, of course, not an absolute rule, since objective statements may be organized in a number of ways.) Here are some examples of objectives in which the role of the verb ending in "ing" is shown:

1. Given an appropriate question, states the provisions of the First Amendment, in *writing*.
2. Given a beaker of water, ringstand, Bunsen burner, and thermometer, demonstrates that water changes state at 100°C., by *recording* several temperature readings.

3. Given a passage of poetry, classifies the similies contained in it by *checking* the words compared.

By using this form, we mean to emphasize that the action verb, while essential for completeness of communication, is not necessarily the most important verb in the objective definition. The major verb is, instead, that which denotes the learned capability. It may be noted that an action verb like "writing" does not in itself identify the intellectual skill involved in the performance, as previous examples have shown. In exhibiting the action of "writing a sentence," for example, a first-grade student might be copying a sentence given in his workbook; a fifth-grade student might be assembling a sentence from a subject, verb, and object supplied by the teacher; an eighth-grade student might be composing a sentence to describe a pictured scene. All are *writing*, yet each is engaged in exhibiting a different kind of learned capability—a different instructional outcome.

Describing Human Capabilities

The major verb of the objective statement has the purpose of communicating the *kind of human capability* one expects to be learned, as it may be observed in some performance exhibited by the student. We undertake to identify in this section the words that can be used for description of these capabilities.

Verbs for Intellectual Skills Our account of the choices of verbs to describe performances implying learned capabilities begins with the types of intellectual skills described in Chapter 3. We need to be concerned with the categories of (1) discriminations; (2) concrete concepts; (3) defined concepts; (4) rules; and (5) higher-order rules.

If five categories of intellectual skills describe learning outcomes in this general domain, it should follow that *these may be described by five verbs*. This is exactly what we propose. We have chosen the verbs with considerable care, so that each denotes an intellectual skill as distinctively as possible. At the same time, these verbs have a degree of abstractness at least one degree greater than verbs for action. This, too, is deliberate, since verbs for intellectual functioning should not be confused with those that simply describe observable actions. The former require an *inference* about behavior, whereas the latter merely permit the observable aspects of the performance to be identified.

The five verbs which can be used to describe intellectual skills in definitions of performance objectives are shown in the first portion of Table 2. The final column of the table provides examples of phrases (not complete statements) for objectives, illustrating their use.

TABLE 2   *Verbs To Describe Human Capabilities, with
Examples of Phrases Incorporating Them*

Capability	Verb	Example
Intellectual Skill		
Discrimination	DISCRIMINATES	discriminates, by matching, the French sounds of "u" and "ou"
Concrete Concept	IDENTIFIES	identifies, by naming, the root, leaf, and stem of representative plants
Defined Concept	CLASSIFIES	classifies, by using a definition, the concept "family"
Rule	DEMONSTRATES	demonstrates, by solving verbally stated examples, the addition of positive and negative numbers
Higher-order Rule (Problem-Solving)	GENERATES	generates, by synthesizing applicable rules, a paragraph describing a person's actions in a situation of fear
Cognitive Strategy	ORIGINATES	originates a solution to the reduction of air pollution, by applying model of gaseous diffusion
Information	STATES	states orally the major issues in the Presidential campaign of 1932
Motor Skill	EXECUTES	executes backing a car into driveway
Attitude	CHOOSES	chooses playing golf as a leisure activity

The statements that result when these verbs are used have a formal character that sometimes makes them seem unduly cumbersome. For example, it may often seem better, in a literary sense, to state simply that the student "finds values of specified variables in algebraic equations," rather than to state, "demonstrates, by transforming algebraic equations, solving to obtain the value of a specified variable." But the latter statement makes clear that the expected performance *requires the use of rules*, whereas the former does not necessarily make this clear. One can imagine a situation in which the student could "find" the value of a specified variable without using such rules; as, for example, in the equation $x = 3$.

Another example of the apparent formal complexity of statements using these verbs may be shown with the verb *classify*. Suppose that, instead of the complete phrase shown in Table 2, one were to be satisfied with "states and gives an example of the definition of 'family'." Neither of these verbs implies an unambiguous meaning for the intellectual skill involved. "States," may very well apply to "stating information," as might be the case if the student repeats the definition "a group consisting of the head of a household and all persons living therein related to him." Further, "giving an example" might be done by identifying one or more family groups by name or in pictures. To convey the full meaning of the desired objective, *classifies* must be included to indicate that the student is expected to show the meaning of the concept "family," including distinguishing it from other concepts.

Perhaps it should also be pointed out that we propose these five verbs, not because we feel wedded to them as words (some surely have approximate synonyms), but because we consider that there are *five necessary distinctions to be made*. Using these five words as verbs for intellectual skills has the desirable effect of preserving these distinctions. Trying to achieve a better "literary" style for statements of objectives can easily lead to nothing better than the introduction of added confusion where there should be as little as possible. If one is inclined to prefer other verbs, their equivalence or lack of equivalence to these should be clearly stated.

Verb for Cognitive Strategy   The next entry in the table shows the suggested major verb of the description of a cognitive strategy, which is *originates*. This verb implies the kind of intellectual process presumed to be involved in tasks requiring thinking or problem solving. When confronted with a truly novel task, without a familiar context, we suppose that the learner must search for applicable rules and applicable information. He then, in effect, formulates a general type of solution, and checks to see how such a solution applies to one or more specific instances. This whole sequence of mental operations is implied by the verb "originate." Actually, there may be more than one cognitive strategy involved in a problem solving process of this sort. However, as previously mentioned, we are unable to identify these strategies more precisely at present. Perhaps someday it will be possible to describe as many or more subtypes of cognitive strategies as is currently possible for intellectual skills.

The example suggests a description for a problem-solving activity in which the learner originates a solution to the problem of reducing air pollution by bringing to bear on this problem a model (that is, a set of complex rules) of gaseous diffusion which he has previously learned. This is, of course, a hypothetical example.

A comment may be in order concerning the difference between the acquiring of a higher-order rule by problem solving, and the application of a cognitive strategy to a problem-solving task. For the former, the suggested phrase is "generate a solution," whereas for the latter it is "originate a solution." The difference is not one we can describe with utter confidence, because additional study of these complex mental processes is badly needed. We speculate, however, that the difference lies in the necessity to reach "out of context" for a solution that is truly a matter of originating. One may, for example, imagine a problem-solving situation in which some higher-order rule must be invented (that is, generated) for a mathematical principle, based upon a combination of previously learned mathematical rules. Such a "generating" process remains within the context of mathematics. In contrast, however, would be an instance in which a thinker came to "see" the applicability of some model of physical science to the occurrence of a social phenomenon such as inflation or population growth. The original set of rules used in such a solution would be "out of context." They would need to be searched for in the individual's memory, and the problem would need to be formulated before its solution could be tested. Thus, to a greater extent, one would expect that "originating a solution" calls upon the internally organized capabilities called cognitive strategies. (Interesting discussions of originating performances are to be found in Bruner, 1971, pp. 52–97.)

Verb for Motor Skill. The major verb suggested for descriptions of motor skill is *executes.* The performance used to illustrate the use of this verb is backing an automobile into a driveway. Obviously, the verb denoting action in this instance is "backing." But we use the verb "executes" to imply the capability of a highly organized skill which is observed by means of a performance possessing appropriate characteristics of smoothness and efficiency.

Verb for Attitude As seen in the preceding chapter, an attitude is a human capability that influences an individual's choice of some personal action. The major verb for a statement of an attitudinal objective, then, is not difficult to find. It is *chooses.* In Table 2, the example used is one which supposes that the student chooses playing golf when given the opportunity of selecting a leisure-time pursuit. Under proper circumstances, it may be supposed that the observation of such a performance (or the self-report of it) can lead to the inference of a positive attitude toward this activity. As is true with other types of objectives, the action verb can be of various sorts, such as "by signing up for golf," or "by selecting golf from a list of sports."

Statements of Objectives and Criteria of Performance

Instructional objectives describe the *class* of performances that may be used to determine whether the implied human capability has been learned. However, they do not state in quantitative terms what *criteria* will be used to judge whether any particular performance class has been learned. That is to say, the objective statements themselves do not describe how many times the student is to "demonstrate the addition of mixed numbers," or how many "errors" will be permitted. They do not state what will be needed for the observer to be confident that the designated capability has been learned. There are two very good reasons why the criterion of performance should not be included in a statement of an instructional objective. First, the necessary criteria are likely to be different for each type of human capability, and it is highly desirable to avoid the error of thinking they can be the same. Second, the question of criteria of performance is a question of "how to measure," and is intimately bound up with the techniques of performance assessment. At the point in instructional planning, when objectives are being described, it is confusing to become concerned with assessment procedures. Such procedures are described in a later chapter of this book.

Statements of objectives prepared in the manner described here *always* imply "mastery" (cf. Bloom, 1971). But what is the criterion of mastery, that is, how is it to be measured? This is a question which needs to be separately decided in connection with specific assessment methods. Sometimes, it is perfectly clear that mastery means that the student will exhibit the performance 100 percent of the time (minus some small percent for "measurement error"). For example, if the objective is defined as "given two or more mixed numbers, demonstrates their addition by writing the sum," one expects the performance of the student to indicate the achievement of this objective for any or all mixed numbers. Such a conclusion might be reached by asking the student to perform a large number of examples of adding mixed numbers, or as few as two or three. The conclusion sought— that the student has or has not mastered this task—is the same in either case.

On other occasions, as when information is being measured, it may be desirable to specify some portion of ideas to be correctly stated, such as three out of five, or four out of six. But this is more appropriately a matter of assessment, rather than a portion of the objective statement itself. For example, the statement implying mastery might be, "states in writing three major economic factors contributing to inflation." For such an objective, an assessment technique must be chosen which specifies a decision concerning what conclusion can be drawn if the student can state only two of three factors, or one of three. Regardless of this latter decision, the objective statement continues in unchanged form to imply mastery.

An exception to the principle of mastery occurs in the case of attitudes. Because of the nature of this kind of human capability, which is one of *modifying* choices, one cannot conceive of an attitude as being "mastered." Instead, attitudes make choices more or less probable. The assessment of attitudes, therefore, although derived from the objective statement, implies only a conclusion concerning the *relative strength* of an attitude. In other words, one does not expect to be able to draw the conclusion from assessment based on an attitudinal objective that "a positive attitude has been mastered," but only that "an attitude has been changed in the positive (or negative) direction."

In the case of intellectual skills, the mastery implied by the statement of the objective has an important theoretical significance. Its function is accounted for in the theory of *learning hierarchies* (Gagné, 1970, pp. 237–276). According to this theory, the learning of any particular intellectual skill is important because it supports the learning of more complex skills. This support by previously learned intellectual skills, however, occurs only when they are readily accessible in memory at the moment the new learning occurs (or is about to occur). In an operational sense, "mastery" means *readily accessible to recall at the time of learning* of the more complex skill. Strictly speaking, therefore, the measurement of mastery must be so designed as to predict the "readily accessible recall" of the intellectual skill which has been learned. From this theoretical view, it is not possible to predict in precise terms how "mastery" should be measured. Nor is it wise to adopt some arbitrary standard like "five out of six correct responses." The criterion of mastery will vary with what is being learned, and needs to be determined as a part of the assessment process.

PREPARING STATEMENTS OF INSTRUCTIONAL OBJECTIVES

Having described the components of complete statements of objectives, we return now to the procedure for preparing these statements.

An Example from Science

Suppose that the instructional designer has in mind, or formulates in a written statement, the purposes to be accomplished by a course of instruction. If the lesson is one in science, the following purposes might be considered. These have been abstracted from a list of objectives for junior high school science instruction prepared by the Intermediate Science Curriculum Study (1972).

1. Understanding the concept of an electric circuit.
2. Knowing that a major advantage of the metric system in science is that its units are related by factors of ten.
3. Taking personal responsibility for returning equipment to its storage places.

Objective No. 1—the concept of an electric circuit. This is a fairly straightforward purpose for instruction. The first question to be asked by an instructional designer is: "What kind of capability am I looking for here?" Do I mean by "understanding" something like "stating what an electric circuit is"? No, that would not be convincing, since it might merely indicate that the student had acquired some verbal information which he could repeat, perhaps in his own words. Do I mean "distinguishing an electric circuit from a noncircuit, when shown two or more instances"? No, I cannot be sure that the student has the understanding I wish in this case, because he may be able simply to pick up the cue of an open wire in the instances shown him and respond on that basis. What I actually want the student to do is to *show me that he can use a rule for making an electric circuit in* one or more specific situations. The rule concerned has to do with the flow of electric current from a source through a connected set of conductors and back to the source. The student could be asked to exhibit this performance in one or more different situations.

The result of this line of reasoning is an objective statement which puts together the necessary components as follows:

[Situation:] Given a battery, light bulb and socket, and pieces of wire [major verb for capability:] demonstrates [object:] the making of an electric circuit [action:] by connecting wires to battery and socket and testing the lighting of the bulb.

Objective No. 2—Knowing something about the metric system. The statement of purpose in this instance implies that some information is to be learned. Again, the first question to be asked by the instructional designer is, "What do I mean by 'knowing' this fact about the metric system? What will convince me that the student 'knows'?" In this instance, the designer may readily come to the conclusion that "knowing" means *being able to state* the particular fact about the metric system. Accordingly, the identification of the required capability as *information* is fairly straightforward.

The resulting objective can then be constructed as follows: [Situation:] Given the question: "What major advantage for scientific work do the units of the metric system have?" [major verb for capability:] states [object:] that its units are related by factors of ten [action:] by writing, in his own words.

Objective No. 3—Taking responsibility for equipment: In thinking over this instructional purpose, the designer will immediately realize that it is not concerned with whether the student is able to put equipment back in its place, but rather with whether he *tends to do so* on all appropriate occasions.

The word "responsibility" implies that the actions of the student may occur at any time, and are not expected to result from any specific direction or question. The designer must ask himself, "What would convince me that the student is 'taking responsibility' of this sort?" The answer to this question implies that the objective in this case deals with choices of personal action, in other words, with an *attitude*.

The standard method of constructing the objective would therefore take this form:

[Situation:] Given occasions when laboratory activities are completed or terminated [major verb for capability:] chooses [object:] courses of action [action:] returning equipment to its storage places.

An Example from English

A second example of the procedure for constructing statements of objectives comes from a hypothetical course in English, concerned with the study of literature. Suppose that a set of lessons in such a course had the following purposes:

1. Identifying the major characters in *Hamlet*.
2. Understanding Hamlet's soliloquy.
3. Being able to recognize a metaphor.

Objective No. 1—Identifying the major characters in Hamlet. This objective, according to our model, involves using definitions to *classify*. In this case the student is being asked to classify characters in *Hamlet* in accordance with their functions within the plot of the play. Under most circumstances, it would be assumed that his doing this by way of verbal statements would be convincing. That is, the student answers a question like: "Who was Claudius?" by defining Claudius as the King of Denmark, Hamlet's uncle, who is suspected by Hamlet of having killed his father. The objective can be constructed as follows:

[Situation:] Given oral questions about the characters of *Hamlet*, as "Who was Claudius?" [major verb for capability:] classifies [object:] the characters [action:] by defining their relationships to the plot.

Objective No. 2—Understanding Hamlet's soliloquy. Here is a much more interesting, and presumably a more important instructional purpose. The instructional designer needs to ask himself, "How will I know if the student 'understands' this passage?" In all likelihood, the answer he will find to this question is "ask the student to express the thoughts of the passage in words that simplify or explain their meaning." (An example would be explaining that "to be, or not to be" means "to remain living or not.") To accomplish such a task, the student must solve a series of problems, bringing to bear upon them a number of intellectual skills such as rules for using synonyms, rules for defining, and concepts of figures of speech. In sum, what he will be asked to do is to *generate* a paraphrase of the soliloquy. It is, then, a *problem-solving* task, or more precisely a whole set of problems, in which subordinate rules must be applied to the generation of higher-order rules. The latter cannot be exactly specified, of course, since one does not know exactly how the student will solve each problem.

As a result of this analysis, the following objective might be composed:

[Situation:] Given instructions to interpret the meaning of Hamlet's soliloquy in simple terms [major verb for capability:] generates [object:] an alternative communication of the soliloquy [action:] by writing sentences of simple content.

Objective No. 3—Recognizing metaphors. Even in its expression, this objective has the appearance of representing a somewhat less complex purpose than No. 2. It may be evident, also, that if a student is able to generate a paraphrased soliloquy, he must be able to detect the metaphoric meaning of such phrases as "to take arms against a sea of troubles." In this simpler example of a purpose, then, the question for the instructional designer is, "What will convince me that the student can 'recognize' a metaphor?" Obviously, a metaphor is a concept, and since it is not something that can be denoted by pointing, it must be a *defined concept*. The performance to be expected of the student, then, will be one of *classifying a metaphor in accordance with a definition.*

The resulting objective might be stated as follows:

[Situation:] Given a list of phrases, some of which are metaphors and some not [major verb for capability:] classifies [object:] the metaphors [action:] by picking out those that conform to the definition, rejecting those that do not.

An alternative objective (and possibly a better one) for this instructional purpose would be:

[Situation:] Given a phrase containing a verb participle and an object (as, "resisting corruption") [major verb for capability:] classifies [object:] a metaphor [action:] by giving an example which accords with the definition (as, "erecting a bulwark against corruption").

An Example from Social Studies

A course in social studies in junior high or high school might have the following purposes:

1. Knowing terms of office for members of the two houses of Congress.
2. Interpreting bar charts showing growth in agricultural production.
3. Applying knowledge of the "judicial review" process of the Supreme Court.

Objective No. 1—Terms of office for Congress. The intended outcome in this case is information. It is, of course, rather simple information, and therefore something that might be learned in grades before high school. As an objective, this purpose may be stated as follows:

[Situation:] Given the question, "What terms of office do members of both houses of Congress serve?" [major verb for capability:] states [object:] the terms for House and Senate members [action:] orally.

Objective No. 2—Interpreting bar charts. Often an important kind of objective in social studies is an intellectual skill. Interpreting bar charts is a rule-using skill. There may be several such skills of increasing complexity to be learned. Consequently, particular attention has to be paid to the description of the situation. More complex charts may require more complex intellectual skills, or a combination of them. This objective may be illustrated by the following example:

[Situation:] Given a bar chart showing production of cotton bales by year during the period 1950–1960 [major verb for capability:] demonstrates [object:] the finding of years of maximal and minimal growth [action:] by checking appropriate bars.

Objective No. 3—Applying knowledge of "judicial review." The statement of this goal is somewhat ambiguous. It might best be interpreted as one of solving problems pertaining to the Supreme Court's judicial review function, and exhibiting knowledge by so doing. Such an objective might be stated in the following way:

[Situation:] Given the statement of an issue of constitutionality contained in a fictitious Act of Congress, and reference to the Constitutional principle to be invoked [major verb for capability:] generates [object:] a proposed judicial opinion [action:] in written form.

USING OBJECTIVES IN
INSTRUCTIONAL PLANNING

When instructional objectives are defined in the manner described here, they reveal the fine-grained nature of the instructional process. This in turn reflects the fine-grained characteristic of what is learned. As a consequence, the quantity of individual objectives applicable to a course of instruction usually numbers in the hundreds. There may be scores of objectives for the single topic of a course, and several for each individual lesson.

How does the instructional designer employ these objectives in his development of topics, courses, or curricula? And how does the teacher use objectives? Can the teacher, as the designer of an individual lesson, make use of lengthy lists of objectives? Many such lists are available, it may be noted, for a variety of subjects in all school grades.*

Objectives and Instruction

The instructional designer, or design team, faces the need to describe objectives as part of each individual lesson. Typically, there will be several distinct objectives for a lesson. Each may then be used to answer the question, "What *kind* of a learning outcome does this objective represent?" The categories to be determined are those corresponding to the major verb indicating capability. That is, the objective may represent information, an intellectual skill in one of its sub-varieties, a cognitive strategy, an attitude, or a motor skill. Having determined the categories of a lesson's objectives, the designer will be able to make decisions about the following matters:

1. Whether an original intention about the lesson's purpose has been overlooked, or inadequately represented;
2. whether the lesson has a suitable "balance" of expected outcomes; and
3. whether the approach to instruction is matched to the type of objective in each case.

Clearly, then, the systematic design of lessons making up a topic or course will result in the development of a sizeable collection of statements of objectives. This collection will grow as lessons are developed, and assembled into topics. Decisions about the correspondence of these objectives with original intentions for the topic and course, and about the "balance" of objectives, can also be made with reference to these larger instructional units. As in the case of the individual lesson, these decisions are made possible by the categorization of objectives into types of capabilities to be learned.

* Lists of objectives may be obtained on order from the Instructional Objectives Exchange, Box 24095, Los Angeles, California, 90024.

The teacher's design of the single lesson also makes use of individual statements of objectives and the classes of capabilities they represent. The instructional materials available to the teacher (textbook, manual, or whatever) may identify the objectives of the lesson directly. More frequently, the teacher may need to (1) infer what the objectives are; and (2) design the lesson so that the objectives represented in the textbook are supplemented by others. For purposes of planning effective instruction, the determination of categories of expected learning outcomes is as important to the teacher as it is to the design team. The teacher, for tomorrow's lesson, needs to make decisions about the adequacy with which the lesson's purpose is accomplished, and about the relative balance of the lesson's several expected outcomes.

Objectives and Assessment

Fortunately, the lists of individual objectives which are developed in a systematic design effort have a second use. Descriptions of objectives, as we have said, are descriptions of what must be observed in order to verify that the desired learning has taken place. Consequently, statements of objectives have direct implications for *assessing* student learning.

The teacher may use objective statements to design situations within which student performance can be observed. This is done to verify that particular outcomes of learning have in fact occurred. Consider the objective: "Given a terrain map of the United States and information about prevailing winds, demonstrates the location of regions of heavy rainfall by shading the map" (applying a rule). This description more or less directly describes the situation which can be used by a teacher to verify that the desired learning has taken place. A student, or a group of students, could be supplied with terrain maps, prevailing wind information, and asked to perform this task. The resulting records of their performances would serve as an assessment of their learning of the appropriate rule.

With comparable adequacy, statements of objectives can serve as bases for the development of teacher-made tests. These in turn may be employed for formal kinds of assessment of student performance, when considered desirable by the teacher. Alternately, they can be used as "self-tests" which students employ when engaging in individual study or self-instruction.

The classes of objectives described in this chapter constitute a *taxonomy* which is applicable to the design of many kinds of assessment instruments and tests. A somewhat different, although not incompatible, taxonomy of objectives is described in the work of Bloom (1956), and of Krathwohl, Bloom, & Masia (1964). The application of this latter taxonomy to the design of tests and other assessment techniques is illustrated in many subject-matter fields by Bloom, Hastings, & Madaus (1971). This work describes in detail methods of planning assessment procedures for most areas of the school curriculum. Further discussion of methods for developing tests and test items based on the categories of learning outcomes described in this chapter is contained in Chapter 9.

SUMMARY

The identification and definition of performance objectives is an important step in the design of instruction. Objectives serve as guidelines for developing the instruction, and for designing measures of student performance to determine whether the course objectives have been reached.

Initially, the aims of instruction are frequently formulated as a set of *purposes* for a course. These purposes are further refined and converted to operational terms by the process of defining the performance objectives. These describe the *planned* outcomes of instruction, and they are the basis for evaluating the success of the instruction in terms of its intended outcomes. It is recognized, of course, that there are often unintended or unexpected outcomes, judged, when later observed, to be either desirable or undesirable.

This chapter has presented a five-component guide to the writing of performance objectives. The five elements named were:

1. Situation
2. Learned Capability
3. Object
4. Action
5. Tools or other constraints

Examples are given, showing how these components can be used to result in unambiguous statements of objectives for different school subjects. The examples chosen also illustrate objectives for various categories of learned capabilities.

Special attention is called to the need for care in choosing action verbs suitable for describing both the learned capability inferred from the observed performance, and for describing the nature of the performance itself. Table 3 presents a convenient summary of such action verbs.

The kinds of performance objectives described for the various categories of learned capabilities play an essential role in the method of instructional design presented in this book. They relate to the evaluation of student performance resulting from instruction, as treated later in Chapter 9. Performance objectives also form a direct link to the topics of the next chapter, Designing Instructional Sequences.

REFERENCES

Bloom, B. S. (Ed.) *Taxonomy of Educational Objectives. Handbook: Cognitive Domain.* New York: David McKay, 1956.

Bloom, B. S. Learning for mastery. In B. S. Bloom, J. T. Hastings, & G. F. Madaus (Eds.), *Handbook on Formative and Summative Evaluation of Student Learning.* New York: McGraw-Hill, 1971.

Bloom, B. S., Hastings, J. T., & Madaus, G. F. *Handbook on Formative and Summative Evaluation of Student Learning.* New York: McGraw-Hill, 1971.

Briggs, L. J. *Handbook of Procedures for the Design of Instruction.* Pittsburgh, Pa.: American Institutes for Research, 1970.

Bruner, J. S. *The Relevance of Education.* New York: Norton, 1971.

Gagné, R. M. *The Conditions of Learning,* 2d Ed. New York: Holt, Rinehart and Winston, 1970.

Krathwohl, D. R., Bloom, B. S., & Masia, B. B. *Taxonomy of Educational Objectives. Handbook II: Affective Domain.* New York: David McKay, 1964.

Mager, R. F. *Preparing Objectives for Instruction.* Belmont, Calif.: Fearon, 1962.

Popham, W. J., & Baker, E. L. *Establishing Instructional Goals.* Englewood Cliffs, N. J.: Prentice-Hall, 1970.

6
DESIGNING INSTRUCTIONAL SEQUENCES

Learning directed towards the goals of school education must of necessity take place on a number of occasions spread over time. The specific accomplishment of a single instructional objective must be preceded and followed by many other individual learning events. Thus there arises a need to plan *sequences* of these learning events. The basic reason for sequences of instruction is simply that the desired learning cannot take place all at once, and therefore must be designed so as to occur in a series of "steps," in other words, in a succession of individual occasions.

Planning sequences of instruction may be conceived as a task relevant to a total course or an entire curriculum, as, for example, a curriculum in social studies for the junior high school. Or, sequencing may represent a problem to be solved for the single course topic, such as "writing descriptive paragraphs," or "using arithmetic operations with whole numbers." A third and critically important reference of the sequence question is to the sequence of events within the individual lesson, such as "constructing sentences with dependent clauses," or "comparing the family in several cultures." And finally, there is the matter of the sequence of events which occurs or is planned to occur, for the purpose of bringing about the acquisition of an individual learning objective, as "identifying initial letters of sentences as capitalized letters." These four different levels of the sequence problem are illustrated in Table 3.

It is important to distinguish among these four levels of the "sequence question," for quite different considerations apply to each one. As will be apparent from the contents of this chapter, we are mainly concerned here with Levels 1 and 2, and will be dealing again in the next chapter with the questions posed by Levels 3 and 4.

Sequence of the Course and Curriculum

It is difficult to find a basis for correct sequencing of the entire set of topics for a course or set of courses other than a kind of "common sense"

TABLE 3   *Four Different Levels of the Problem of Instructional Sequence*

	Unit	*Example*	*Sequence Question*
Level 1	Course or Course Sequence	Essay Composition	How shall the topics of "achieving unity," "paragraph arrangement," "writing the paragraph," "summarizing," etc., be arranged in sequence?
Level 2	Topic	Writing the Paragraph	How shall the sub-topics of "topic sentence," "arranging ideas for emphasis," "expressing a single idea," etc., be arranged in sequence?
Level 3	Lesson	Composing a topic sentence	How shall the subordinate skills in composing a topic sentence be presented for learning in sequence?
Level 4	Lesson Component	Constructing a complex sentence	How shall the communications and other events in the learner's environment be arranged in a sequence resulting in learning of the desired single capability?

logical ordering. Presumably, one wants to insure that prerequisite intellectual skills and verbal information that are necessary for any given topic have been previously learned. For example, the topic of adding fractions is introduced in arithmetic after the student has learned to multiply and divide whole numbers, because the operations required in adding fractions include these "simpler" operations. In a science course, one is concerned that a topic like "representing relations between physical variables graphically" has been preceded by a topic such as "measuring physical variables," because it is these measures which are to be represented in the graph. Similarly, one attempts to insure that a social studies topic on "comparison of family structures across cultures" has been preceded by a topic on "the family" and one on "What is a culture?"

Presumably, the primary basis for the design of such topic sequences within courses or sets of courses rests upon judgments of *how much* can be accomplished within any single topical unit. If the topic is conceived as "small" (such as "Roman numerals"), it can be planned as a single topic. If it is large, this means it will take more time, and therefore must be designed as a succession of topics, or possibly as a sequence of common "threads" within a succession of topics.

Course and curriculum sequences are typically represented in *scope and sequence charts*, which name the topics to be studied in a total course or set of courses and lay them out in matrices, often indicating the topics suggested for each grade level. More elaborate methods for representing both topics and lessons have been attempted, notably by *Science—A Process Approach* (AAAS Commission on Science Education, 1967). The chart which accompanies this elementary science curriculum not only suggests a set of topics and a sequence of lessons within each, but also indicates the set of prerequisite relationships which may be presumed to exist among them.

It may be that some theoretical basis will one day be proposed to replace the "common-sense logic" which now underlies the design of sequences of topics for courses. The idea of the "spiral curriculum" (Bruner, 1960, p. 52), for example, proposes that content topics be systematically reintroduced at periodic intervals. Two purposes are served by such a scheme. First, the previously learned knowledge of the topic is given a review, which tends to improve its retention. And second, the topic may be progressively elaborated when it is reintroduced, leading to broadened understanding and transfer of learning. The conception of the spiral curriculum has not as yet been explicated in detail, but it appears to hold much promise for future curriculum design efforts.

Sequence of the Topic

Designing a sequence of instruction within a topic is a problem on which some systematic techniques can be brought to bear. As an initial step, it may be recognized that a topic may, and often does, have several components—several different purposes. A topic on "the family," for example, is likely to include purposes like (a) "understanding the definition of 'family'," (b) "knowing differences in the characteristics of families of different cultures," and (c) "appreciating cultural differences in families." It may be noted that we use the word "purpose" to represent the aims of a topic. This word is used to imply an instructional unit of intermediate size—a size which is typical in the planning of topics. Note also that statements of purpose are not usually phrased in terms of human performance, as is true of the unitary objectives described in the previous chapter.

A mathematics topic, such as "understanding the addition of integers," may likewise have more than one purpose. One may be "finding the sum of positive and negative numbers," while another within the same topic may be "deriving the properties of a number system from basic axioms." Further, the designer of instruction for such a topic may even have in mind the purpose of "appreciation of the precision of mathematical reasoning."

The probability is high that when differing purposes (stated in terms similar to those employed in these examples) can be identified as part of a single topic, one must be prepared to deal with different kinds of *learning outcomes* (that is, different types of *learned capabilities*). Unfortunately, though, the existence of different learning outcomes and their number cannot be established with certainty simply by the statement of more than one purpose for a topic. The difficulty lies in the ambiguities of language. Thus, a statement like "appreciation of family differences" may imply one, or two, or even three different kinds of learned capabilities, when examined more thoroughly.

Analyzing Goal Statements to Determine Learning Outcomes   To overcome the difficulty of language ambiguity in statements of topic purposes, one must move in the direction of *performance objectives*. It is often recommended that the entire process of stating a total set of performance objectives, including those for each lesson in the topic, be carried out. Such an effort would be likely to yield a fairly large number of specific performance objectives, such as "classifies the functions of a mother" (for a topic on the family), and many others as specific. This manner of proceeding is surely not incorrect in any basic sense. The specific objectives can then be grouped and categorized into types of learned capabilities, which is the desired aim.

However, it may be recognized that, although correct, the method of defining an entire set of performance objectives may be inconvenient at this stage of the game. The designer of instruction within a topic may well not want to be bothered with the details of performance objectives in order to plan the various component lessons on which his attention is focused. He wishes to answer the question, "What lessons are needed?" rather than, "What objectives are to be contained within each lesson?" He therefore is likely to search for a shortcut.

How can one "move in the direction of performance objectives" without actually stating all of them in detail? One possible answer is to attempt to analyze each topic purpose in terms of some *representative* performance objectives, rather than all of them. "Appreciation of family differences"— what does that mean in terms of human performance? It might mean "classifying the characteristics which make families differ, from one culture to another"—a reasonably good performance objective. Or, it might mean "generating a definition of family which takes account of cultural differences"—a different but equally good performance objective. At this point it may be clear to the designer that there is still another possibility latent in this topic statement. This is "choosing not to make prejudicial statements about families or members of families from different cultures"—again, a reasonably good performance objective.

When analyses of this sort are carried out, yielding objectives in performance terms, even if only representative examples, the process of identifying learning outcomes becomes quite clear. With just a little thought, one can readily identify the kind of learned capability which is being demanded, as follows:

"classifying the characteristics which make families differ from one culture to another"	type of capability—an intellectual skill, more specifically, a defined concept
"generating a definition of family which takes account of cultural differences"	type of capability—a different intellectual skill, namely, problem-solving
"choosing not to make prejudicial statements about families or members of families from different cultures"	type of capability—an attitude

It is evident from this example, then, that statements of topic purposes are simply too ambiguous to be dealt with in analytical fashion. They may serve a satisfying purpose for the person who enunciates them (who may, of course, be a parent or school-board member). The instructional designer, however, cannot work with such ambiguity. He must find at least representative examples of the performance objectives which reflect the single or multiple meanings of the topic statement. In these terms, he will readily be able to categorize them as types of capabilities to be learned.

The previously stated mathematics example, "understanding the addition of integers," can as readily be analyzed to yield types of learning outcomes as follows:

"finding the sum of positive and negative numbers"	type of capability—intellectual skill (rule)
"deriving the properties of a number system from basic axioms"	type of capability—(1) intellectual skill (problem solving) and (2) cognitive strategy
"preference for using the precision of mathematical reasoning"	type of capability—attitude

Identifying the Lessons Required for a Topic   Once the learning outcomes have become clear, it is possible to proceed with planning for the topic in terms of the lessons required. Often, one tries to have a single lesson deal with a single learning outcome. The reason for this procedure, of course, is that each type of learning outcome (motor skill, verbal information, intellectual skill, cognitive strategy, attitude) requires a different set of critical learning conditions, as described in Chapters 3 and 4. However, a hard-and-fast rule should probably not be suggested, since in many instances the designer may think it better to include more than one type of learning outcome in each lesson, or even to shift back and forth between different types of outcomes. The implication is that planning for lessons within a topic should be done in terms of learned capabilities. These are likely to be the stable elements in the total plan, rather than the lessons themselves.

The components of the topic, then, can be planned as sets of lessons (if relatively lengthy instruction is implied), individual lessons (if instruction is of moderate length), or parts of lessons (if small). In any case, these components of the topic need to be conceived as *differentiated types of learning outcomes*, each of which requires a different set of critical conditions in order for the desired learning to occur. Of course, it is possible that a topic might have only one type of capability to be learned; but it is not uncommon for several types to be present within a given topic.

Sequencing Lessons in Topics   Now it is possible to return to the main subject of this section, which is the sequencing of lessons within topics. In view of the fact that different learning outcomes may be involved, this is not an entirely simple matter, and it is one in which, again, common sense plays a part.

Table 4 summarizes the major considerations regarding the arrangement of sequence within a topic for each of the types of learned capability.

TABLE 4   *Desirable Sequence Characteristics*
Associated with Five Types of Learning Outcome

Type of Learning Outcome	Major Principles of Sequencing	Related Sequence Factors
Motor Skills	Provide intensive practice on part-skills of critical importance and practice on total skill.	First of all, learn the "executive routine" (rule).
Verbal Information	For major sub-topics, order of presentation not important. Individual facts should be preceded or accompanied by meaningful context.	Prior learning of necessary intellectual skills involved in reading, listening, etc. is usually assumed.
Intellectual Skills	Presentation of learning situation for each new skill should be preceded by prior mastery of subordinate skills.	Information relevant to the learning of each new skill should be previously learned or presented in instructions.
Attitudes	Establishment of respect for source as an initial step. Choice situations should be preceded by mastery of any skills involved in these choices.	Information relevant to choice behavior should be previously learned or presented in instructions.
Cognitive Strategies	Problem situations should contain previously acquired intellectual skills.	Information relevant to solution of problems should be previously learned or presented in instructions.

The central column of the table indicates sequencing principles applicable to the particular kind of capability that represents the central focus of the learning. The right-hand column lists sequence considerations relevant to this learning, but arising in other domains.

Sequencing Lessons for Motor Skills   In the case of motor skills, there is evidence to the effect that the learning of an "executive routine" (Fitts & Posner, 1967, p. 11) is of critical importance to learning. Such a routine represents the "procedure" of the motor performance and governs the sequence of actions involved in it. The executive routine is actually a rule, the intellectual-skill component of a motor skill. For example, in learning to put the shot, the performer must learn to follow the sequence of taking some running steps, stopping at a line, taking a stance with the shot, and then ejecting the shot. In carrying out these actions in order, he is following a rule, which he must learn as an early part of his total learning task, perhaps first of all. The more specifically motor components must then be practiced. Generally, the evidence does not indicate that the total skill will always be more quickly or readily learned if the components are practiced as "parts" before being put together into the total skill (Bilodeau, 1966, p. 398). Highly complex motor skills appear to be best learned when practiced as "wholes." However, there may in some instances be an advantage to providing intensive practice on some part-skill which plays a particularly critical role in determining good performance in the whole skill. An example is the intensive practice of the "flutter-kick" by swimmers who are aiming at competitive swimming of the "crawl."

Sequencing Lessons for Information   When outcomes of information learning are intended, sequence is not of outstanding importance. For example, if a text in history is presenting the political events leading up to the election of President Lincoln, it is not of great importance for learning that these events be discussed in a strict temporal order, so long as this order is indicated (cf. Payne, Krathwohl, & Gordon, 1967). The presentation of these facts within a meaningful context, however, is an important consideration for effective learning. Ausubel (1968) suggests that the meaningful context in the form of an "advance organizer" should come first, and he has obtained evidence to this effect (Ausubel, 1960; Ausubel & Fitzgerald, 1961).

When the topic or subtopic requires the learning of *intellectual skills*, sequence in the sense of the mastery of prerequisite skills becomes a most important consideration, as we have seen in Chapter 3 (cf. Gagné, 1970, pp. 237–276). The learning of each skill representing a lesson objective will occur most readily when the learner is able to bring to bear those recalled, previously acquired skills which are relevant to the new task. The learning of such tasks also requires information, which may either be recalled or presented as a part of instructions for the learning task (Gagné, 1970b). For example, if the intellectual skill being acquired involves the balancing of a chemical equation, the learner may need either to recall, or to be told by instructions, such facts as the valence of hydrogen (H^+), sulfur (S^{--}), and other elements.

Sequencing Lessons for Attitudes   The learning of attitudes appears to occur best under circumstances in which a respected "source" (that is, a person) makes a verbal communication to the learner regarding desirable choices of action, or perhaps displays these choices directly. For example, the model may indicate by his behavior a preference for counting to ten before losing his temper. To be effective, however, it is clear that the person acting as the model must be admired, respected, or otherwise well thought of. Respect for the model may of course already be present in the learner, for example, when that person is a teacher, a parent, or a friend. If such respect is not present, as when the source is not well known to the learner, it must be established as a first step in the sequence of events leading to attitude learning or change.

The desired attitude may involve choice of some action which in turn requires intellectual skills. Again, the implication is that such skills must have been previously learned; and if they are not, they should be acquired before the learning of the attitude is undertaken. For example, the desired learning may concern a consumer attitude governing the tendency to compare prices of packaged foods in terms of ratios, or cost per ounce. But such an attitude will not be successfully established, regardless of how well the other conditions of instruction may be arranged, if the learner has not acquired the capability of forming ratios to obtain comparative costs. In a similar manner, it may be determined that information relevant to the desired course of action is needed. Such information may be recalled from prior learning, or may be presented as part of the learning situation, usually before the communication which centers on the attitude to be learned.

Sequencing Lessons for Cognitive Strategies   In the learning of cognitive strategies, problem situations are presented to the learner which call upon his self-management skills of organizing, analyzing, and thinking. In arranging such problem situations within a topic, one is often concerned with designing them with suitable variety, so that the strategy being learned will become generalizable to many new situations in the future. Variations in successively presented problems need not occur in any particular sequence so far as is now known. However, it would seem best to avoid variations which appear too extreme, which have the effect of making the problem too "difficult" and scare the learner away. Even more important, the designer of instruction must avoid presenting problems which actually *are* too difficult for the reason that they demand intellectual skills or information which the learner does not possess. For instance, a geometrical problem may challenge the learner to engage in the kind of thinking which improves certain of his cognitive strategies; but if he fails to solve the problem because he is missing some component skill or piece of information about a particular geometrical relationship, the learning will not be effective, and the occurrence may contribute to the learner's discouragement. Prior learning of both relevant intellectual skills and relevant information (when not supplied by instructions) accordingly becomes a matter of consequence to the design of sequences for the learning of cognitive strategies.

Opportunities for application of cognitive strategies to varied problem situations are important to the learning of this kind of capability. Such varied "practice" appears to be essential for acquiring strategies which are broadly generalizable. In addition, success in solving problems has the effect of establishing and maintaining positive attitudes toward this kind of activity. In successfully solving novel problems, the learner may be acquiring confidence in his own capabilities. Thus he may be increasingly ready to trust his resources of cognitive strategies in meeting new problems.

Sequence of Events within the Lesson

The principles governing the design of sequences of instruction within lessons are essentially similar to those for various kinds of learning outcomes as they occur in topics, and as shown in Table 4. These types of learned capabilities typically appear as smaller "chunks" in lessons than they do in topics. Sometimes, of course, a particular "chunk" may require more than one time period, and thus need two or more lessons for complete coverage.

As we have seen, more than one type of learning outcome—intellectual skill, cognitive strategy, information, motor skill, or attitude—may occur within a lesson. Each of these kinds of outcome implies certain prerequisite learnings, and therefore an instructional sequence. Following the procedure we have outlined previously, the designer of a lesson will be placing emphasis on what the student can *do* as a result of instruction. Usually this means that the designer will need to make a somewhat detailed analysis of the *intellectual skills* involved in a lesson. The planning of a lesson can often best be undertaken by making intellectual skills the major organizing factor. In any case, the method of analyzing these skills to reveal the requirements of sequencing needs to be described in greater detail.

Table 4 indicates, for intellectual skills, that each new skill should be preceded by prior mastery of subordinate skills. The way this influences the planning of events of a lesson is described in the following chapter. Before reaching that point, however, we need to deal more fully with the pattern of skills and subordinate skills which is fundamental to instructional planning, as seen in *learning hierarchies*.

DERIVING LEARNING HIERARCHIES FOR INTELLECTUAL SKILLS

The structure of intellectual skills makes it possible to design with considerable precision effective conditions for learning them. When this is done, the learning of intellectual skills becomes a process which is easy for a teacher to manage. In addition, the process of learning becomes highly reinforcing for the learner, because he is frequently realizing that with apparent and satisfying suddenness he knows how to do some things that he didn't know before. Thus the activity of learning takes on for him an excitement which is at the opposite pole from "drill" and "rote recitation."

The key to the design of conditions for this effective kind of learning is the *learning hierarchy* (Gagné, 1970, pp. 237–276). The learning hierarchy is an arrangement of intellectual skill objectives into a pattern which shows the prerequisite relationships among them. Beginning with a particular objective (often a lesson objective), the learning hierarchy shows which intellectual skills are prerequisite; having identified this second set of skills, the prerequisites of each of these is in turn indicated, and this process continues until one has displayed in a bottom "row" the most elementary intellectual skills with which one needs to be concerned. An example of a learning hierarchy for a skill of elementary mathematics is shown in Figure 3.

Here the lesson objective (for a prekindergarten or kindergarten child) is one of dividing a group of objects into halves, and a similar group of objects into thirds. In order to learn to perform such a task correctly, the child must have some prerequisite skills, which are indicated on the second "line" of the hierarchy. Specifically, he must be able (1) to look at a set of

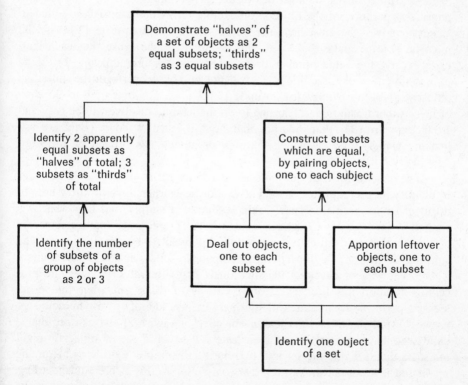

FIGURE 3   A learning hierarchy for a task in elementary mathematics. (From Gagné, R. M., 1970, Figure 17; adapted from Resnick and Wang, 1969.)

objects which the teacher has divided into halves and be able to identify them (as by pointing) as "halves," and similarly for a set of objects divided into thirds. Also, he must be able (2) to make subsets of objects which are equal by a one-to-one pairing process. These two prerequisite skills, then, are considered to be essential for the learning of the skill represented by the target objective with which the hierarchy was begun. Each of these prerequisite skills (1) and (2) has its own prerequisites, which are indicated on the next "line" of the hierarchy.

What is meant by a prerequisite? Evidently, a prerequisite is a "simpler" intellectual skill, but such a characterization is quite inadequate to identify it properly, since one could name many intellectual skills pertaining to sets of objects which are simpler than the lesson objective described in the figure. A prerequisite skill is *integrally related* to the skill which is superordinate to it, in the sense that the latter skill cannot be done if the prerequisite skill is not available to the learner. Consider what the child is doing when he "demonstrates 'halves' of a set of objects as two equal subsets." He makes a physical separation of the objects, on a table top. But he must know that to achieve "halves" he must have *two* subsets; this is prerequisite (1). And he must be able to make these two subsets equal, in the sense that each contains exactly the same number of members; this is prerequisite (2). If he *fails* to do either of these things, he will not be able to perform the milestone objective. Now turn this idea around: If he *already knows* how to do each of these subordinate things, learning to do the lesson objective will be easy and straightforward. The likelihood is that he will learn to do it (once we ask him to) rapidly, and even with the kind of immediacy implied by the word "discovery."

The general form of question one needs to ask about any skill, in order to identify its prerequisites, is "What would the learner have to know how to do in order to learn this (new) skill, assuming I simply told him what was wanted?" (cf. Gagné, 1968). In other words, prerequisite intellectual skills are those that are critically required to be recalled by the learner, if the learning of the new skill is to proceed most rapidly and without a hitch. There is a way of checking whether one's first attempt to answer the preceding question has been successful. This is to think out what the to-be-learned performance requires of the learner, and identify "how he could go wrong." Applying this to the lesson objective of Figure 3, one can see that a child who is attempting to "demonstrate halves of a set of objects" might fail if he didn't divide the set into two parts (this is prerequisite (1)); or, he might fail if he didn't make these two parts equal (this is prerequisite (2)). Thus the specification of prerequisite skills should provide a complete description of those previously learned skills needed by the learner in order to acquire the new skill most readily.

Incidentally, the fact that prerequisite skills may be checked by considering ways in which the learner can fail serves to emphasize the direct relevance of learning hierarchies to the teacher's task of *diagnosis*. If one finds a learner who is having trouble acquiring a new intellectual skill, the first diagnostic question should probably be, "What prerequisite skills has he failed to learn?" The contrast between such a question and those of, "What genetic deficiency does he have?" or "What general intelligence does he have?" will be apparent. The latter questions may suggest solutions which merely serve to remove the learner from the learning environment by putting him in a special group or class. Responsible diagnosis, in contrast, attempts to discover what the learner needs to learn. The chances are high that this will turn out to be a prerequisite intellectual skill, as indicated by a learning hierarchy. If it is, suitable instruction can readily be designed to get the learner "back on the track" of a learning sequence which continues to be positively reinforcing.

Relation to Types of Learning   Further consideration of the learning hierarchy of Figure 3 may be of interest, for the purpose of relating the objective represented there to the types of learned capabilities described in Chapter 3.

The varieties of capabilities represented by the lesson objective and subordinate objectives of the hierarchy correspond to the "levels" of learning described as rules, defined concepts, and concrete concepts. The target objective "demonstrate halves as two equal subsets" may readily be recognized as a *rule*. The first prerequisite skill, tracing down the left-hand branch, is "identify two apparently equal subsets as 'halves.'" This is an example of a *defined concept*. (Note that the major verb should be "classify," in accordance with the method of Chapter 5). When we ask the child to show us that two subsets represent "halves" (or that three represent "thirds"), his performance includes the demonstration that there are two (or in the case of thirds, three). He is thus classifying subsets in accordance with a definition that includes "two" (or "three"). Now consider the intellectual skill subordinate to this one—here the child identifies two subsets as two, and three subsets as three. These are *concrete concepts*, which the child can identify by some action equivalent to pointing. One says "show me the set which is a two," and the child indicates it by pointing, or by placing his hand on the set. Or, one may have various sets, and say "show me all those that are two," and the child points to each set of two successively.

A similar description, in terms of types of intellectual skills, can be made for the branch of the hierarchy lying on the right. When the child "constructs subsets which are equal, by pairing objects," he is obviously following a *rule*. (It is, of course, a simpler rule than that of the lesson objective). Prerequisite to it is the skill "deal out objects, one to each subset," which is still another *rule*. The skill "apportion leftover objects, one to each subset," may be considered a *defined concept*. What the child is doing in this case is classifying sets for equality; in other words, he is showing that he knows the concept of set equality, under conditions in which the numerical size of the sets is made to vary. Since both of these prerequisite skills involve identifying "one," we arrive finally at the simplest skill at the bottom of the hierarchy, which is a *concrete concept*.

Can even simpler prerequisites be identified, representing simpler types of learning? It is easy to see that this is indeed the case. "Identifying the number of subsets as two or three" must obviously have been preceded by a *discrimination*, in which the child distinguishes things which are two and things which are three (not by name, but simply by "seeing them as different"). As another example, "dealing out objects, one to each subset," requires the prior learning of some *motor chains*, having to do with the movements involved in picking up the objects and dealing them into piles. Obviously, the designer of this hierarchy made the reasonable assumption that, for the group of children to be instructed in this instance, these simpler intellectual skills had been previously learned. Thus it may be seen that there is a fairly simple answer to the question of where the process of deriving a hierarchy should stop. One proceeds with the analysis of prerequisite skills to the point at which the reasonable assumption can be made that subordinate skills have been already learned, for the group of learners with which one is dealing. This does not mean that prerequisite skills down to the level of simple chains cannot be identified; it merely means they do not need to be.

It may be noted that the process of deriving a hierarchy does not set out to represent the kinds of learned capabilities described in Chapter 3; it merely ends up doing so. One does not proceed by saying to oneself, this lesson objective is a rule, therefore it must have defined concepts as prerequisites, and these in turn must have concrete concepts as prerequisites, and so on. Instead, as previously indicated, one proceeds by considering what the critical subordinate skills must be for specific tasks of learning. However, the fundamental logic of the arrangement of skills from simple to complex still applies, and that is the basic reason why the nature of intellectual skills needs to be understood. An attempt to design a hierarchy which indicates a rule as prerequisite to a defined concept, or a defined concept as prerequisite to a concrete concept, or any other inversion of this sort, is surely wrong. If one arrives at such inversions in deriving a hierarchy, it is a sure sign of the necessity for rethinking the entire structure.

Some Cautions   Deriving a learning hierarchy for intellectual skills is not necessarily an easy matter. Mistaken approaches can be taken, unless one attends closely to the necessity for thinking out as clearly and comprehensively as possible what the learner is doing when he solves a problem, applies a rule, uses a definition, identifies an object quality, distinguishes differences, or executes a chain of responses. Some of the wrong roads that are easily chosen may be identified as follows:

1. Identifying prerequisite information rather than prerequisite skills. Of course, such information may indeed be needed. But it does not fit into the scheme of a learning hierarchy (cf. Gagné, 1968). Suppose the lesson objective is "converting Fahrenheit to Centigrade temperature readings." It is easy to suppose that a prerequisite might be "knowing that $C = 5/9$ $(F-32)$." But this is an item of information, and not in itself a skill. Prerequisite information cannot be analyzed in the manner of prerequisite skills because it simply doesn't behave the same way in learning. Further thought about this objective, with this caution in mind, leads to the identification of prerequisite skills as "finding numerical values of an unknown variable by solving equations," and "substituting numerical values of variables in equations," and "simplifying equations to yield a single numerical value for a variable," and others subordinate to these.

2. Identifying as prerequisites skills that are "simpler" rather than those which are "integral components." An example is as follows: Suppose that the lesson objective is "subtracting multiple digit numbers, with borrowing," as in the example 53242 minus 178. One might readily imagine that a subordinate skill is "subtracting two-digit numbers, with borrowing," as in 42 minus 17. But this identification of a subordinate skill leaves out a great deal. It fails to include, for example, the prerequisite skill of "double borrowing," as exhibited in a task such as 317 minus 149. Neither does it include the skill of "subtracting when 'bringing down' is required," as in the example 3467 minus 42. Correct identification of subordinate skills thus requires the thinking out of all the component mental operations, and cannot depend merely upon the finding of skills that are "simpler."

Other Examples of Learning Hierarchies

Using the principles just described, several learning hierarchies have been developed in a number of different subject-matter areas. It will be recognized in these examples that full statements of the objectives of each capability to be learned cannot be included in the "boxes" of the hierarchy, owing to space limitations. Accordingly, abbreviated statements are used. The reader should experience little difficulty, however, in classifying the subordinate intellectual skills by type should he wish to do so.

A Hierarchy for Subtraction   Figure 4 illustrates a hierarchy for acquiring the complex skill of subtracting whole numbers. (In this case, the subordinate skills are identified by Roman numerals, to facilitate the discussion of lesson planning contained in the following chapter). It is evident that learning this skill requires the learner to combine a number of simpler rules.

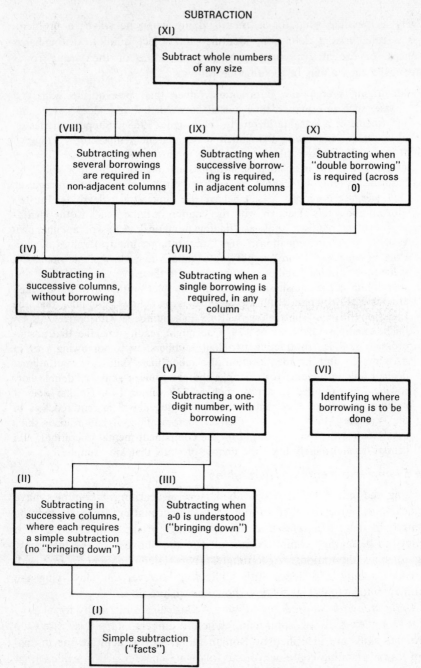

FIGURE 4   A learning hierarchy for subtracting whole numbers.

A Hierarchy for a Beginning Reading Skill   Another example of an analysis of learning structure may be selected from the field of reading. A hierarchy describing the skills composing an important beginning reading skill is illustrated in Figure 5. The target skill in this case requires that the child read orally words of any length, familiar or unfamiliar, which conform to regular pronunciation rules (for example, words such as "sensitizing," "contaminate," "distended").

A Hierarchy for a Science Problem   Figure 6 presents an example of a learning hierarchy developed by Wiegand (1970) for a study of problem-solving in science with sixth-grade students. In this case, the target higher-order skill to be learned involved the solving of a problem to derive a general expression for a relationship of physical variables presented in an inclined plane demonstration.

A Hierarchy for a Lesson in Social Studies   Figure 7 shows a learning hierarchy developed as a basis for instruction in a problem-solving lesson in social studies for sixth graders. The task in this instance required the students to make "new" categories of agricultural products from various countries, when presented with variegated lists of such products which were not categorized. This particular lesson was part of a set in which the students were discovering how to compare and contrast the exports of different countries (Coleman and Gagné, 1970).

These various examples of hierarchies will serve the purpose of indicating the meaning of lesson objectives for the learning of intellectual skills. Other varieties of hierarchies are contained in Briggs (1972). These include (a) art criticism for prospective art teachers, (b) for sixth grade children, how to analyze the effects of heredity and environment upon people and animals, and (c) how to write a news story for a newspaper.

SUMMARY

This chapter has suggested ways of deciding upon instructional sequences at the levels of the course and the topic. Course planning for a sequence of topics is typically done by a kind of "common-sense" logic. One topic may precede another because it describes events prior in time, or because it is a component part, or because it provides a meaningful context for what is to follow.

In proceeding from course purposes to performance objectives, it may not always be necessary to describe all the intermediate levels of planning in terms of complete lists of performance objectives for the topic. The method suggested here involves choosing representative samples of objectives within each domain of learning outcomes. It may be noted, however, that the

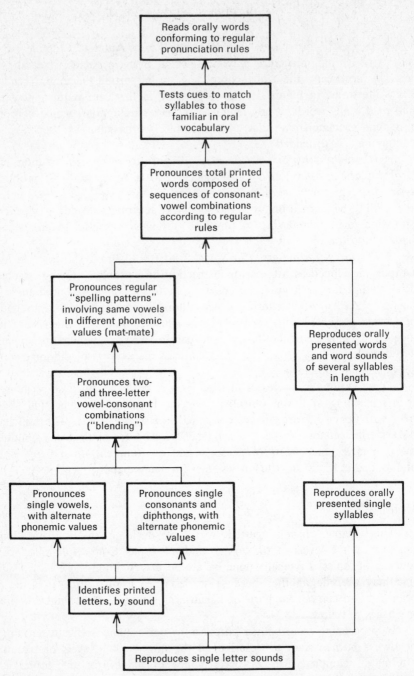

FIGURE 5   A learning hierarchy for a basic reading skill. (From Gagné, R. M., 1970, Figure 20.)

VARIABLES IN AN INCLINED PLANE

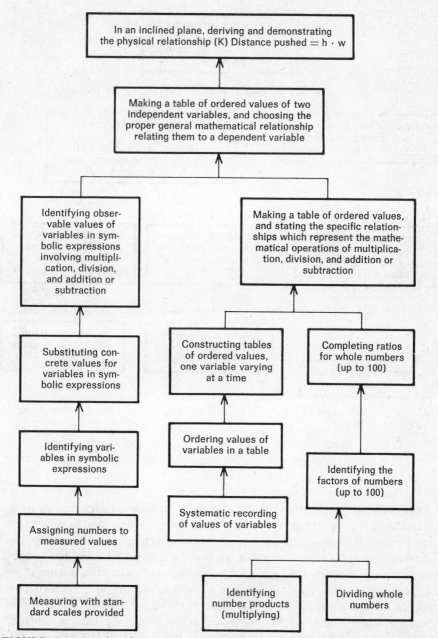

FIGURE 6   A learning hierarchy for a science problem. (From Wiegand, V. K., 1970.)

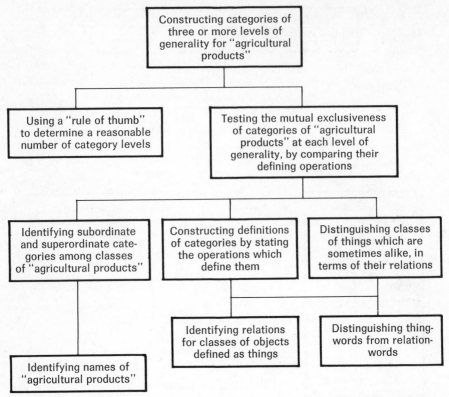

CATEGORIZING AGRICULTURAL PRODUCTS

Constructing categories of three or more levels of generality for "agricultural products"

Using a "rule of thumb" to determine a reasonable number of category levels

Testing the mutual exclusiveness of categories of "agricultural products" at each level of generality, by comparing their defining operations

Identifying subordinate and superordinate categories among classes of "agricultural products"

Constructing definitions of categories by stating the operations which define them

Distinguishing classes of things which are sometimes alike, in terms of their relations

Identifying relations for classes of objects defined as things

Distinguishing thing-words from relation-words

Identifying names of "agricultural products"

FIGURE 7   A learning hierarchy for a social studies problem. (Adapted from Coleman and Gagné, 1970.)

more complete procedure can be followed, and may sometimes be desirable, as is illustrated in Briggs (1972).

The designing of sequences for intellectual skills is described in greater detail than is the case for other types of capabilities. Learning hierarchies are derived by "working backwards" from target objectives to analyze the component skills involved. When complete, learning hierarchies represent sequences of skills to be learned in an order suggested by their arrangement. The learning of a new skill will be done most readily when the learner is able to recall the subordinate skills which compose it. When an instructional sequence has been designed for an intellectual skill, related learning of other kinds of capabilities may be interjected at appropriate points, as when the learning of information is required, or when the modification of an attitude is desired. In other instances, instruction aimed at other domains of capabilities may come before or after the intellectual skill represented in the learning hierarchy.

Designing sequences for other kinds of learned capabilities also requires an analysis of prerequisite learnings. Examples are given to illustrate how such prerequisites may be identified and incorporated into sequences of instruction.

The following two chapters describe how the plans for instructional sequence are carried into the design of a single lesson or lesson component. It is in the latter context that the "events of instruction" are introduced. These events pertain to the external supports for learning provided by the teacher, the course materials, or by the learner himself. They depend upon the prior learning which has been accomplished in accordance with a planned sequence.

REFERENCES

AAAS Commission on Science Education. *Science—A Process Approach.* Hierarchy Chart. New York: Xerox, 1967.

Ausubel, D. P. *Educational Psychology: A Cognitive View.* New York: Holt, Rinehart and Winston, 1968.

Ausubel, D. P. The use of advance organizers in the learning and retention of meaningful verbal material. *Journal of Educational Psychology*, 1960, *51*, 267–272.

Ausubel, D. P. & Fitzgerald, D. The role of discriminability in meaningful verbal learning and retention. *Journal of Educational Psychology*, 1961, *52*, 266–274.

Bilodeau, E. A. *Acquisition of Skill.* New York: Academic Press, 1966.

Briggs, L. J. *Student's Guide to Handbook of Procedures for the Design of Instruction.* Pittsburgh: American Institutes for Research, 1972.

Bruner, J. S. *The Process of Education.* Cambridge, Mass.: Harvard University Press, 1960.

Coleman, L. T. & Gagné, R. M. Transfer of learning in a social studies task of comparing-contrasting. In R. M. Gagné (Ed.), *Basic Studies of Learning Hierarchies in School Subjects.* Berkeley, California: University of California, 1970. (USOE Contract No. OEC–4–062949–3066, Final Report).

Fitts, P. M. & Posner, M. I. *Human Performance.* Belmont, California: Brooks/Cole, 1967.

Gagné, R. M. Learning hierarchies. *Educational Psychologist*, 1968, *6*, 1–9.

Gagné, R. M. *The Conditions of Learning*, 2d Ed. New York: Holt, Rinehart and Winston, 1970.

Payne, D. A., Krathwohl, D. R., & Gordon, J. The effect of sequence on programmed instruction. *American Educational Research Journal*, 1967, *4*, 125–132.

Resnick, L. B. & Wang, M. C. *Approaches to the Validation of Learning Hierarchies.* Pittsburgh, Pa.: Learning Research and Development Center, University of Pittsburgh, 1969 (Preprint 50).

Weigand, V. K. A study of subordinate skills in science problem solving. In R. M. Gagné (Ed.), *Basic Studies of Learning Hierarchies in School Subjects.* Berkeley, California: University of California, 1970. (USOE Contract No. OEC–4–062949–3066, Final Report).

7
THE EVENTS OF INSTRUCTION

Planning a course of instruction makes use of the principles described in the preceding chapters: determining what the outcomes of instruction are to be, defining performance objectives, and deciding upon a sequence for the topics and lessons which make up the course. When these things have been done, the fundamental "architecture" of the course is ready for more detailed planning in terms of both teacher and student activities. It is time to give consideration to the bricks and mortar of the individual lesson.

Supposing, then, that the course of instruction has been planned so that the student may reasonably progress from one lesson to the next. How does one insure that he takes each learning step, and that he does not falter along the way? How is the student coaxed along during the lesson itself? How does one, in fact, *instruct* him?

THE NATURE OF INSTRUCTION

In designing the "architecture" for the course, we have said virtually nothing about how instruction itself may be done. In making progress from one moment to the next during a lesson, a set of events takes place which acts upon the student, and in which he becomes involved. This set of events is specifically meant by *instruction*.

The instructional events of a lesson may take a variety of forms. They may require the teacher's participation to a greater or lesser degree; and they may be determined by the student to a greater or lesser degree. In a basic sense, these events constitute a set of *communications to the student*. Their most typical form is as verbal statements, whether oral or printed. Of course, communications may be made to young children which are not verbal, and which instead use other media of communication such as gestures or pictures. But whatever the medium, the essential nature of instruction is most clearly characterized as a set of communications.

The communications which make up instruction have the sole aim of aiding the process of learning—that is, of getting the student from one state of mind to another. It would be wrong to suppose that their function is simply "to communicate" in the sense of "to inform." Sometimes it appears that teachers are inclined to make this mistake—they "like to hear themselves talk," as has sometimes been said. There is perhaps no better way to avoid the error of talking too much than to keep firmly in mind that communications during a lesson have this purpose of facilitating learning, and that anything beyond this is mere chatter. Much of the communicating done by a teacher is essential for learning. Sometimes a fairly large amount of teacher communication is needed; on other occasions, however, none may be needed at all.

Self-Instruction and the Self-Learner

Any or all of the events of instruction may be put into effect by the learner himself when he is "self-instructing." Students engage in a good deal of self-instruction, not solely when they are working on "programmed" materials, but also when they are studying textbooks, performing laboratory exercises, or completing projects of various sorts. Skill at self-instruction may be expected to increase with the age of the learner as he gains in experience of learning tasks. Events of the lesson, designed to aid and support learning, require teacher activities to a much greater extent in the first grade than they do in the tenth. As a learner gains experience and continues to pursue learning activities, he acquires more and more of the characteristics of a "self-learner." That is, he is able to use skills and strategies by which he manages his own learning.

The events of instruction to be described next, therefore, should not be viewed as being invariably required for every lesson and every learner. In practice, a judgment must be made concerning the extent of self-instruction the learner is able to undertake. A more extensive consideration of self-instruction in systems of individualized instruction is contained in Chapter 10.

Instructional Events

The events of instruction are designed to make it possible for the learner to proceed from "where he is" at the beginning of a lesson to the achievement of the capability identified as the lesson's objective. In some instances, these events occur as a natural result of the learner's interaction with the particular materials of the lesson; as, for example, when the beginning reader comes to recognize an unfamiliar printed word as something familiar in his oral vocabulary, and thus receives *feedback* (a significant kind of instructional event). Mostly, however, the events of instruction must be deliberately arranged by a lesson designer or teacher as events which are initiated externally to the learner.

The exact form of communications to the learner is not something that can or should be specified in general for all lessons, but rather it must be decided for each lesson. The particular communications chosen should fit the circumstances and be designed to have the desired effect upon the learner. The functions served by the various events of instruction in a lesson are as follows, listed in the approximate order in which they are employed (cf. Gagné, 1968):

1. Gaining attention
2. Informing the learner of the objective
3. Stimulating recall of prerequisite learnings
4. Presenting the stimulus material
5. Providing "learning guidance"
6. Eliciting the performance
7. Providing feedback about performance correctness
8. Assessing the performance
9. Enhancing retention and transfer.

It should be realized at the outset that these events of instruction do not invariably occur in this exact order, although this is their most probable order. Even more important, by no means all of these events are provided for every lesson. Sometimes, one or more of them may already be obvious to the learner, and therefore may not be needed. Frequently, too, one or more of these kinds of communication are provided by the learner himself, particularly when the learner is a sophisticated "self-learner."

Gaining Attention   Various kinds of events are employed to gain the learner's attention. Basic ways of commanding attention involve the use of stimulus change, as is often done in moving display signs or in the rapid "cutting" of scenes on a television screen. Beyond this, a fundamental and frequently used method of gaining attention is to appeal to the learner's interests. A teacher may appeal to some particular child's interests by means of a verbal question such as "Wouldn't you like to know what makes a leaf fall from a tree?" in introducing a lesson dealing with leaves. A boy's interest may be captured by such a question as, "How do you figure a baseball player's batting average?" in connection with a lesson on percents. Naturally, one cannot provide a standard content for such questions—quite to the contrary, since every student's interests are different. Being skillful at gaining attention is a part of the teacher's art, involving insightful knowledge of the students with whom he deals.

Communications which are partially or even wholly non-verbal are often employed to gain attention for school lessons. For example, the teacher may present a demonstration, perhaps exhibiting some physical event (a puff of smoke, an unexpected collision, a change in color of liquid) which is novel and appealing to the student's interest or curiosity. Or, a motion picture or television scene may depict an unusual event and thus command attention.

A good preplanned lesson provides the teacher with one or more options of communications designed to gain attention. When instruction is individualized, the teacher is able to vary the content and form of the communication whenever necessary, in order to appeal to individual student interests.

Informing the Learner of the Objective   In some manner or other, the learner should know the kind of performance which will be used as an indication that learning has, in fact, been accomplished. Sometimes this aim of learning is quite obvious, and no special communication is required. For example, it would be somewhat ridiculous to make a special effort to communicate the objective to a novice golfer who undertakes to practice putting. However, there are many performance objectives which may not be initially obvious to students in school. For example, if the subject under study is the Preamble to the United States Constitution, being able to recite it verbatim is not at all the same objective as being able to state its major ideas. If decimals are being studied, is it obvious to the student during any given lesson whether he is expected to learn to (1) read decimals, (2) write decimals, or perhaps, (3) add decimals? The student should not be required to solve the puzzle of what is in the mind of his instructor. He needs to be told (unless, of course, he already knows).

On the whole, it is probably best not to take the chance of assuming that the student knows what the objective of the lesson is. Such a communication takes little time, and may at least serve the purpose of preventing the student from "getting entirely off the track." Communicating the objective also appears to be an act consistent with the frankness and honesty of a good teacher. In addition, the act of verbalizing the objective may help the teacher to stay "on target."

Of course, if objectives are to be communicated effectively, they must be put into words (or pictures, if appropriate) that the student can readily understand. For a six-year-old, an objective like "given a noun subject and object, and an active verb, formulate a correct sentence" must be translated into a communication which runs somewhat as follows: "Suppose I have the words 'boy,' 'dog,' and 'caught.' You could make them into a sentence, like 'The boy caught the dog.' This is called 'making a sentence,' and that's what I want you to do with the words I point to." Performance objectives, when used to describe a course of study, are typically stated in a form designed to communicate unambiguously to teachers or to instructional designers. The planning of instruction for a lesson, however, includes making the kind of communication of the lesson's objective which will be readily understood by students.

It is sometimes speculated that communicating an objective to a student may tend to keep him from trying to meet still other objectives which he may formulate himself. No one has ever seen this happen, and the chances are it is a highly unlikely possibility. When one communicates a lesson's objective to a student, the student is hardly inclined to think that such a statement forbids him from giving further thought to the subject at hand. Working with an objective of "reading decimals," for example, it is not uncommon for a teacher to ask the question, "What do you suppose the sum of these decimals might be?" Thus still another objective is communicated, which the student is perfectly free to think about, while making sure that he has achieved the first-mentioned objective. Naturally, one also wants the student to develop in such a way that he will think of objectives himself and learn how to teach them to himself. Nothing in the communication of a lesson's objectives carries the slightest hint that such activities are to be discouraged. The basic purpose of such communication is simply to answer the student's question, "How will I know when I have learned?"

Stimulating Recall of Prerequisite Learned Capabilities   This kind of communication may be critical for the essential event of learning. Much of new learning (some might say, all) is, after all, the combining of ideas. Learning a rule about *mass* (Newton's Law) involves a combination of the ideas of *acceleration* and *force*, as well as the idea of *multiplying*. In terms of modern mathematics, learning the idea of *eight* involves the idea of the *set seven*, the *set one*, and *joining*. Component ideas (concepts, rules) must be previously learned if the new learning is to be successful. At the moment of learning, these previously acquired capabilities must be highly accessible in order to take part in the learning event itself. Their accessibility is insured by having them recalled just before the new learning takes place.

The recall of previously learned capabilities may be stimulated by a communication which asks a recognition, or better a recall, question. For example, when children are being taught about rainfall in relation to mountains, the question may be asked, "Do you remember what the air is like in a cloud which has travelled over land in the summer?" (The air is warm.) The further question may then be asked, "What is the temperature likely to be of the land on a high mountain?" (Cold.) This line of questioning recalls previously learned rules, and obviously leads to a strand of learning which will culminate with the acquisition of a new rule concerning the effects of cooling on a warm, moisture-laden cloud.

Presenting the Stimulus Material   The nature of this particular event is relatively obvious. The stimuli to be displayed (or communicated) to the learner are those involved in the performance which reflects the learning. If the learner must learn a sequence of facts, such as the events of history, then it is these facts which must be communicated, whether in oral or in printed form. If the learner is engaged in the task of pronouncing aloud printed words, as in elementary reading, then the printed words must be displayed. If he must learn to respond to oral questions in French, then these oral questions must be presented, since they are the stimuli of the task to be learned.

Although seemingly obvious, it is nevertheless of some importance that the proper stimuli be presented as a part of the instructional events. For example, if the learner is acquiring the capability of answering questions delivered orally in French, then the proper stimuli are *not* English questions, nor printed French questions. (This is not to deny, however, that such tasks may represent subordinate skills which have previously been used as learning tasks.) If the learner is to acquire the capability of using positive and negative numbers to solve verbally stated problems, then the proper stimuli are verbally stated problems, and not something else. If one neglects to use the proper stimuli for learning, he may end up observing the learner acquire the "wrong" skill.

A number of features of stimulus presentation are of special importance in the learning of the simpler kinds of intellectual skills, such as verbal and motor chains and discriminations. As indicated in Chapter 3, it is in connection with these kinds of capabilities that one finds the *timing* and *ordering* of stimulus events playing a particularly important role in learning. For example, suppose the student is learning the short motor chain of pronouncing a German sound (such as umlauted u) that is not made in speaking English. The teacher first makes the sound, and then asks the learner to repeat it. In successive trials, the learner's attempts to pronounce must come soon after the teacher says the sound, and the student must be told whether he is improving or not, until he can judge this for himself. It may take several repetitions of this process before acceptable mastery is achieved. This situation, then, involves *repeated close pairings* (in a time sense) of the teacher's sound, the student's response, and feedback from the teacher. The characteristics of this kind of stimulus presentation include *contiguity* of the stimulus with the student's response; *reinforcement* of correct student responses; and *repetition*.

In the learning of long verbal chains, an example of which is memorizing a poem, clearly one needs to read or hear the lines in the correct *order* before he attempts to repeat them. The student is in this case memorizing a series of words having a fixed sequence. Such memorization is enhanced by the meaningful nature of the poem, as contrasted to the case in which a set of semantically unconnected words are to be learned. The student's attempt to recite is the response, and is followed by feedback which may come from glancing at the printed poem, or may come from the teacher. When a student gets "stuck" while reciting, the teacher may supply the next word or line, thus giving what is called a "direct prompt." Other fixed sequences may be learned which are not meaningfully connected; for example, the names of United States presidents in a time order. In such instances, it is sometimes recommended that the order be learned *backwards*, beginning with the last member of the chain, and proceeding to add new links (presidents' names) in successive trials until the beginning of the sequence is reached (Gilbert, 1971). The recitation by the student, of course, is always in the forward direction. More research will be needed to determine clearly whether this backwards method of presentation has a distinct advantage over the more usual forward method.

In establishing discriminations, the use of *distinctive features* is often a useful feature of stimulus presentation. Pointing out the differences between a triangle and a square, or a "b" and a "d," can help in establishing the discrimination. Typically, such discriminations are learned immediately prior to the learning of the concrete concepts. Many programs of beginning-reading are designed so that the discrimination of letters is mastered before the names of the letters are introduced.

Stimulus presentation for the learning of concepts and rules requires the use of a *variety of examples*. When the objective is the learning of a concept such as "circle," it is desirable to present not only large and small circles on the chalkboard or in a book, but also green circles, red ones, and ones made of rope or string. One might even have the children stand and join hands so as to form a circle. For young children, the importance of this event can hardly be over-emphasized. The failure to provide such a variety of examples accounts for the classic instance related by William James in which a boy could recognize a *vertical* position when a pencil was used as the test object, but not when a table-knife was held in that position.

Comparable degrees of usefulness can be seen in the use of variety of examples as an event for rule learning. To apply the formula for area of a rectangle, $A = x \cdot y$, the student must not only be able to recall the statement which represents the rule, but he must know that A means area; he must understand what area means; he must know that x and y are the dimensions of two non-parallel sides of the rectangle, and he must know that the dot between x and y means multiply. But even when all these subordinate concepts and rules are known, the learner must do a variety of examples to insure that he understands and can use the rule. Retention and transfer are also likely to be enhanced by presenting problems stated in words, in diagrams, and in combinations of the two, over a period of time.

Once such rules are learned, groups of them need to be selectively recalled, combined, and used to solve problems. Employing a variety of examples in problem solving might entail teaching the learner to break down odd-shaped figures into known shapes, like circles, triangles, and rectangles, and then to apply rules for finding the area of these figures as a way to arrive at the total area of the entire shape.

In learning of both concepts and rules, one may proceed either inductively or deductively. In learning concrete concepts, like circle or rectangle, it is best to introduce a variety of examples before introducing the definition of the concept. (Imagine teaching a four-year-old the formal definition of a circle before exposing him to a variety of circles!) But for the older learners who are learning defined concepts, a simple definition might best come first, such as: "A root is the part of a plant below the ground." Assuming the learner understands the component concepts that are contained in the statement, this should be a good start, perhaps followed at once by a picture.

Providing Learning Guidance   Suppose one wishes a learner to acquire a rule (or it might be called a defined concept) about the characteristics of prime numbers. He might begin by displaying a list of successive numbers, say, 1 through 25. He then might ask the learner to recall that the numbers may be expressed as products of various factors; $8 = 2 \times 4 = 2 \times 2 \times 2 = 8 \times 1$, etc. The learner could then be asked to write out all the factors for the set of whole numbers through 30. What is wanted, now, as a learning outcome, is for the learner to discover the rule that there is a certain class of numbers whose only factor (or divisor) other than the number itself is 1.

The learner may be able to "see" this rule immediately. If not, he may be led to its discovery by a series of communications in the form of "hints" or questions. For example, such a series might run somewhat as follows: "Do you see any regularities in this set of numbers?" "Do the original numbers differ with respect to the number of different factors they contain?" "In what way are the numbers 3, 5, and 7 different from 4, 8, and 10?" "In what way is the number 7 like the number 23?" "Can you pick out *all* the numbers which are like 7 and 23?"

These communications and others like them may be said to have the function of *learning guidance*. Notice that they do not "tell the learner the answer"; rather, they suggest the line of thought which will presumably lead to the desired "combining" of subordinate concepts and rules so as to form the new to-be-learned rule. Again, it is apparent that the specific form and content of such questions and "hints" cannot be spelled out in precise terms. Exactly what the teacher or textbook says is not the important point. It is rather that such communications are performing a particular function. They are stimulating a direction of thought and thus are helping to keep the learner "on the track." In performing this function, they contribute to the efficiency of learning.

The amount of learning guidance, that is, the number of questions and the degree to which they provide "direct or indirect prompts," will obviously vary with the kind of capability being learned (Wittrock, 1966). If what is to be learned, for example, is an arbitrary matter such as the name for an object which is new to the learner (say, a pomegranate), there is obviously no sense in wasting time with indirect hinting or questioning in the hope that somehow such a name will be "discovered." In this case, "just telling him the answer" is the correct form of guidance for learning. At the other end of the spectrum, however, are cases where less direct prompting is appropriate, because this is a logical way to discover the answer, and such discovery may be more permanent than being told the answer.

The amount of questioning or hinting needed will also vary with the learner. Some learners require less of learning guidance than do others in most situations. They simply "catch on" more quickly. Prior learning can never reduce such individual differences to the zero point. For this reason, learning guidance needs to be adapted to the individual learner. Too much of it may seem condescending to the quick learner, whereas too little of it can simply lead to frustration on the part of the slow learner. The best practical solution would seem to be, apply learning guidance a little at a time, and allow the student to use as much as he needs. Only one "hint" may be necessary for a fast learner, whereas three or four may work better with a slower learner. In memorizing a poem, one would give the actual word which the learner cannot recall, but in learning a principle one might just supply a hint.

Eliciting the Performance   Presumably, having had sufficient learning guidance, the learner will now be carried to the point where the actual internal "combining" event of learning has taken place. Perhaps the learner's brow has cleared, or some indication of pleasure has appeared on his face. He has "seen" how to do it! We must now ask him to *show* that he knows how to do it. We want him not only to convince us, but to convince himself also.

Accordingly, the next event is a communication that in effect says "show me," or "do it." Usually, this first performance following learning will use the same example (that is, the same stimulus material) with which the learner has been interacting all along. For example, if he has been learning to make plurals of words ending in ix, and has been presented with the word *matrix*, his first performance is likely to be production of the plural *matrices*. In most instances, the instructor will follow this with a second example, like *appendix*, in order to make sure the rule can be applied in a new instance.

Providing Feedback   Although in many situations it may be assumed that the essential learning event is concluded once the correct performance has been exhibited by the learner, this is not universally the case. One must be highly aware of the aftereffects of the learning event and their important influence on determining exactly what is learned. In other words, as a minimum, there should be feedback concerning the correctness or degree of correctness of the learner's performance. In many instances, such feedback is automatically provided—for example, an individual learning to throw darts can see almost immediately how far away he has come from the bull's-eye. Similarly, a child who has managed to match a printed word with one that he has in his oral vocabulary, and which at the same time conveys an expected meaning, receives a kind of immediate feedback which has a fair degree of certainty. But, of course, there are many tasks of school learning which do not provide this kind of "automatic" feedback. For example, in practicing using the pronouns *I* and *me* in a variety of situations, is the student able to tell which are right and which are not? In such instances, feedback from an outside source, usually a teacher, may be an essential event.

There are no standard ways of phrasing or delivering feedback as a communication. In an instructional program, the confirmation of correctness is often printed on the side of the page or on the following page. Even standard textbooks for such subjects as mathematics and science customarily have answers printed in the back of the book. When the teacher is observing the learner's performance, the feedback communication may be delivered in many different ways—a nod, a smile, or a spoken word. Again in this instance, the important characteristic of the communication is not its content but its function: providing information to the learner about the correctness of his performance.

Assessing Performance The immediate indication that the desired learning has occurred is provided when the appropriate performance is elicited. This is, in effect, an assessment of learning outcome. Accepting it as such, however, raises the larger questions of *reliability* and *validity* which relate to all systematic attempts to assess outcomes or to evaluate the effectiveness of instruction. These are discussed in a later chapter, and we shall simply state here their relevance to the single learning event.

When one sees the learner exhibit a single performance appropriate to the lesson objective, how does he tell that he (the observer or teacher) has made a *reliable* observation? How does he know the student didn't do the required performance by chance, or by guessing? Obviously, many of the doubts raised by this question can be dispelled by asking the learner to "do it again," using a different example. A first-grader shows that he can distinguish the sounds of *mat* and *mate*. Has he been lucky, or can he exhibit the same rule-governed performance with *pal* and *pale*? Ordinarily, one expects the second instance of the performance to raise the reliability of the inference (concerning the student's capability) far beyond the chance level. Employing still a third example should lead to practical certainty so far as the observer is concerned.

How is the teacher to be convinced that the performance exhibited by the learner is *valid*? This is a matter which requires two different decisions. The first is, does the performance in fact accurately reflect the objective? For example, if the objective is "recounts the main idea of the passage in his own words," the judgment must be made as to whether what the student says is indeed the *main* idea, not just any old idea. The second judgment, which is no easier to make, is whether the performance has occurred under conditions which make the observation *free of distortion*. As an example, the conditions must be such that the student could not have "memorized the answer," or remembered it from a previous occasion. The teacher must be convinced, in other words, that the observation of performance reveals the learned capability in a genuine manner.

Obviously, the single, double, or triple observations of performance that are made immediately after learning may be conducted in quite an informal manner. Yet they are of the same sort, and part of the same piece of cloth, as the more formally planned assessments described in a later chapter. There need be no conflict between them, and no discrepancies.

Enhancing Retention and Transfer   When information or knowledge is to be recalled, the existence of the meaningful context in which the material has been learned appears to offer the best assurance that the information can be reinstated. The network of relationships in which the newly learned material has been embedded provides a number of different possibilities as cues for its retrieval.

Provisions made for the recall of intellectual skills often include arrangements for "practicing" their retrieval. Thus, if defined concepts, rules, and higher-order rules are to be well retained, course planning must make provision for systematic *reviews* spaced at intervals throughout weeks and months. The effectiveness of these spaced repetitions, each of which requires that the skill be retrieved and used, contrasts with the relative ineffectiveness of repeated examples given directly following the initial learning (Reynolds & Glaser, 1964).

As for the assurance of transfer of learning, it appears that this can best be done by setting some *variety* of new tasks for the learner—tasks which require the application of what has been learned in situations that differ substantially from those used for the learning itself. For example, suppose that what has been learned is the set of rules pertaining to "making the verb agree with the pronoun subject." Additional tasks which vary the pronoun and the verb may have been used to assess performance. Arranging conditions for transfer, however, means varying the entire situation more broadly still. This might be accomplished, in this instance, by asking the child to compose several sentences in which he himself supplies the verb and the pronoun (rather than having them supplied by the teacher). In another variation of the situation, the student may be asked to compose sentences using pronouns and verbs, to describe some actions shown in pictures. Ingenuity of the teacher is called for in designing a variety of novel "application" situations for the purpose of insuring transfer of learning.

Variety and novelty in problem-solving tasks are of particular relevance to the continued development of cognitive strategies. As has previously been mentioned, the strategies used in problem solving need to be developed by the systematic introduction of occasions for problem solving interspersed with other instruction. An additional event to be especially noted in the presentation of novel problems to the student is the need to make clear the general nature of the solution expected. For example, "practical" solutions may be quite different from "original" solutions, and the student's performance can easily be affected by such differences in the communication of the objective (cf. Johnson, 1972).

THE EVENTS OF INSTRUCTION
IN A LESSON

In using the events of instruction for lesson planning, it is apparent that they must be organized in a flexible manner, with primary attention to the lesson's objectives. What is implied by our description of these events is obviously not a standardized, routine, set of communications and action. The invariant features of the single lesson are the functions which need to be carried out in instruction. Even these functions are adapted to the specific situation, the task to be accomplished, the type of learning represented in the task, and the students' prior learning. But each one of these functions needs to be specifically considered, and not overlooked, in lesson planning.

It is now possible to consider how these events are exemplified within an actual lesson. We have chosen as a model a first-grade lesson in elementary science, entitled *Linear Measurement*, from *Science—A Process Approach* (AAAS Commission on Science Education, 1967). The objective of this exercise is "demonstrating a procedure for finding the length of an object in units on an agreed-upon scale." The following columns show, on the left, the suggested activity for the lesson; and on the right, a description of the instructional event being served by each of these activities.

Lesson Activities as Given in Science—A Process Approach, Part B *Measuring 2—Linear Measurment*	*Instructional Event*
A large cardboard box is placed on one side of the room, a table on the other. Children are asked how they could tell, without moving box or table, whether the box would fit under the table. Suggestions are asked for, discussed, and verified.	*Gaining attention* by introducing a novel situation, appealing to children's motive for mastery of their environment.
Children in groups are given "measuring sticks" varying in length from 5 to 100 cm. They are asked to think about how they could use the sticks to measure the height of the box.	*Stating the objective.*
Measurements obtained by different groups of children are found to be different. The suggestion is made that different "units" be given different names. A table is made of measurements obtained by children, report-	During this activity, there is *recall* of a previously learned capability, in which lengths of unit sticks are ordered from shortest to longest. In addition, the children are being asked to *recall* the counting of numbers, in reporting how

ing the number of units they obtained in measuring a designated length.

Children are asked to measure strips of tape placed on the floor (a little over 1.5 meters long); and also to measure the length of new pencils. Different groups of children have different-sized measuring units (5 cm. to 100 cm.). The children discuss the appropriateness of different lengths being measured.

Finally, they are asked to compare the suitability of 15 cm. sticks and the 100 cm. sticks in measuring the tapes on the floor. The 15 cm. sticks and the 100 cm. sticks are laid end-to-end on each side of the tapes, and the children are asked which units are more suitable.

Following the learning, additional appraisal is carried out by marking different chalk-lengths on the floor, and asking the children to select appropriate unit sticks to report their measurements in number of stick-lengths.

A "generalizing experience" is suggested, consisting of measurements of the span of the child's outstretched arms, and also his height. The children must choose the "stick units" and make the measurements.

many units are contained in the length they measure. They are learning to select shorter or longer units and to place them end-to-end, both subordinate skills which will be readily *recalled* in the next activity.

The *stimulus materials* for the learning are presented: the sticks and the lengths to be measured.

The "tries" made by the children, which are more or less successful, depending on the units they work with, provide for discussions in which some amount of *learning guidance* is given.

The *performance* sought is elicited by the question "Which is more suitable for measuring these tapes?" The selection of appropriate units is the objective in this case.

Feedback is given for selection of units that result in more successful and less successful measurement attempts.

Assessment of the learning has been carried out in an immediate sense, in this lesson, by asking for the measurement of (1) pencils, and (2) tapes on the floor. The assessment is continued, in order to increase confidence in its reliability, by the additional "appraisal" portion of the exercise.

Transfer of learning is the functional aim of this and other measurements which might be employed. Note the intention of using varied situations for these additional activities.

Retention is provided for in these materials by scheduling review in a subsequent lesson. For example, Measurement 4 is entitled "Linear Measurement Using Metric Units."

It is evident, then, that this lesson in elementary science has been carefully planned in the sense that it reflects each of the instructional events described in this chapter. Of course, it should be understood that the lesson itself has only been summarized here; the reader who wishes to gain a fuller understanding of its suggested procedures should refer to the original source. Obviously, it is an exercise in which the teacher's art can be given considerable opportunity to flourish, within the framework of events which generate confidence that the desired learning will be accomplished.

SUMMARY

This chapter is concerned with the events that make up instruction for any single performance objective, as they may occur within a lesson. These are the events that are usually external to the learner, supplied by the teacher or text, or other materials with which the learner interacts. When self-instruction is done, the events may be made to occur by the learner himself. Their purpose is to activate and support the internal processes of learning.

Instructional events listed and discussed are as follows:

1. Gaining attention
2. Informing the learner of the objective
3. Stimulating recall of prerequisite learnings
4. Presenting the stimulus material
5. Providing "learning guidance"
6. Eliciting the performance
7. Providing feedback about performance correctness
8. Assessing the performance
9. Enhancing retention and transfer.

These events apply to the learning of all of the types of learning outcomes we have previously described. Examples are given to illustrate how each is planned for and put into effect.

The order of these events for a lesson or lesson segment is approximate, and may vary somewhat depending upon the objective. Not all of them are invariably used. Some are made to occur by the teacher, some by the learner, and some by the instructional materials. An older, more sophisticated learner may supply most of these events by his own study effort. For young children, the teacher would arrange for most of them to occur.

Some of the examples of instructional events given here anticipate another matter expanded upon in Chapter 8. As our discussion moved from one type of learning outcome to another, we noted certain variations in the nature of particular learning events. Thus, presenting the stimulus (Event 4) for the learning of discriminations requires learning conditions of repetition and reinforcement; whereas concept learning needs the condition of variety of examples. Similarly, conditions of learning guidance (Event 5) required for the learning of rules differ from those needed in the learning of information. The following chapter deals more fully with ways in which conditions of learning are blended into the events of instruction.

REFERENCES

AAAS Commission on Science Education. *Science—A Process Approach, Part B*. New York: Xerox, 1967.

Gagné, R. M. Learning and communication. In R. V. Wiman & W. C. Meierhenry (Eds.), *Educational Media: Theory into Practice*. Columbus, Ohio: Merrill, 1968, pp. 93–114.

Gilbert, T. F. Mathetics: The technology of education. In M. D. Merrill (Ed.), *Instructional Design: Readings*. Englewood Cliffs, N. J.: Prentice-Hall, 1971.

Johnson, D. M. *A Systematic Introduction to the Psychology of Thinking*. New York: Harper & Row, 1972, pp. 272–338.

Reynolds, J. H. & Glaser, R. Effects of repetition and spaced review upon retention of a complex learning task. *Journal of Educational Psychology*, 1964, *55*, 297–308.

Wittrock, M. C. The learning by discovery hypothesis. In L. S. Shulman & E. R. Keislar (Eds.), *Learning By Discovery: A Critical Appraisal*. Chicago: Rand McNally, 1966.

8
DESIGNING THE INDIVIDUAL LESSON

Goals of instructional programs, and the objectives derived from them, need to be defined at several different levels. In previous chapters we have described techniques for planning goals and objectives for courses, for topics or units within courses, and for particular kinds of learning objectives within a unit or topic. Instruction itself must also be planned at correspondingly different levels. Prior chapters have provided a groundwork of principles and strategies for the planning of courses and topics. Continuing the direction of increasing specificity, Chapter 7 has introduced those events of instruction which ultimately must be incorporated into the planning of the day-to-day process of teaching, in other words, into the design of the *individual lesson*.

In the context of the present chapter, instruction is to be designed with reference to performance objectives and the prerequisite capabilities they imply. Often the lesson has only a single objective, which itself may represent a single capability subordinate to a more inclusive objective. Thus the *lesson* is the level at which instruction is designed in detail. In planning for individualized instruction, as will be seen in Chapter 10, the level of planning comparable to the lesson is the *module*. Designing instruction at this level means getting to the moment-by-moment events of instruction.

Most of the characteristics of human capabilities which have been discussed earlier are used as a basis for planning the lesson. So, too, are the events of instruction described in Chapter 7. These events apply to the design of all kinds of lessons, irrespective of the domain of the learning outcome intended. In this chapter, we emphasize the variations among lessons which are introduced to correspond with *different* domains of learning outcomes. These variations are first considered in terms of their implications for designing *sequences* of instruction, and later with respect to the establishment of *effective learning conditions* for the different domains.

In designing a lesson, one needs first to insure that the events of instruction in their general form are provided for. In addition, it is necessary to classify the lesson as having a particular type of learning objective. This step having been accomplished, it will then be possible (1) to place the lesson properly in a sequence relating it to its prerequisites, and (2) to incorporate into the instructional events of the lesson the conditions for effective learning appropriate to the domain of its intended outcome. These events are made to occur by whatever media are selected as most appropriate for the purpose.

LESSON PLANNING

Before launching into a description of the many details a lesson designer must keep in mind, we provide a general orientation which may help in giving the individual lesson a proper setting. Whether planning a lesson, a topic, or an entire course, it is necessary to achieve internal consistency among three important components of instruction:

(1) objectives or goals;
(2) methods, materials, media, and learning experiences or exercises; and
(3) evaluation of the success of the learners.

These three components are referred to here as the "anchor points" in the design of instruction. Past experience has suggested that frequent referral to these anchor points while planning instruction aids in keeping an entire instructional plan "on target." That is, it helps the designer to keep from "wandering around" too much. In addition, it helps in checking to be sure that what is to be taught agrees well with the objective of the lesson and with the kind of test or other evaluation device used to decide whether the teaching has been successful.

Mager (1968) has expressed these three components of instruction in a way that appears easy to remember. The following guide for lesson planning presents the three anchor points posed as questions, each accompanied by a suggested answer:

Question	*How To Answer the Question*
1. "Where am I going?" (in this lesson)	1. State the performance objective for the lesson, showing what the students can do when they have mastered the lesson.
2. "How will I get there?" (how to achieve the objective)	2. Select methods, materials, and exercises which will implement the instructional events and learning conditions appropriate for each subordinate capability.
3. "How will I know when I've arrived?" (achieved success)	3. Administer an appropriate test or other appraisal of student performance to determine when students have achieved the objective.

These three questions and their answers can profitably be used when planning the lesson, when checking the plan, and when replanning the lesson for the future. It also appears desirable for teachers to keep these in mind while teaching. These anchor points are not mere "gimmicks," or mnemonic devices. Evidence can be cited to show that when these three components are used in systematic planning, the resulting instruction has usually been found to be successful (Briggs, 1970, 1972).

Steps in Lesson Planning

A systematic application of these three anchor points to the design of a lesson results in the following expanded set of actions:

Step 1 Organize the entire course into major units and topics, so that objectives for individual lessons can be justified as needed to achieve a larger (topic or unit) objective.

Step 2 Define objectives so that the human capabilities they represent can be clearly identified, whether intellectual skills, cognitive strategies, information, motor skills, or attitudes. These categories will in turn imply the necessity of certain prerequisites, or subordinate capabilities.

Step 3   Design a teaching sequence to take account of the subordinate capabilities necessary to facilitate the attainment of the objective by the learner. How this is done is to be described in the next section.

Step 4   Identify each type of subordinate learned capability represented in the sequence (discriminations, concepts, rules, information, etc.).

Step 5   Choose a single "target" capability as a lesson objective, fitting the estimated learning time to the length of periods available for instruction.

Step 6   For each objective, organize a teaching plan by considering the instructional events and effective learning conditions needed for each learning outcome.

Step 7   After the list of instructional events, including those for learning effectiveness, has been determined for an objective to be learned, choose a medium of instruction for each instructional event; following this, the materials can be selected or designed especially for each event.

Step 8   After the first use of the lesson, assess student performance to see if the objective of the lesson has been met. When lessons are short, one may wish to test student performance only over groups of lessons, or even over objectives for an entire topic. The latter plan is efficient when the lessons have been successful, but if some students fail the test over the entire topic, then diagnostic testing is required to determine which capabilities or lessons were not mastered. As a compromise, teachers often do informal evaluations of lessons, but give carefully prepared tests over the entire topic. A safe but more time-consuming procedure is to give a formal test after each lesson. In any case, the test results can then be used as a guide in revising those lessons which were less successful. This procedure is often called "formative evaluation."

In so-called "adaptive" forms of instruction, pre-tests may be given to see which capabilities the student has already mastered. Students are then exempted from instruction they do not need.

In the following section, attention will be especially directed to how the nature of the learning objective may affect the details of the lesson plan. Referring to the eight steps which have been outlined, it is assumed that earlier chapters have provided the information necessary for conducting the first two steps in lesson planning. We proceed next to deal with step three, describing a procedure for making a sequence of instruction which leads up to the target objective of the lesson. When such a sequence is found to involve several different *prerequisite* learning outcomes, it is often necessary to plan for other lessons which precede the given lesson.

ESTABLISHING A SEQUENCE
OF OBJECTIVES

A lesson objective is seldom so simple that it cannot stand analysis to reveal a desirable teaching sequence (Steps 3 and 4). Lesson objectives often turn out to specify the learning of fairly complex skills, which require the prior learning of simpler skills in order for instruction to be effective. This is particularly true if one begins lesson planning with an objective representing an intellectual skill such as a defined concept, rule, or a problem-solving task. The skills to be learned in such tasks typically suggest a preceding sequence of objectives for simpler skills and related information. The sequences implied for lesson objectives representing information, motor skills, and attitudes present quite a different picture, as Chapter 4 has indicated. Yet each of these kinds of learned capability has its own prerequisites, and accordingly its own implications for instructional sequence.

Planning a Sequence
for Intellectual Skill Objectives

We begin our account of lesson sequence planning with objectives representing *intellectual skills*. The subordinate skills required to attain an objective of this sort can be derived as a learning hierarchy. Suppose that one does indeed want to establish the skill of subtracting multiple-digit numbers, and that a pattern of subordinate skills has been worked out as in Figure 4 (page 114). The hierarchy indicates that if the target objective is to be achieved by efficiently planned learning, all of the subordinate objectives (I through X) must have been learned at some previous time. A sequence of previous instruction is also implied by the indication that skills IV, VIII, IX, and X are the ones that the student needs to have readily available for recall when he undertakes to learn the final skill; whereas other skills are subordinate to these, and should be learned at still earlier times.

Determining a Starting Point   In order to plan a sequence of lessons, the designer must first decide upon a starting point among the skills to be acquired (I through X). This is a matter of determining what the student (or set of students) already knows how to do. It would not be unusual, for example, if students for whom instruction was planned had already mastered simple subtraction "facts" (I). They might even have progressed as far as skill IV, or V. Obviously, one needs to begin the planning of a sequence of lessons at a point where mastery of necessary skills can be assumed. A brief review of these subordinate skills can, of course, be undertaken as an initial step of any lesson.

Specifying a Sequence of Lessons   The sequence of lessons which will be most effective is depicted by the learning hierarchy. Notice, however, that several options for specific sequences are readily available. While the hierarchy implies that skills II and III need to be learned before IV, it implies nothing about the ordering of II and III. Skill II may be learned before or after III, since no dependency is shown. Similarly, both Skills V and VI need to be learned before VII, according to the hierarchy, but either V or VI may be learned first in a sequence.

The hierarchy, then, implies several possible optimal lesson sequences. The skill relationships which indicate prerequisites need to be maintained in planning such sequences—otherwise no particular sequence is implied, and other considerations of convenience may apply.

Achievement of Skills in Sequence   The planning of lessons designed to attain the final skill (XI) makes the assumption that each student will display *mastery* of prerequisite skills before being asked to learn the next higher skill. For example, before tackling Skill VII (illustrated by an example such as 47185 — 2634), the planning assumption is made that the student has mastered Skill V (illustrated by the example of 46 — 9). He should also have mastered Skill VI, in which he shows, in an example such as 327 — 194, that borrowing from the 3 must be done in order to subtract in the column containing 2 and 9.

The notion of mastery needs to be taken with complete seriousness when one is dealing with intellectual skills. The lessons must be so designed that skills such as V and VI can be performed with perfect confidence by the student, before he tries Skill VII. It is not enough that he simply be "told about" Skills V and VI, or that he be able to do them sometimes. The difference between confident mastery and mere acquaintance or indifferent performance of these subordinate skills will be revealed by what happens when the student undertakes to learn Skill VII. If the student has indeed mastered the prerequisite skills, Skill VII will be learned with a minimum of hesitation or perceived difficulty. If he has not mastered the subordinate skills, his learning of Skill VII is likely to be characterized by puzzlement, delay, and inefficient trial-and-error.

Provisions for Diagnosis and Relearning   Lesson planning with the use of the hierarchy of intellectual skills may also make provision for diagnosis of learning difficulties. If it is found that a student has difficulty learning any given skill, the most probable diagnostic indication is that he cannot recall how to perform one or more prerequisite skills. Any given lesson may make provision for diagnosis by requiring that prerequisite skills be recalled. If one or more cannot be recalled, then relearning of these prerequisites must be undertaken. Thus the assessment of mastery for any given skill, occurring as a part of a lesson on that skill, may be followed by further diagnosis of prerequisite skills, in case mastery is *not* achieved. Following this, provision should be made for a "relearning loop" in the sequence of lessons, which gives the student an opportunity to relearn and to display mastery of the necessary prerequisites before proceeding.

Sequence in Relation to Cognitive Strategies

The use of cognitive strategies by a learner is indicated by his solution of one or more novel problems with answers of greater or lesser quality. In such problems, however, there are many "right" answers, not just one. Accordingly, one cannot specify a particular sequence of prior learning leading up to the presentation of a problem situation. What must be recognized, nevertheless, is that novel problem solution depends upon previously learned information and intellectual skills. To the extent that relevant capabilities are unavailable to the learner, he will be restricted in the variety of adequate solutions that are possible for him to invent.

Planning for a sequence of instruction designed to improve the quality of problem solving (and the inferred effectiveness of the learner's thinking strategies) usually takes the form of *repeated opportunities* for problem solving. Such occasions may be interspersed with instruction having other intended outcomes, and typically are made to reoccur over relatively long periods of time. In this way, it is expected that gradual improvement in cognitive strategies will be possible. However, it does not seem likely that observable amounts of improvement in this type of capability can occur within the space of a single lesson or two.

Planning a Sequence for Information Learning

As indicated in Chapter 5, the most important prerequisite for the learning of information is the provision of a meaningful context within which the newly learned information can be "subsumed," or with which it can be in some meaningful sense "associated." The principles applicable to sequencing differ somewhat depending on whether the objective concerns learning a set of names (labels), learning an isolated fact, or learning the sense of a logically organized passage.

Names or Labels   The learning of a set of names (such as the names of a number of trees) is facilitated by the use of previously learned organized structures which the learner has in his memory. A variety of structures may be used by the learner to "encode" the newly acquired information. The encoding may take the form of a simple association, as when a new French word "la dame" is associated with the English word "dame," which thus becomes a somewhat humorous association for "lady." Sometimes, encoding may involve the use of a sentence, such as that which associates "starboard" with "right," in "the star boarder is always right." Frequently, too, the method of encoding may involve the use of visual images, as would be the case if the learner associated an image of a crow with a person's name "Crowe." The imagery employed for encoding may be quite arbitrary, as when a learner uses the shops on a well-known street as associates for newly acquired names of things having nothing to do with the shops themselves (cf. Crovitz, 1970).

It is clear, then, that the learning of new names or labels calls upon previously learned entities stored in the learner's memory. Yet, in this kind of information learning, it does not seem reasonable that a *specific* sort of previous learning, implying a sequence of instruction, can be recommended. While it is possible to facilitate the learning of new labels by prescribing some particular "codes" for the learner to use, such a procedure is generally found to be less successful than permitting the learner to use an encoding system of his own. What the learner mainly needs to have learned previously, aside from the various meaningful structures he may have in his memory, is "how to encode." This would be a particular kind of *cognitive strategy*. The possibilities of long-term instruction designed to improve such a strategy have not been explored. The lesson designer, therefore, typically assumes that both the strategy and the encoding structures have been previously learned, and makes no specific provision for them in the lesson sequence.

Individual Facts   The learning of individual "facts," as they may occur, for example, in a chapter of a history text, also involves an encoding process. In this case, the encoding is usually a matter of relating the facts to larger meaningful structures—larger organized "bodies of knowledge" which have been previously learned.

Two kinds of procedures are available for instructional sequencing when one is dealing with factual information. Both of them should probably be employed, with an emphasis determined by other factors in the situation. The first is the prior learning (in a sequence) of what Ausubel (1968) calls "organizers." If the learner is to acquire facts about automobiles, for example, an "organizing passage" may first be presented which informs the learner about the major distinctive categories of automobile description—body style, engine, frame, transmission, and so on. The specific facts to be learned about particular automobiles then follow.

The second procedure, not entirely unrelated to the first, involves the use of questions or other statements to identify the major categories of facts for which learning is desired (cf. Frase, 1970; Rothkopf, 1970). Thus, if the learning of the names of persons described in a historical passage is the most important information to be learned, prior experience with questions about such names in a "sample" passage will facilitate the learning and retention of names. Should the lesson have the objective of stating dates, then dates could be asked about in a prior passage.

Organized Information   Most frequently, an objective in the category of information states an expectation that the learner will be able to state a set of facts and principles in a meaningfully organized manner. For example, an objective in social studies might be to trace the steps involved in the passage of a bill by the United States Congress. The learning of organized information of this sort is also subject to an encoding procedure which calls upon previously learned structures in the student's memory. However, the existence of such prior information, as well as relevant language skills, is usually assumed by the lesson designer, rather than being specifically provided in an instructional sequence. Sometimes, the learning of new information can take advantage of the prior learning of a related class of information. An example is cited in the work of Ausubel (1968); he speaks of the process of "correlative subsumption," occurring when information about Buddhism is acquired following the learning of information about a different religion, Zen Buddhism.

Planning a Sequence for a Motor Skill

The capabilities that constitute prerequisites for the learning of a motor skill are the part-skills that may compose the skill to be learned, and the executive subroutine (the complex rule) which serves to control their execution in the proper order. Of course, the relative importance of these two kinds of prerequisites depends largely upon the complexity of the skill itself. To attempt to identify part-skills for dart-throwing, for example, would not be likely to lead to a useful sequencing plan; but in a complex skill such as swimming, practice of part-skills is usually considered a valuable approach.

Typically, the learning of the executive subroutine is placed early in the sequence of instruction for a motor skill, before the various part-skills have been fully mastered. Thus, in learning to put the shot, the learner may at an early stage acquire the executive subroutine of approaching the line, shifting his weight, bending his arm and body, and propelling the shot, even though at this early stage his performance of the critical movements is still rather poor.

The learning of particular part-skills may themselves have important prerequisites. For example, in the skill of firing a rifle at a target, the concrete concept of a correct sighting "picture" is considered to be a valuable subordinate skill to the execution of the total act of target shooting. Accordingly, a plan of instruction for a motor skill must provide not only for the prior practice of part-skills, when this is appropriate, but also on some occasions for a sequence relevant to the individual part-skills themselves.

Planning a Sequence for Attitude Learning

As is true for other kinds of learned capabilities, the learning or modification of an attitude calls upon previously acquired entities in the learner's memory. A positive attitude toward reading poetry, for example, could scarcely be established without some knowledge of particular poems on the learner's part, or without some of the language skills involved in interpreting the meaning of poetic writing. Thus, for many attitudes with which school learning is concerned, the planning of an instructional sequence must take into account these kinds of prerequisite learning.

The basis for an instructional sequence aimed at establishing an attitude is to be found in the particular information and intellectual skills that become a part of the personal action expected to be chosen by the learner, following instruction. If the learner is to have a positive attitude, for example, toward associating with people of races different from his own, such an attitude must be based upon information concerning what these various "associations" (playing games with, working with, dining with, etc.) are about. Or, if the learner is to acquire a positive attitude towards the methods of science, this must be based upon some capabilities (skills) of using some of these methods.

An instructional sequence for learning an attitude, then, often begins with the learning of intellectual skills and information relevant to that attitude. It proceeds then to the introduction of a procedure involved in establishing the "positive" or "negative" tendency which constitutes the attitude itself, as described in Chapter 5.

When the method of human modeling is employed for attitude modification, another prerequisite step in the sequence may be necessary, depending on the circumstances. Since the "message" which represents the attitude needs to be presented by a respected source (usually a person), it may in some instances be necessary to establish or to build up respect for the source. "A famous scientist" is likely not to command the respect that a particular scientist, such as Lavoisier, does; and Lavoisier as a pictured person is more likely to be respected if the learner knows of his accomplishments. In contrast, a living "famous person," perhaps a sports hero, may not require a "build-up."

LESSON PLANNING FOR LEARNING OUTCOMES

The sequence of capabilities exemplified by the learning hierarchy (for intellectual skills) or by a set of identified prerequisites (for other types of outcomes) is used as a basis for planning a *series* of lessons. The single implication it has for the design of a *single* lesson is that one or more prerequisite capabilities need to be available to the learner. Obviously, though, there is more than this to the planning of each lesson. How does the student proceed from the point of having learned some subordinate knowledge or skills to the point of having acquired a new capability? This interval, during which the actual learning occurs, is filled with the kinds of instructional events described in the previous chapter. These events include the actions taken by the students and by the teacher, in order to bring about the desired learning. In terms of the planning steps previously outlined, the present discussion centers on Step 6.

Effective Learning Conditions
for Instructional Events

The most general purpose which can be stated for what we have called the events of instruction is that of arranging the external conditions of learning in such a way as to insure that learning will occur. Instructional events, as described in Chapter 7, are typically incorporated into the individual lesson. These events apply in a general sense to all types of lessons, irrespective of their intended outcomes. Just as we have found it necessary to describe particular sequencing conditions that pertain to different lesson outcomes, we also recognize a need to give an account of the particular events that affect the learning effectiveness of lessons having different kinds of outcomes. This makes it possible to recall the *conditions of learning* for various classes of learning outcomes, as described in earlier chapters, and to make application of these principles to the arrangement of effective learning within a lesson.

Tables in the sections to follow have the purpose of consolidating several ideas bearing upon lesson design. First, they assume the general framework of instructional events described in the previous chapter, without developing these ideas further. Second, they describe procedures for implementing optimal learning conditions that are specifically relevant to each class of learning objective. These have been referred to in Chapters 3 and 4 as the *external conditions* of learning. And third, they take account of the problem of lesson sequencing by representing as *internal conditions* the recall of prerequisite capabilities appropriate for each kind of learning outcome.

The result of this integrating exercise is a kind of checklist of distinctive conditions for effective learning which need to be incorporated into the general framework of instructional events in order to accomplish particular learning objectives.

Lessons for Intellectual Skill Objectives   Effective learning conditions for the varieties of intellectual skills, as they may be reflected in planning the events of a lesson, are given in Table 5. Each list of conditions given in the

TABLE 5   *Effective Learning Conditions for Incorporation into Lessons Having Intellectual Skill Objectives*

Type of Lesson Objective	Learning Conditions
Discrimination	Recall of S-R connections ("responses") Repetition of situations presenting "same" and "different" stimuli, with feedback Emphasis on distinctive features
Concrete Concept	Recall of discrimination of relevant object qualities Presentation of several concept instances, varying in irrelevant object qualities Identification of concept instances by student
Defined Concept	Recall of component concepts Demonstration of the components of the concept, *or* verbal statement of the definition Demonstration of concept by the student
Rule	Recall of component concepts or subordinate rules Demonstration or verbal statement of the rule Demonstration of rule-application by student
Higher-Order Rule	Recall of relevant subordinate rules Presentation of a novel problem Demonstration of new rule in achieving problem solution

second column begins with a statement designating the recall of a capability which has been previously learned, often from a previous lesson in a sequence. The list then proceeds with conditions which are to be reflected in other instructional events (such as those of presenting the stimulus, providing learning guidance, eliciting the student performance, etc.). In interpreting the information in this column, the reader may find it useful to review the statements of internal and external conditions of learning for these types of objectives, as described in Chapter 3.

Lessons for Cognitive Strategy Objectives   Conditions designed to promote effective learning for cognitive strategies are listed in the beginning portion of Table 6. The list pertains particularly to the learning of strategies

TABLE 6 *Effective Learning Conditions for Incorporation into Lessons Having Objectives of Cognitive Strategies, Information, Attitudes, and Motor Skills*

Type of Lesson Objective	Learning Conditions
Cognitive Strategy	Recall of relevant rules and concepts Successive presentation (usually over an extended time) of novel problem situations with class of solution unspecified Demonstration of solution by student
Information	
Names or Labels	Recall of verbal chains Encoding (by student) by relating name to image or meaningful sentence
Facts	Recall of context of meaningful information Performance of reinstating fact in the larger context of information
Knowledge	Recall of context of related information Performance of reinstating new knowledge in the context of related information
Attitude	Recall of information and intellectual skills relevant to the targeted personal actions Establishment or recall of respect for "source" (usually a person) Reward for personal action either by direct experience or vicariously by observation of respected person
Motor Skill	Recall of component motor chains Establishment or recall of executive subroutine (rules) Practice of total skill

of productive thinking and problem solving. External and internal conditions for learning cognitive strategies have been previously discussed in Chapter 3.

Lessons for Objectives of Information, Attitudes, Motor Skills. The design of instructional events for lessons having objectives of the classes of outcome designated as Information, Attitudes, and Motor Skills needs to take into account the particular conditions for effective learning shown in the corresponding portions of Table 6. These lists are derived from the fuller discussion of internal and external conditions of learning contained in Chapter 4.

SELECTING MEDIA AND ACTIVITIES

In the 8-step method of lesson design outlined earlier in this chapter (p. 139), planning the events of instruction is Step 6. We now proceed to Step 7, selection of media, materials, and exercises.

Often, of course, a teacher selects materials and exercises for the lesson, rather than writing or developing all the materials to be used for implementing each instructional event. In the elementary science lesson used earlier as an illustration, no printed materials were to be read by the pupils, in view of their age. The teacher conducted the various events by talking with the children and providing the materials they needed to solve the problem posed to them. However, in order to take account of the entire range of learners, varying in age and in sophistication, there is need to consider all types of media and materials that are available or that could be produced for the lesson.

When asking, "How can effective learning conditions best be accomplished for each instructional event?", the designer has available many bases on which to choose media, materials, and exercises. These criteria include cost, availability, ease of use, estimated effectiveness for the purpose, practicality for use and storage, familiarity with the kinds of media available, anticipated maintenance problems, and probable acceptability to the learners.

Choosing Media

One method for making media selection is to ask "What type of stimuli would be needed for this instructional event?". If this can be decided, some media alternatives at once present themselves for further consideration. At the same time, other media can at once be excluded. In this approach, one makes a tentative, separate medium choice for each instructional event, and then reviews the list of tentative media before making final media choices. By this method, the selection of media is based upon the instructional events *within* lessons, rather than at the level of the lesson, topic, or course. Completed examples of this method of media selection are given by Briggs (1972).

The following list shows how the identification of type of stimuli presented in a lesson implies certain options of media choice.

Type of Stimuli	*Media Options*
1. Printed words	books; programmed instruction; handouts; charts; slide projectors; posters; chalkboard; checklists;

2. Spoken words	teacher; tape recording;
3. Still pictures and spoken words	slide-tapes; voice slide; lecture plus posters;
4. Motion, spoken words, and other sounds	motion pictures; television; live demonstration;
5. Pictoral portrayal of theoretical concepts	animated motion pictures; puppets and props.

Another aid in media selection is to consider Dale's (1969) "Cone of Experience." Twelve categories of media and exercises are listed, roughly in an age-related fashion. Thus, at level 1, "Direct purposeful experience," a child would come into physical contact with objects, animals, and people, using all his senses to "learn by doing." As one goes up the age scale, pictoral and other simulated substitutes can be employed for some of the experiences. At the top of the cone is the use of "verbal symbols," which suggests learning by reading, an efficient method for sophisticated learners. A good rule in using Dale's Cone is: "Go as low on the scale as you need to in order to insure learning, but go as high as you can for the most efficient learning."

By considering the opposing factors of "slow but sure" (time-consuming direct experience) and "fast but risky" (typically occurring when learners are not skillful readers), one may decide just where on the scale is the best decision point for media selection.

Dale's categories are as follows:

12. Verbal symbols
11. Visual symbols—signs; stick figures
10. Radio and recordings
9. Still pictures
8. Motion pictures
7. Educational television
6. Exhibits
5. Study trips
4. Demonstrations
3. Dramatized experiences–plays, puppets; role-playing
2. Contrived experiences—models; mock-ups; simulation
1. Direct purposeful experience.

Unfortunately, research has not yielded data permitting sweeping generalizations about media, such as "the best medium for learning biology is _____," or "the best medium for slow learners is _____." Individual differences among learners and among teaching topics are too many and diverse to permit such simple rules for decision-making. Consequently, good judgment must be used in planning just how to accomplish each instructional event for the lesson plan. In doing this, it may be found desirable to make a separate medium selection for each event; alternatively, it may be possible to use a single medium in such a way as to introduce all the events for a lesson.

The Assumed Learning Environment   Another set of factors in media selection is based upon administrative considerations rather than resting on technical grounds. The practicality of use of media varies with such features of the learning environment as: (1) size of school budget; (2) size of class; (3) capability for developing new materials; (4) availability of radio, television, and other media equipment; (5) teacher capabilities and availability for an instructional design effort; (6) availability of modular materials for individualized, performance-based instruction; (7) attitudes of principal and teachers towards innovations; and (8) school architecture.

When performing as instructional designers, some teachers dare to be innovators in a tradition-bound school; others avoid "rocking the boat." It is sensible to find out what the attitudes are of those in power, and to gently find out whether those attitudes can be changed. A teacher in such a position may even have to make a deliberate decision whether to risk job security in favor of innovative teaching. Many a discharged teacher has been the most innovative one in the school. This is an unfortunate fact of life that is hard to change. But by observing what goes on, one can discover whether innovation is welcome.

Selecting or Developing Materials and Learning Exercises

Once the desired kinds of media, materials, and learning exercises have been identified, one of course has to ask, "Are they available, or must they be developed?" Often the answer is that some are available, but perhaps not in the form desired. This leads to a decision point as to whether to use the lesson as it is, modify it, or develop a new item. Sometimes some "on the shelf" items can be put together as a "module" for the capability to be learned. This often requires the design and preparation of some supplementary components, such as objectives, practice exercises, and tests. Making part of a module is less work than making the entire module, and there may not always be time available to develop entirely new materials. Often a compromise has to be made. Whether purchased, developed, or modified, the purpose of the entire set of resources is to implement the instructional events that have been identified, to insure that the students attain the objective.

Tryout and Formative Evaluation

The final step is to use the assembled materials and plans for teaching the lesson. Such tryouts provide the information needed for revising the material, or for changing the organization of instructional events. These procedures will be discussed in Chapters 9 and 12.

AN EXAMPLE OF LESSON DESIGN

An example of lesson design to be described here is a condensed and modified version of a plan by Carol Robb, which is presented in full detail elsewhere (Briggs, 1972, p. 140–177).

This lesson is intended as a part of a high school course sequence in journalism, defined as "the work of gathering news, writing news reports, editing, and publication of a newspaper." The course, "Introduction to Journalism," is a prerequisite for students who wish to work on the school newspaper. A required entering competency is the ability to type well enough to present the student's own news story to an editor or printer. Speed is not essential, but accuracy and neatness are.

The *course objective* is as follows: "The student will be able to gather news, write it in acceptable form, and edit the copy for publication. He will employ standard practices in newspaper layout and placement of stories according to their 'newsworthiness.' He will be able to differentiate between news and feature stories. He will be able to write headlines; to avoid libel; and to formulate a philosophic position of a newspaper in our society. He can identify the duties of each position in a standard newspaper organization."

As might be expected from the above course description, an early topic of the course deals with the following capabilities: "The student will be able to view an event, decide whether it is newsworthy, record the pertinent facts, write an acceptable news story based on the 'who, what, when, where, why?' criteria, and edit his copy and type it for setting into type." Components of this topic are expressed in performance terms as topic purposes, including:

1. Observing and taking notes on an actual event or a simulated event (motion picture or videotape);
2. Deciding newsworthiness, and if such criteria are met, recording necessary facts and checking their accuracy;
3. Using the notes to write a news story;
4. Editing in a form to be sent in for type setting.

For topic purpose 3, a learning hierarchy was constructed which contained, among others, the following performance objectives:

a. Given notes on a newsworthy event, demonstrates the writing of a good lead.
b. Given notes and a lead, demonstrates the organization of the story in "pyramid" form.
c. Given (a) and (b), generates the story, using standards of brevity and reader interest.

It is evident that the writing of a good lead requires the component capability of classifying a "lead," and distinguishing it from the remainder of the story. In this case, the designer indicated the form of a single lesson for the subordinate objective *"given a news story, classifies the 'lead' by underlining."* In other words, this particular lesson was designed for the learning of the defined concept "lead." Keeping in mind the events of instruction, and the conditions of learning appropriate to such an objective (Table 5, p. 148), the following events of the lesson were arranged:

(1) State the objective of the lesson

(1) The teacher explains that the class will learn what a "lead" is. The ultimate goal is to *write* leads; but for now the students need only to *recognize leads.*

(2) Inform the learner of the objective by providing a model of performance

(2) The teacher projects a slide containing a short news story. The sentences which are underlined constitute the lead. Students are told that at the end of the lesson they will be asked to underline the lead in other news stories.

(3) Learning guidance

(3) The teacher asks the class to try to explain why the underlined part of the slide is the "lead." They speculate on what lead means in this context; some attempt to define "lead."

(4) Learning guidance: providing a verbal definition

(4) The teacher now defines the lead as the *first part* of a news story which gives a *skeleton outline* of the *entire story* in the *fewest possible words.*

(5) Learning guidance: providing a variety of examples

(5) The teacher next projects several other slides and hands out some one-page news stories.

(6) Present the stimulus, and elicit performance

(6) The teacher asks the students to identify leads to "practice" stories. The students respond by pointing on the screen or by underlining on paper.

(7) Provide feedback

(7) The teacher provides confirmation and corrective feedback as needed.

(8) Assess attainment of objective

(8) A group of three short news stories is given. Students underline the lead as a performance test over the lesson.

Discussion of the Example

It is clear that this sample lesson could have been presented somewhat differently, without departing from its objective as the learning of a defined concept. Some teachers might spend much time on Step 3, expecting that the students will "discover" the definition of a lead. This plan permits such an approach. It provides, however, that in case the student discussion is not adequate, the teacher next gives the verbal definition as a time-economical step in the lesson.

The use of a variety of examples is usually important for such a lesson, in which one wishes to insure the generalizability of the learned capability to new situations. It is conceivable, of course, that the verbal definition alone might be enough to enable some students to apply the rule consistently.

An alternate version of the lesson is somewhat more prescriptive, depending upon applying *formal criteria* for identifying an acceptable lead. In this alternate plan, one would insert, after Step 2, the event "stimulate recall of prior learning." Here the teacher would elicit recall of the six criteria: who, what, when, where, why, and how. The teacher would suggest that a good lead must contain most of these or all of them. Formal criteria for a lead are listed in the designer's plan for this form of the lesson (Briggs, 1972, p. 173).

It may be noted that since the objective of this lesson is "classifying the lead of a story in accordance with a definition," the assessment requires an appropriate performance, not the statement of a definition of a lead. The latter statement could be learned as an item of information, and would not meet the objective of the lesson. Nowhere in the lesson are the learners asked to state the definition; but they are asked to identify several "practice" leads before their performance is assessed.

SUMMARY

In this chapter, we describe a procedure to be followed by the designer of an individual lesson. The steps in lesson design are outlined as follows:

Step 1   Organize the course into major units and topics, and define lesson objectives for each.

Step 2   Identify the human capabilities represented in the lesson's objectives.

Step 3   Design a teaching sequence to take account of prerequisite learnings.

Step 4   Identify the type of capability represented in each subordinate lesson objective.

Step 5   Choose a single "target" objective to fit available lesson time.

Step 6   Design a teaching plan for each objective, considering the appropriateness of instructional events and the effective learning conditions associated with them.

Step 7   Identify a medium of instruction which can best achieve the effective conditions of learning for each event; and choose the medium or media combination which will best do the total job.

Step 8   Assess learning outcomes in terms of student performance and make the revisions that are implied, until a satisfactory degree of effectiveness is attained.

The purpose of lesson planning is to bring into harmony a learning objective, a way to teach it, and a way to evaluate the outcome. Tryouts and revisions (formative evaluation) are then undertaken, if necessary, to improve the lesson for the next group of learners, or when possible, to make adjustments while the first group is being taught. Bringing congruence among objectives, teaching materials and procedures, and evaluation procedures, are viewed here as the accomplishment of the "three anchor points" in lesson planning: (1) Where am I going? (2) How will I get there? and (3) How will I know when I've arrived?

When the design procedures described in this book are used in a large curriculum-development enterprise, the separate steps identified help in managing and organizing the work of a large team of people. One way to manage this is to assign certain clusters of objectives to each team member. Another way is to have members of the team specialize in the different design steps. Some combination of the two plans may be feasible in other instances. Special formats for such efforts can aid in the total team effort (Briggs, 1970, 1972).

Up to this point in the book, we have described techniques some of which would be appropriate to a large team effort, and some of which would fit the situation of the teacher-designer working alone. In this chapter on the lesson, we have had the teacher especially in mind. In contrast, Chapters 10 and 11 deal with total systems of instruction, and for these we assume a design team which can mount a larger effort.

REFERENCES

Ausubel, D. P., *Educational Psychology: A Cognitive View*. New York: Holt, Rinehart and Winston, 1968.

Briggs, L. J. *Handbook of Procedures for the Design of Instruction*. Pittsburgh, Pa.: American Institutes for Research, 1970.

Briggs, L. J. *Student's Guide to Handbook of Procedures for the Design of Instruction*. Pittsburgh, Pa.: American Institutes for Research, 1972.

Crovitz, H. E. *Galton's Walk*. New York: Harper & Row, 1970.

Dale, E. *Audiovisual Methods in Teaching*, 3d Edition. New York: Holt, Rinehart and Winston, 1969.

Frase, L. T. Boundary conditions for mathemagenic behaviors. *Review of Educational Research*, 1970, *40*, 337–347.

Mager, R. F. *Developing Attitudes Toward Learning*. Belmont, Calif.: Lear Siegler/Fearon, 1968.

Rothkopf, E. Z. The concept of mathemagenic activities. *Review of Educational Research*, 1970, *40*, 325–336.

9
ASSESSING STUDENT PERFORMANCE

Instruction is designed to bring about the learning of several kinds of capabilities. These exhibit themselves as improved performance on the part of the student. While much learning goes on outside the school, and much results from the student's own effort, the responsibility of the school is to organize and provide instruction directed toward specific goals—goals which might not be achieved in a less organized manner.

The outcomes of this planned instruction consist of student performances which show that various kinds of capabilities have been acquired. Five domains of such capabilities have been identified and discussed in previous chapters: intellectual skills, cognitive strategies, information, motor skills, and attitudes. Performance objectives in these categories, applicable to a course of instruction, may be further analyzed to discover their internal "learning structure." This in turn can become the basis for deciding upon a sequence of individual lessons, and for the design of the lessons themselves.

Both the designer of instruction and the teacher need a way to determine how successful the instruction has been, in terms of the performance of each individual student, and in terms of entire groups of students. There is a need to assess student performance to determine whether the newly designed instruction has met its (design) objectives. Assessment may also be done to learn whether each student has achieved the set of capabilities defined by the instructional objectives. Both these purposes can be served by the development of procedures for assessing student performance, which is the topic of this chapter.

DEVELOPMENT PROCEDURES
FOR OBJECTIVE-REFERENCED ASSESSMENT

The term *objective-referenced assessment* is used with a distinctly literal meaning in the context of this book. It is intended to imply that the way to assess student learning is to build tests or other assessment procedures which measure directly the human performances described in the objectives for the course. Such measures of performance make it possible to infer that the intended capability to perform has indeed been developed as a result of the instruction provided. Similar tests can be administered before the instruction is given (pretests), and provisions made to allow students to bypass instruction which they do not need. Normally, a teacher tests only for the "assumed entering capabilities" before introducing the instruction, and assesses performance on the objective itself only following the instruction (that is, by a post-test). A convenient compromise practice might be for the teacher to permit any student who thinks he has mastered the objective before instruction to take the test reflecting that objective as a pretest, and to excuse the student from that portion of the instruction if he passes it.

The performance *objective* is the keystone in planning assessment of performance. We have indicated the critical importance of the *verb* in the statement for correctly describing the objective (Table 3, Chapter 5). The verb is equally crucial as a basis for planning the performance assessment. Such verbs tell what the student should be asked to *do* when taking the performance-assessment test. While the part of the test consisting of "directions to the student" may employ synonyms for this verb, a valid assessment must ask the student to do the performance implied in that objective.

Congruence of Objective and Test: Validity

The objective-referenced orientation to assessment greatly simplifies the concept of "validity" in performance measurement. This approach to assessment results in a direct rather than an indirect measure of the objective. Thus it eliminates the need to relate the measures obtained to a criterion by means of a correlation coefficient, as must usually be done when indirect measures are used, or when tests have been constructed without reference to any explicit performance objectives. Accordingly, one can address the matter of test validity by inspection to obtain an answer to this question: "Is the performance required during assessment the same performance as that described in the objective?" If the answer is a clear "yes," then the test is valid. In practice, it is desirable for more than one person to make this judgment, and for consistency to be attained among them.

Validity is assured when the assessment procedure results in measurement of the performance described in the objective. This occurs when the test and the objective are *congruent* with each other. In terms of our previous discussion in Chapter 8, two of the three "anchor points" in instructional design have been achieved when the tests are made congruent with the objectives.

A caution may be interjected here, however. This method of determining validity assumes that the statement of the objective is itself valid, in the sense that it truly reflects the purposes of the topic or lesson. The procedures described for defining objectives in Chapter 5 are intended to insure that this is the case. Nevertheless, there may be an additional need to recheck the consistency of specific objectives and more broadly stated purposes. Sometimes, inconsistencies become apparent when statements of objectives are transformed into tests of student performance.

It should be recognized that the word "test" is used here in a generic sense to mean any procedure for assessing the performance described in an objective. Thus the use of the brief word "test" can cover all forms of written and oral testing as well as procedures for evaluating student products such as essays, musical productions, constructed models, or works of art. We choose the term "assessment" to refer to the measurement of student performance, rather than the alternative of "achievement testing." The latter term is often associated with norm-referenced measurement, which will be the subject of a later discussion in this chapter. At this point, however, "test" and "assessment" are used to refer to objective-referenced performance measurement.

Some of the performance objectives given in Chapter 5 can be used to illustrate how judgments about test validity may be made. Initially, we shall be concerned primarily with two of the five parts of an objective statement, the two verbs which describe the *capability* to be learned, and the *actions* the student takes in demonstrating this capability. Later on, other parts of the objective will be related to performance assessment.

First, consider the example of *generating* a letter by typing (p. 81). The word "generate" is the clue that in the test situation the student must compose his own letter, rather than typing a different form of a letter composed by someone else. It is clear that the learner must use his capability of generating a particular kind of letter within the constraints of the situation described in the objective. In the alternative objective relating to typing, the learner receives a written longhand letter composed by someone else. These two objectives relating to business letters are very different. One requires only the skill of typing a letter already composed, while the other requires also the problem-solving capability of composing the letter. Thus two domains (motor skills and intellectual skills) are sampled.

In a second example drawn from Chapter 5, the student must *demonstrate* the use of a rule by supplying the missing factor in an equation. Simply copying the missing value from a book, or remembering the value from having seen the problem worked before, would not constitute a valid test for this capability. In designing a test, care must be taken to use different examples for testing than those used for teaching, so as to minimize the chance that the correct response can be supplied by any means other than the intended intellectual process.

In any example of demonstrating mastery of a concept, the learner may *identify* the concept by printing the first letter of the concept (name) in a blank. This is not the same as either copying the first letter, or spelling the name of the concept. It is also different from the performance of explaining how the concept may be used. Any or all of these latter instances may be useful performances, but they do not reflect the intent of the objective, either as to the capability required or the action which signifies that the capability is present.

Exercises on judging the validity of test items by comparing them with the corresponding performance objectives are given by Briggs (1970, Chapter IV).

Designing the Test Situation

The form of performance objectives described in Chapter 5 serves as the basis from which the test situation can be derived. It will be recalled that the five components of an objective statement are given as: (1) situation; (2) learned capability; (3) object; (4) action; and (5) tools and constraints. Such a statement also provides a description of the situation to be used in testing.

For certain types of objectives and for learners who are not too young, the change of only a few words may convert the objective statement to a test. For example, one could give the objective on generating and typing a letter to the learner as "directions for taking the test." All that would be needed in addition would be to supply the "received letter," and to provide an electric typewriter, typing paper, and carbon paper. The person administering the test would further be instructed to insure a favorable (monitored) test environment, and to record and call "time." For the objective of demonstrating the substitution of factors from one equation to another, about all the test administrator (teacher) would need to do would be to supply two equations of the proper form and make clear whether the student was expected to write his answers on the same page or on a separate answer page. The objective itself should be communicated so that the learner understands how he is to solve the "problems," that is, by using the commutative property of multiplication.

It is clear, then, that the more closely objectives are prepared to follow the outline given in Chapter 5, the fewer decisions remain to be made in planning the test, and the fewer "directions" must be given to the student. Statements of objectives as prepared for the use of the instructional designer or teacher also are used to define most of the test situation for the student. Of course, both objectives and test items derived from them have to be presented in simpler terms for young children, either for communicating to them the purpose of the lesson or for testing their performance after the lesson is completed.

Some Cautions   In using objectives to plan tests, a few cautions should be noted. The more incomplete are the statements of objectives, the more these cautions may be needed, because more must be "filled in" in moving from the objective to the test situation.

1. Substitute verbs which change the meaning of either the *capability* or the *action* described in the objective should be avoided. When synonyms or more simple explanations are needed to translate the objective into a test, these restatements must be reviewed for agreement with the intent of the objective. Particular care should be taken not to change from an answer the student must somehow construct or develop for himself, to an answer he must merely choose, select, or recall. If an objective says "generate a position and a defense for the position," he can only do this orally or in writing—not by selecting answers from a multiple-choice test. Avoidance of ambiguity in "guessing at" what vague verbs mean in poorly stated objectives can be achieved by using the standard verbs from Table 3. But careful attention needs to be given to deciding upon unambiguous meanings for verbs such as "summarize," "describe," "list," "analyze," "complete," except as "ing" verbs

denoting the particular action expected. Review of an objective in these terms sometimes reveals that the objective itself needs to be changed. In that case, it should be changed before planning the instruction, and before using the statement either as a lesson objective or as a part of the directions for a test.

2. Changes in other elements of the objective should be avoided, except when needed to simplify directions to the student as to how to take the test. That is, unless a deliberate change is intended, the situation, the object, and the tools and other constraints, as well as the two verbs denoting the capability and the action, should be congruent between the objective and the test. It is possible that changes might be so great as to make the test call for capabilities the students have not yet been taught. In a "worst possible" mismatch between objective and test, capabilities in different domains of learning outcomes might be specified in the objective and in the test. In such a situation, if the teaching were to be directed to an objective in still a third domain, there would be maximum non-congruence among the three anchor points. A revealing instance pertaining to this caution might be obtained by asking teachers or designers, on three separate occasions, to produce their "objective," their "examinations," and their "lesson plans." Is it an inconceivable finding that the objectives might call for "appreciate," while the teaching contains "facts," and the examination calls for "use of concepts and rules"?

3. Tests should not be made either more "easy" or more "difficult" than the objectives. These terms need not enter into testing of the objective-referenced variety. The aim is one of accurately representing the objective, rather than one of estimating how to make tests sufficiently difficult.

4. The test should not try to achieve a large range in scores or a "normal" distribution of scores. The aim of such testing is not that of "discriminating" among the students. That is to say, testing does not have the purpose of finding that student A scores higher or lower than student B. Rather, its purpose is to discover which objectives both students have learned.

THE CONCEPT OF MASTERY

The introduction of the idea of *mastery* of learning outcomes (Bloom, 1968) requires a change in viewpoint towards the conduct of instruction, as well as towards its assessment. In conventional instruction, both the teacher and the students expect that only a few students will learn so well as to receive an *A* in the topic or course. The rest will either do fairly well, as represented by a *C*, for example, or they will "fail." When test scores are plotted as frequency distributions, a "normal curve" is formed, and certain percentages of students are assigned to various letter grades.

In commenting on the impact of this system of assessment, Bloom, Hastings & Madaus (1971, p. 43) observe that the expectations so established tend to fix the academic goals of teachers and students at inappropriate low levels, and thus reduce both teacher and student motivation. The particular educational practice which produces these effects is "group-paced" instruction, in which all students must try to learn at the same rate and by the same mode of instruction. When both pace and mode are fixed, the achievement of each student becomes primarily a function of his aptitude. But if both mode and rate of instruction can vary among learners, the chances are that more students can become successful in their learning.

It is easier to set up means by which *rate* of learning is allowed to vary among learners than it is to predict the *mode* of learning which will benefit each student the most. And of course there are economical and other limits— one cannot provide a different mode for every single student. Modularized, individualized instruction can largely take care of the rate problem, and to some extent (when alternate materials or modes are available) the problem of learning "style" as well. The diagnostic features of individualized assessment also make it possible to help a student redirect his efforts properly.

Mastery learning means essentially that if the proper conditions can be provided, perhaps 90 to 95 percent of the students can actually master most objectives to the degree now only reached by "good students." Thus the mastery learning concept abandons the idea that students merely learn more or less well. Rather, an effort is made to find out why students fail to reach mastery, and to remedy the situation for such students. The resolution of a learning problem by a student usually requires one of the following measures: (a) more time for learning, (b) different media or materials, or (c) diagnosis to determine what missing prerequisite knowledge or skills he must acquire to master the objective. Within this context, the personal knowledge of the teacher can be added to form decisions concerning students whose performance is exceptional even when these methods have been fully utilized. The general aim implied by the notion of mastery includes the resolution to provide materials and conditions by means of which most learners can be successful at most tasks, in a program that is reasonable for each individual.

Determining Criteria for Mastery

How can it be known when a student has performed satisfactorily, or attained mastery, on a test applicable to any particular objective? The student needs to be told he was successful, so that he can then move on to work toward achieving the next objective he chooses or has assigned to him. In case he has not been successful in attaining the objective, the teacher needs to determine what remedial instruction is needed.

A remedial decision for an objective in the intellectual skill domain can best be made by administering a diagnostic test over the capabilities subordinate to the objective. In other instances, the teacher may use oral testing methods to find out where in the teaching sequence the failure to learn first began to occur. When instruction is individualized, the individual lessons often include such diagnostic tests on subordinate capabilities. For a known slow-learner, such "diagnostic" tests of subordinate competencies may be used as "assessments of performance" so that the learner is known to have mastered each capability before he goes on to the next. This procedure detects "small failures" before they accumulate into "large failures" of entire lessons, topics, or courses. Certainly consistent use of frequent testing could often prevent the "year after year" failures, or at least alert the school earlier than usual to a need to reappraise the program for a particular student.

When "mastery" is defined for a test assessing performance on an objective, this also defines the "criterion of success" for that objective. The first step is to define *how well* the learner must perform on the test to indicate success on that objective. Then a record is made of *how many* students have reached the criterion (mastery). This makes it possible to decide whether the instruction over that objective has reached its design objective. Later, at the end of an entire course, the percentage of students who reached the criterion of mastery on all the objectives (or any specified percentage of the objectives) can be computed. From such data, one can determine whether the course-design criterion has been met. A frequently used course-design criterion is that 90 percent of the students achieve mastery of 90 percent of the objectives, but other percentages than these may of course be used. Sometimes three design criteria are set, one to indicate minimal acceptable success, while others represent higher degrees of success. In general, this means of representing course-design criteria can be used to give *accountability* for the performance of students following instruction.

The administration of tests applicable to course objectives, and the definition of "mastery level" for each objective, provide the means for evaluating both the course itself and the performance of individual students. Thus students can be "promoted" on the basis of such tests, and the test results can be used in the *formative evaluation* of the course, showing where revisions are needed, if any (see Chapter 12). This built-in capability for course improvement is compatible not only with "fair promotion standards" for students, but also with the individualization of instruction, and with the development and evaluation of entire instructional systems.

While the action of defining mastery on each objective, when objective-referenced tests are employed, is intended primarily for the purpose of monitoring student progress and for discovering how successful the course is, data from the same tests can be used for "assigning grades" when that is required by the school.

CRITERIA FOR OBJECTIVE-REFERENCED ASSESSMENT

The question next to be addressed concerns the matter of deciding upon criteria of mastery for each kind of learning objective. Typical procedures for each domain of learning outcomes are described in the following section.

Intellectual Skill Objectives

Problem Solving   As an illustration of criteria for assessing performance for this type of learning outcomes, we begin with the objective for the learning of a *higher-order rule (problem-solving)*, briefly described in Table 2 (p. 85). The statement of this objective is "generates, by synthesizing applicable rules, a paragraph describing a person's actions in a situation of fear."

To "score" such a paragraph as acceptable, a list of features the paragraph should include would be prepared. In this case no "verbatim key" is possible, and mechanical scoring is out of the question (at least with technology currently available). Since no grammatical requirements are reflected in this abbreviated statement of the objective, it may be assumed that an adequate description of a case of fear need only be "descriptive" and not necessarily error-free in grammar and punctuation. If several teachers are using the same objective, they might work together to define assessment criteria more precisely, and to agree upon *how many actions* must be described and how to judge that they describe a *fearful reaction* of the person. The minimum number of rules to be "synthesized" in developing the description could be agreed upon. The application of some rules might be mandatory, and some optional, in a satisfactory paragraph.

As in many appropriate tests, the test for this objective is not to be judged simply as "8 out of 10 questions right." The criteria to be looked for may be both qualitative and quantitative in nature. Whatever the checklist for scoring may contain, its application will require judgment, not a clerical checking of an answer with an "answer key." Consequently, degree of agreement among teachers in applying the checklist to determine "acceptable" or "not acceptable" paragraphs is a relevant factor in determining the reliability of the measure of performance obtained. The criteria employed for judging such a performance might be (a) expression, (b) one action of the large muscles, and (c) two statements of rules governing emotional expression in behavior.

Rule Learning   For the learning of a *rule*, the example given in Table 2 is "demonstrates, by solving verbally stated examples, the addition of positive and negative numbers." In order to examine the matter of performance criteria more exactly, one needs to begin with an expanded version of this objective, which is: "Given verbally stated examples involving physical variables which vary over a range of positive and negative values, demonstrates the addition of these values by writing appropriate mathematical expressions yielding their sum." Obviously, this more complete statement adds to the specification of the situation, and therefore to the adequate formulation of a test item. Such an item, for example, might say, "The temperature in Greenland on one day was 17°C. during the day and decreased by 57° during the night. What was the nighttime temperature?"

Thus the "situation" part of the objective statement defines the class of situations from which particular test items are to be drawn. Suppose the objective is: "Given a verbal statement defining values of length and width of a rectangularly shaped face of an object, finds the area of the face." From such a statement, an item such as the following could readily be derived: "A box top is 120 cm. in length and 47 cm. in width; what is its area?" It may be noted that the statement of the objective in this case implies that the performance will be measured in a situation including a verbal statement of the problem. A different statement beginning "Given a diagram of a rectangle with values of length and width indicated . . ." would of course imply a different form of test item.

A remaining decision pertaining to the criterion of performance measurement has to do with the question of how many items to employ. Obviously, the aim is to achieve measurement to which the ideas of "mastered" versus "not mastered" can be applied. It may need to be determined empirically how many items must be used in order to make such a decision correctly. By convention, ten or twenty items might be considered necessary as a number of examples for a test of the learning of an arithmetic rule. While there is no strong argument against this practice, except for the time required, it is difficult to see why more than three or four examples are needed. The aim in using multiple examples is primarily one of avoiding "errors of measurement" which may arise because of one or more undesirable idiosyncratic features of a single item.

Defined Concepts   To derive an illustration of performance criteria for the measurement of a *defined concept*, the following example of an objective may be used: "Given a picture of an observer on the earth and the sky above him, classifies the zenith as the point in the sky vertically above the observer." Again it is apparent that the situation described in this statement may be directly represented in the form of a test item. For example, such an item might first depict (in a labeled diagram) the earth, the sky, and an observer standing on the earth. Going on, it could say: "Show by an angular diagram the location of the *zenith*." For answer, the student would draw a vertical line pointing from the observer to the sky, indicate that it made a 90° angle with the earth's surface at the point at which the observer was located, and label the point in the sky to which the line was directed as the "zenith."

An item of this type would not be highly dependent on the verbal abilities of the student, and might be a desirable form of measurement for that reason. Alternatively, providing verbal facility of the student could be assumed, an item might be based upon a differently stated objective, as follows: "Asked to define, classifies zenith as the point in the sky vertically (or 90° to the surface) above an observer on the earth, by stating a definition orally." It is evident that measurement in this case is subject to distortion. Unless one is entirely convinced that the student has mastered the subordinate concepts (earth, sky, observer, 90°), the resulting response of the student may have to be interpreted as a memorized verbal chain. Nevertheless, it is noteworthy that verbal statements are often employed as criteria for assessment of defined concepts.

Concrete Concepts The assessment of *concrete concept* learning involves the construction of items from an objective statement like the following: "Given five common plants and asked to name the major parts, identifies for each the root, leaf, and stem, by pointing to each while naming it." For such an assessment to be made, the child would be provided with five plants laid out on the table. In response to the teacher's question, he would point to and name the root, leaf, and stem for each plant. Of course, an objective with a somewhat different statement of the "situation" would lead to a corresponding difference in the test item. For example, the objective statement: "Given pictures of five common plants, identifies the root, leaf, and stem of each by placing labels bearing these names opposite the appropriate part," implies a specifically different kind of test item. Whereas the previous example assumes only that the oral responses "root," "leaf," and "stem" can be made without error, the latter example requires the assumption that the labels containing these words can be read.

A very simple example of assessment for a concrete concept is provided by the task of identifying a common geometrical shape, as it may occur in an early grade. The objective statement might read: "Given a set of common geometrical shapes, and oral directions 'show me the circles,' identifies the circles by pointing." From this statement may be derived an assessment item which involves giving the child a piece of paper on which appear figures such as the following:

○□△○○□□○□△○

Upon being given the oral directions, "Point to each one that is a circle," the child would make the appropriate response to each circular figure, in order to be counted as having attained the concept.

Verbal and Motor Chains   Measuring *verbal* or *motor chains* requires a fairly self-evident process. In the case of a verbal chain, for example, one might simply say, "Recite 'Old Ironsides.'" Decisions would need to be made as to whether hesitations or promptings would be acceptable for criterion performance. A time limit might be set for hesitations; and the learner should be informed whether enthusiasm, voice inflection, gestures, or aspects of performance other than the correct verbal chain itself are to be expected. Such criteria should preferably be known before practice starts, as well as at the time of the test.

Shorter verbal chains often are tested as an incidental part of a test whose aim is primarily a more complex form of learning. Having a student work with chemical equations without reference to a listing of symbols of any kind would constitute an example.

Motor chains have for many years been evaluated by "comparison with standards," as in the case of handwriting. Many years ago, a familiar scene in the elementary school room was the Palmer Scale for grading handwriting. A sample of the pupil's writing was compared with ideal samples on a board containing various degrees of "correct" penmanship, each having a numeral such as 90, 80, 70, etc., indicating the "standard" for each level of skill in writing. This was a "criterion-referenced" form of grading in that standards were stable and always meant the same thing; and also in the sense that teachers could say that 60 was "passing" at the third grade, 70 at the fourth grade, and so on.

Cognitive Strategies

While it would seem desirable to extend the notion of mastery learning to all domains of instructional objectives, its application to the measurement of cognitive strategies cannot readily be achieved. Since such strategies as we deal with them here are primarily relevant to performances of novel problem solving, it is apparent that the *quality* of the mental process is being assessed, and not simply its presence or absence. Sometimes, novel problems have many solutions, rather than a single solution. In such instances, cognitive strategies will have been used by the student in achieving the solution, whatever it may be. Accordingly, assessment becomes a matter of judging how good the solution is, and it is unlikely that a "pass-fail" decision will be made.

It is noteworthy that standards of originality and inventiveness are applied to the assessment of such student products as theses and dissertations in university undergraduate and graduate education. Besides being thorough and technically sound, a doctoral dissertation is expected to make "an original discovery or contribution" to a field of systematic knowledge. Exact criteria or dimensions for judging this quality are typically not specified. Varying numbers of professionally qualified people usually arrive at a consensus concerning the degree of originality exhibited by a dissertation study, and its acceptability as a novel contribution to an area of knowledge or art.

Productive Thinking The measurement of productive thinking, and by inference the cognitive strategies that underlie such thinking, has been investigated by Johnson and Kidder (1972) in psychology classes at the undergraduate level of education. Students were asked to invent novel hypotheses, questions, and answers in response to problem statements which go beyond the information obtained from lectures and textbook. The problems employed included (1) predicting the consequences of an unusual psychological event; (2) writing an imaginative sentence incorporating several newly learned (specified) concepts; (3) stating a novel hypothesis related to a described situation; (4) writing a title for a table containing behavioral data; and (5) drawing conclusions from a table or graph. When items such as these were combined into tests containing 10–15 items, reasonably adequate reliabilities of "originality" scores were obtained. Quality was judged by two raters whose judgments were found to agree highly after a short period of training.

Assessments of originality can presumably be made of students' answers, compositions, and projects at precollege levels. In fact, such judgments are often made by teachers incidentally, or at any rate informally, concerning a variety of projects and problems undertaken by students in schools. It seems evident that systematic methods of assessment can be applied to cognitive strategies at these lower levels of the educational ladder, although this has not as yet been done.

It should be pointed out that the assessment of cognitive strategies, or the originality of thought, as an *outcome* of learning does not necessarily have the same aim, nor use the same methods, as those employed in the measurement of creativity as a *trait*. Creativity has been extensively studied in this latter sense (Torrance, 1963; Guilford, 1967; Johnson, 1972), and the findings go far beyond the scope of the present discussion. When assessment of the quality of thought is to be undertaken as a learning outcome, two main characteristics must be sought. First, the problem (or project) that is set for the student must require the utilization of knowledge, concepts, and rules which have been recently learned by the student, rather than calling upon instances of skills and information which may have been acquired an indeterminate number of years previously. Second, it must be either assumed, or preferably shown, that students have in fact learned relevant prerequisite information and skills, before the assessment of "originality" is undertaken. This condition is necessary to insure that all students have the same opportunity to be original, and that their solutions are not handicapped by the absence of necessary knowledge and intellectual skills.

Information

In this domain, the concept of mastery must be related to a predetermined set of facts, generalizations, or ideas, an acceptable number of which the student can state in acceptable form or degree of completeness and accuracy. The conventional "norm-referenced" measurement is often closely related to assessment of information. The fundamental distinction to be held in mind, however, is that of *objective versus content-referenced* measurement. The aim of assessment is to determine whether certain objectives have been attained, rather than to discover whether some content has been "covered."

Objective-referenced assessment may be achieved for the information domain of learning outcomes by specifying what information is to be learned as a minimum standard of performance. Objectives pertaining to information should state clearly *which* names, facts, and generalizations should be learned. They thus differentiate the core content of information to be recalled, from the incidental information which may be in the book and which some students may be able to recall, but which represents learning beyond the required level.

It would be a mistake to make the objectives in the information domain so exhaustive as to leave no time for objectives in other domains. Instead, one should deliberately seek out and identify those informational outcomes which are likely to contribute most to the *attainment of objectives in other domains*. While masses of information should be acquired over years by the well-educated person, this goal should not be allowed to interfere with the attainment of objectives in the areas of intellectual skills and problem-solving strategies.

When students are provided with information objectives (names, facts, or generalizations and condensed substance to be learned), it is possible for them to undertake the learning of these objectives with the same confidence that pertains to learning objectives in other domains, *simply because they know what they are expected to learn.* When the possibility of doing this is recognized, the testing of students for information can become as fair and humane as are tests on intellectual skills.

Examples of Information Items   Some typical items for information assessment are as follows:

1. Describe at least three of the causes of the Revolutionary War, as discussed in the textbook.
2. Tell briefly what was the role of each of these men in the affair at West Point. (This statement to be followed by names of the men, and further identification of the affair as Benedict Arnold's treason).
3. State the chemical symbols for the following compounds.
4. Write a paragraph summarizing how a president is elected when the electoral college fails to elect.
5. Show in one page or less the major advantages of objective-referenced measurement, by simply *listing* them.
6. Name any 15 of these 20 animals from seeing their pictures.
7. What is the boiling point of water?
8. Read this report and write a summary of the four main themes developed in the report.

As these examples indicate, objective-referenced testing of information requires the exact identification of what information is to be learned and retained. If the listing of names or dates is to be acquired, this should be made clear. Alternatively, if the substance of a passage is to be recounted, this objective should be made equally apparent to the student. These procedures make learning for mastery feasible, and also fair and reasonable.

Attitudes

As Chapter 4 has indicated, attitudes vary in the intensity with which they influence the choice of personal actions. Since the strength of attitudes is what one wishes to assess, it is evident that "mastery" cannot be identified. The assessment of strength of an attitude toward or against a class of action choices may be obtained in terms of the proportion of times the person behaves in a given way in a sample of defined situations. For example, attitude toward using public transportation might be assessed by observing the likelihood of a student's choosing various forms of public (rather than private) transportation in the various situations in which such choices are made. The observed incidents would be the basis for inferring the degree to which the person *tends* to use or not to use public conveyances.

In assessing an attitude like "concern for others," it is evident that no "pass-fail" criterion of mastery can be set. However, a teacher might adopt the objective that all her second-grade pupils will improve in the positive direction of this attitude during a year's period. In addition, it would be possible to adopt the standard that each child will exhibit concern for others, either in verbal expression or overt actions, more times per month in May than during the previous October. Anecdotal records may be kept recording such actions, and reports of "improved" or "not improved" made at the end of the school year. Such reports can be quantified in terms of number of positive actions and in terms of proportion of positive to total (positive plus negative) actions. Behaviors representing neither kind of action would simply not be recorded, in recognition of the fact that some of the child's time is spent in study periods offering little opportunity for behaving either way toward other people.

The following examples suggest some actions which might be recorded in relation to such an attitude as "concern for others": any act or word directed to comforting a child who is upset; expression of condolence for illness or other misfortune; helping locate lost articles; suggesting that the class write letters to an ill classmate; offering encouragement to any child experiencing a difficulty whether relating to learning or otherwise; offering to tutor a child who missed work due to absence or failure; offering to share a discovery about materials or methods for learning; helping to obtain first aid for a playground injury.

Attitudes are often measured by obtaining "self-reports" of the likelihood of actions, as opposed to direct observations of the actions themselves. As is well known, the most serious limitation in the use of questionnaires for this purpose is the possibility of bias resulting from students' attempts to answer questions in ways that will win approval, as opposed to a manner that reflects their choices accurately. There appears to be no simple solution to the problem of obtaining truly accurate information from self-reports, although many investigations have been carried out with this purpose (cf. Fishbein, 1967). Best results appear to be achieved when students are first assured that the assessment being done is not intended as an "adversary" process; that is, when they are relieved of the anxiety of reporting only what will (they think) be approved. When questionnaires are administered to groups, the additional precaution is frequently taken to insure that responses are anonymously recorded.

Motor Skills

Assessment of motor skills, like that for information, typically requires the setting of certain standards of performance. Usually such standards refer to the *precision* of the performance, but often also to its *speed*. Since motor skills are known to improve in either or both of these qualities with extended practice, it is unrealistic to expect that mastery can be defined in the sense of "learned" or "not-learned." Accordingly, a standard of performance must be decided upon in order to determine whether mastery has been achieved.

Typing skill provides a good example of assessment methods in this domain. A number of different standards of performance are set at progressively higher levels for practice which has extended over increasingly long periods of time. Thus a test standard of 30 words per minute with a specified minimum number of errors may be adopted as a reasonable standard in a beginning course, while 40 or 50 words per minute may be expected for an advanced course after more time has been given for additional practice.

Reliability of Objective-Referenced Measures

Choosing criteria for items and tests designed to accomplish objective-referenced measurement requires the selection of standards of performance which are appropriate to the stated objective, as the preceding discussion has shown. In addition, the items employed for assessment need to yield measurement which is *dependable*. This latter feature of the assessment procedure is referred to as *reliability*, and it has two primary meanings.

Consistency   A first meaning of reliability is *consistency* of measurement. It is necessary to determine that the student's performance in answering or completing one particular item designed to assess his performance on an objective is consistent with his performance on other items aimed at the same objective. A pupil in the second grade may be asked by one item to demonstrate his mastery of an arithmetic rule by means of the item: $3M + 2M = 25$; $M = ?$ Obviously, the purpose of assessment is to discover whether he is able to perform a *class* of arithmetic operations of this type, not simply whether he is able to do this single one. Accordingly, additional items belonging to the same class (for example, $4M + 3M = 21$; $5M + 1M = 36$) are typically employed in order to insure the dependability of the measurement.

In informal testing situations, as when the teacher "probes" by asking questions of one student after another, single items may be employed to assess performance. However, it is evident that no measure of consistency is available in such situations. On any single item, a student may make a successful response because he happens to have seen and memorized an "answer." Alternatively, his response may be incorrect because he has inadvertently been misled by some particular characteristic of the item. The single item does not make possible a confident conclusion that the student has mastered the performance implied by the objective.

In those instances in which the class of performances represented by the objective is well defined (as in the arithmetic example previously given) the procedure of selecting additional assessment items of the same class is fairly straightforward. It is essential to bear in mind that the conclusion aimed for is not "how many items are correct?", but rather "does the number correct dependably indicate mastery?" While two items are obviously better than one, they may yield the puzzling outcome, half right-half wrong. Does this mean that the student has attained mastery, or does it mean he got one item right only because he somehow managed to memorize an answer? Three items would seem to provide a better means of making a reliable decision about mastery. In this case, two out of three correctly answered leads to a certain confidence that reliability of measurement has been achieved. More items can readily be employed, but three seems a reasonable minimum on which to base a reliable assessment of mastery.

When cognitive strategies are the aim of assessment, the "item" selected for the purpose of assessment may actually be a rather lengthy problem-solving task. For example, such a task might be to "write a 300-word theme on a student-selected topic, within one hour." Assessing performance consistently may require several items, since it is necessary to disentangle the prior learning of information and intellectual skills from the quality of original thought. A number of occasions must be provided on which the student can display the quality of his performance within this domain of learning outcome. The aim is to make it unlikely that a student could meet the criteria set for such tasks without possessing a genuine, generalizable capability of writing original themes on other topics.

Temporal Dependability   The second meaning of reliability is dependability of the measurement on temporally separated occasions. One wishes to be assured that the student's demonstration of mastery of the objective as assessed on Monday is not different from what it would be on Tuesday, or on some other day. Is his performance an ephemeral thing, or does it have the degree of permanence one expects of a learned capability? Has his performance, good or bad, been determined largely by how he felt that day, by a temporary illness, or by some adventitious feature of the testing situation?

Reliability of measurement in this second meaning is usually determined by a second testing separated from the first by a time interval of days or weeks. This is the test-retest method, in which good reliability of the tests is indicated by a high degree of correspondence between scores obtained by a group of students on the two occasions. Often this procedure is used in the formative evaluation of the test, but it may also be employed in practical assessment to determine whether what has been learned has a reasonable degree of stability.

NORM-REFERENCED MEASURES

Tests designed to yield scores which compare each student's performance with that of a group, or with a norm established by group scores, are called *norm-referenced*. Characteristically, such tests are used to obtain assessments of student achievement over relatively large segments of instructional content, such as topics or courses. They differ from objective-referenced tests in that they typically measure performance on a *mixture* of objectives, rather than being confined to assessment of single, clearly identifiable objectives. Thus, a norm-referenced test is more likely to have the purpose of assessing "reading comprehension" than it is to measure the attainment of the individual skills involved in reading, considered as specific objectives.

Because of this characteristic of comprehensive coverage, norm-referenced tests are most useful for *summative* kinds of assessment and evaluation (see Chapter 12). They provide answers to such questions as, "How much American history does a student know (compared to others at his grade level)?" "How well is the student able to reason using the operations of arithmetic?" "What proficiency does the student have in using grammatical rules?" Obviously, such assessment is most appropriate when applied to instruction extending over reasonably long periods of time, as in mid-course or end-of-course examinations.

At the same time, the characteristics of norm-referenced measures imply some obvious limitations, as compared with objective-referenced tests. Since their items usually represent a mixture of objectives, often impossible to identify singly, they cannot readily be used for the purpose of diagnostic testing of prerequisite skills and knowledge. For a similar reason, norm-referenced tests typically do not provide direct and unambiguous measures of what has been learned, when the latter is conceived as one or more defined objectives.

Often a norm-referenced test presents questions and tasks which require the student at one and the same time to utilize learned capabilities of intellectual skills, information, and cognitive strategies. In so doing, they make possible assessments of student capabilities which are "global" rather than specific to identifiable objectives. For this reason they are particularly appropriate for assessing outcomes of learning in a set of topics or in a total course. Since the scores obtained are also representative of a group (a single class, or a larger "referenced" group such as ten-year-old children), the score made by each student may conveniently be compared with those of others in the group. Percentile scores are often used for this purpose; the score of a student may be expressed, for example, as "falling at the 63d percentile."

Teacher-Made Tests

Tests constructed by teachers are sometimes of the norm-referenced variety. The teacher may be interested in learning how well students have learned the content of a course, which may represent a number of different objectives and several categories of learning outcome. Mid-course and end-of-course examinations often have this characteristic of mixed purposes of assessment. These may also be conceived as being aimed at testing the student's "integration" of the various skills and knowledges he is expected to have learned.

At the same time, a norm-referenced test makes possible the comparison of student's performances within a group, or with a referenced group (such as last year's class). Often, such tests are refined over periods of years, using methods of item analysis to select the most "discriminating" items (cf. Wood, 1960; Payne, 1968). This means that items which do not discriminate—those that many students answer correctly and those that few answer correctly—are progressively discarded. Tests refined in this manner tend increasingly to measure problem-solving and other cognitive strategies. They may also, in part, measure "intelligence," rather than what has been directly learned. While this may be a legitimate intention when the aim is to assess the total effects of a course of study, it is evident that this quality of norm-referenced tests makes them very different from objective-referenced tests.

When assessment is aimed at the outcomes of individual lessons or parts of lessons, little justification can be seen for the use of norm-referenced tests. When such tests are used to assess student performance resulting from the learning of defined objectives, they are likely to miss the point of assessment entirely. When instruction has been designed so as to insure the attainment of objectives, tests should be derived directly from the definition of the objectives themselves, as indicated in the earlier portion of this chapter. Unless objective-referenced tests are used for this purpose, two important purposes of assessment will likely be neglected: (1) the assessment of mastery of the specific capabilities learned; and (2) the possibility of diagnostic help for students in overcoming particular learning deficiencies by retrieving missing prerequisite skills and knowledges.

Standardized Tests

Norm-referenced tests intended for broad usage among many schools within a school system, a region, or in the nation as a whole, may have norms that are *standardized*. What this means is that the tests have been given to large samples of students in specified age (or grade) groups, and that the resulting distributions of scores obtained become the standards to which any given student's scores, or those of any class of students, may be compared. Sometimes the standard norms are expressed as percentiles, indicating what percent of the large sample of students attained or fell below particular scores. Often, too, such standards are expressed as grade-equivalent scores, indicating the scores attained by all children in the group who were in the first grade, the second grade, and so on. Procedures used in the development and validation of standardized tests are described in many books on this subject (cf. Cronbach, 1970; Thorndike & Hagen, 1969; Tyler, 1971).

Standardized tests are generally norm-referenced tests—the development of objective-referenced tests has not yet proceeded to the point of availability for a variety of objectives and for a variety of "levels" of instruction. Accordingly, standardized tests typically exhibit the characteristics previously described. They are usually mixed in their measurement of particular objectives, since their items have not been directly derived from such objectives. Their items are selected to produce the largest possible variation in scores among students, and thus their scores tend to be rather highly correlated with intelligence, rather than with particular learning outcomes. With few exceptions, they fail to provide the identification of missing subordinate capabilities which is essential to diagnostic aims.

Obviously, then, standardized tests are quite inappropriate for use in the detailed assessment of learning outcomes from lessons having specifiable objectives. Their most frequent and most appropriate use is for the purpose of summative evaluation of total courses or of several years of instruction. When employed for these purposes, standardized tests can provide valuable information about the long-term effects of courses and of larger instructional programs.

SUMMARY

Up to this point, we have been concerned primarily with goals and performance objectives, with the domains of learning they represent, and with the design of lessons which employ instructional events and conditions of learning suitable for the chosen objectives. In this chapter we turn our attention to the assessment of student performance on the objectives. Thus we proceed from the *what* and the *how* to the *how well* aspect of learning.

For the purpose of assessing student performance on the planned objectives of a course, *objective-referenced tests employing a criterion-referenced interpretation* constitute the most suitable procedure. Such tests serve several important purposes:

1. They show whether each student has mastered an objective, and hence may go on to study for another objective.
2. They permit early detection and diagnosis of failure to learn, thus helping to identify the remedial study needed.
3. They provide data for making improvements in the instruction itself.

4. They are "fair" evaluations in that they measure performance on the objective that was given to the student as an indication of what he was supposed to learn. This kind of testing is consistent with the honesty of the relation of teacher to learner.

Objective-referenced tests are direct rather than indirect measures of performance on the objectives. They deal with each objective separately, rather than with very large units of instruction, such as an entire year of study. For this reason they have diagnostic value, as well as value for formative evaluation of the course.

The *validity* of objective-referenced tests is found by determining the congruence of test with objective. *Reliability* is obtained by measuring the consistency of the performance assessment, and its dependability over time. The concept of *mastery* is relevant for objective-referenced tests in the domains of intellectual skills, motor skills, and information. For these types of learning outcomes, mastery levels can be defined as error-free performances. In the case of cognitive strategies and attitudes, since assessments deal with "how well" or "how much," the use of criteria of mastery is less clearly applicable. Examples are given of how criteria of performances can be chosen for each learning domain.

Another type of test is called *norm-referenced*. Such tests do not measure separate, specific objectives of the course. Rather, they measure mixtures or composite sets of objectives, whether these are identified or not. When a norm-referenced test is a standardized test, it has been carefully designed and revised to yield high variability of scores. The interpretation of the scores is made by reference to norms, which represent performance on the test for large groups of learners. Such tests permit comparison of a score of one pupil with that of others; they also permit comparing the average score for a group with the scores of a larger norm group.

REFERENCES

Bloom, B. S. Learning for mastery. *Evaluation Comment*, 1968, I, No. 2.
Bloom, B. S., Hastings, J. T., and Madaus, G. F. *Handbook on Formative and Summative Evaluation of Student Learning*. New York: McGraw-Hill, 1971.
Briggs, L. J. *Handbook of Procedures for the Design of Instruction*. Pittsburgh, Pa.: American Institutes for Research. 1970.
Cronbach, L. J. *Essentials of Psychological Testing*. 3d Ed. New York: Harper & Row, 1970.
Guilford, J. P. *The Nature of Human Intelligence*. New York: McGraw-Hill, 1967.
Johnson, D. M. *A Systematic Introduction to the Psychology of Thinking*. New York: Harper & Row. 1972.

Johnson, D. M. & Kidder, R. C. Productive thinking in psychology classes. *American Psychologist*, 1972, *27*, 672–674.

Payne, D. A. *The Specification and Measurement of Learning Outcomes*. Waltham, Mass.: Blaisdell, 1968.

Thorndike, R. L. & Hagen, E. *Measurement and Evaluation in Psychology and Education*. New York: Wiley, 1969.

Torrance, E. P. *Education and the Creative Potential*. Minneapolis: University of Minnesota Press, 1963.

Tyler, L. E. *Tests and Measurements*. 2d Ed. Englewood Cliffs, N.J.: Prentice-Hall, 1971.

Wood, D. A. *Test Construction; Development and Interpretation of Achievement Tests*. Columbus, Ohio: Merrill, 1960.

THREE
INSTRUCTIONAL SYSTEMS

10
INDIVIDUALIZED INSTRUCTION

Instruction may be designed in units of various sizes and lengths. It may be sequenced in a number of ways, which take into account the necessity of prerequisite learning. It may also be managed in different forms, in the sense of being delivered to the students who are its major participants. In other words, instructional design in its total meaning includes consideration of the *delivery system* by means of which students become involved with the process of instruction.

In this chapter we deal with an important kind of delivery for instruction, called *individualized instruction*. The units of instruction corresponding to the lesson are the primary focus of the design effort, signifying the small segments of instruction which normally occupy relatively small time periods.

We choose here to use the term "module" to identify the unit of individualized instruction corresponding to the lesson in conventional instruction. Both "lessons" and "modules" may often relate to only a single hour or class period; or they may relate to both in-class and out-of-class learning for some limited period of time, such as two weeks.

The basic principles in designing a lesson are the same as in designing a module. Accordingly, what has been said previously about performance objectives, learning hierarchies, sequencing, instructional events, and the arrangement of effective learning conditions, is equally applicable to modules and to lessons.

Why, then, is there need for a separate chapter on individualized instruction? The need occurs because there are some very fundamental differences between conventional group instruction and individualized instruction. These differences pertain not so much to how learning takes place, but rather to how the learning environment is controlled and managed to achieve the desired instructional events, resulting in the outcomes described in the objectives. Differences pertain primarily to the matter of how the instructional events are presented. In individualized instruction (as compared to conventional instruction):

1. The teacher provides fewer of the instructional events.
2. The materials provide more of the instructional events.
3. Time is thus made free so that the teacher can do more personalized work with students in deciding what to learn and how to learn it. The teacher also monitors pupil progress more closely and does more diagnosis of difficulty and remedial teaching.
4. There is more opportunity for variations among learners in what to learn, how to learn, and which materials to use for learning.
5. Time to learn is allowed to vary among students. There is no need for all learners to work at the same pace.

VARIETIES OF INDIVIDUALIZED INSTRUCTION

While the differences listed are typical, not all of them are found in all variations of individualized instruction. Some of these variations need to be further described, in order to show how they are brought about and managed in the classroom.

Although the term individualized instruction has been widely employed in education for a long time, it has no single widely accepted meaning. It has been used in reference to such a diverse array of educational methods as the following:

1. *Independent study plans*, in which there is agreement between a student and a teacher on only the most gross level of stating objectives to indicate the purpose of studying. The student works on his own to prepare for some form of final examination. No restrictions are placed upon the student as to how he may prepare for the examination. A course outline may or may not be provided. The task may be described at the course level in such terms as "preparing for an examination in differential calculus," or at the degree level as in "honors programs" in English universities. A similar procedure in American practice is preparing for the doctoral comprehensive examination in psychology, English, or other named field.

2. *Self-directed study*, which may be undertaken with specific objectives agreed upon, but with no restriction upon how the student learns. Here the teacher may supply a list of objectives which define the test performances required to receive credit for the course; the teacher may also supply a list of readings or other resources available, but the student is not required to use them. If he passes the test, he receives credit for the course.

3. *Learner-centered programs*, in which the student decides a great deal for himself: within broadly defined areas what his objectives will be, how he will learn, and when he will decide to terminate one task and go to another. This degree of "openness" is sometimes found in public schools, and has been the customary style of operation for a few private, special schools. Usually in public schools, learner choice is permitted only for "excursions" or "enrichment" exercises, and then only after certain required or "core" skills have been mastered. Often such excursions are offered as an incentive to the student to learn the core skills. This is an application of contingency management—offering a preferred activity contingent upon the prior mastery of a required activity.

4. *Self-pacing*, in which the learner works at his own rate, but upon objectives set by the teacher and required of all students. In this case all students may use the same materials to reach the same objectives—only the rate of progress is individualized.

5. *Student-determined instruction*, providing for student judgment in any or all of the following aspects of the learning: (a) selection of objectives; (b) selections of the particular materials, resources, or exercises to be used; (c) selection of a schedule within which work on different academic subjects will be allocated; (d) self-pacing in reaching each objective; (e) self-evaluation as to whether the objective has been met; and (f) freedom to abandon an objective in favor of another one. Obviously this description in itself implies the possibility of over twenty different ways in which instruction may be said to be "individualized" or "learner-determined."

Rationale for Individualized Instruction

It is evident, then, that individualized instruction has a great variety of meanings as it relates to procedures for managing the instructional situation. Most of these varieties of educational practice have been tried out in school settings, and many of them have been the subject of evaluation studies. Concrete examples of these procedures and their effects have been reported (cf. Edling, 1970; Weisgerber, 1971). We turn our attention now to some essential features of individualized instruction.

It is perhaps unfortunate that the most common connotation of school learning is that which takes place in a group situation. While everyone knows that learning is an individual matter, the fact that most schools place one teacher with a group of 30 to 40 students can easily lead to the uncritical thought that school learning, at least, is a social, group matter. The fact is that while "teaching" may be most commonly a group activity, "learning" takes place within the individual learner. This fact accords with the emphasis in earlier chapters, on the "internal conditions of learning," such as the student's desire to learn, willingness to follow directions, attention to the task, attempts to recall relevant information or skills, and receptivity to the guidance of the teacher. As important as all these are, perhaps a most critical internal condition arises from the effects of prior learning which the student brings to the new lesson—his "entering competencies," both those peculiar to the new learning objective, and his general skills such as reading ability and study habits. Several stages of activity internal to the individual are required even in the most simple forms of school learning.

Since learning is an individual matter, why is so much of school learning undertaken as a group activity? Probably in part because the economics of the situation requires one teacher to have many pupils; partly because that is the way the teacher was taught; and partly because of the mistaken notion that pupils learn *better* by group activity. But even a little reflection will suggest that pupils, once they can read well, learn many skills and acquire most information better and faster from a printed source than from orally delivered group instruction. It may be true that only attitudes are more efficiently learned in a group, supervised by a teacher, rather than by solitary study or practice.

It may be expected that sophisticated learners such as university students will be more capable of arranging conditions for their own effective learning than is the case with less mature students. If this is so, why is lecturing more common in the university than it is in the elementary school? Quite probably, both tradition and a lack of suitable materials and resources must be listed as reasons. Many professors like to give lectures; that was the method used when they were in college. In view of the greater capability of older students for self-instruction, if suitable resources can be provided, there is probably more reason now to employ individualized methods in college-level instruction than at any other level. Looking to future benefits in the long range, the earlier that students are taught to accomplish and practice independent learning the more successful will they become as mature learners.

Experience with programmed instruction and other modes of delivery suggests that individualized instruction is often not only more effective and more efficient than group instruction, but is also more responsive to the needs of the learner. It therefore may also be characterized as more humane than group methods, because it: (1) allows realistic goals to be set for each learner; (2) provides various materials or resources for a given goal, thus adapting to individual competencies and backgrounds; (3) provides privacy when difficulty is encountered; (4) permits the learner to work at his own rate; and (5) provides consistent individual feedback rather than hit-or-miss or inappropriate feedback.

Except on those occasions when socializing or exchange of views is the purpose of the lesson, there is every reason to favor individualized over group instruction, not only for enrichment but also for the attainment of basic skills. This is not to say that both large-group and small-group exercises should not be made a part of an overall individualized instruction plan. Teacher-led group instruction provides variety, contributes to long-range social goals, and is especially appropriate for arranging certain instructional events, such as gaining attention, motivating, and providing a model of performance. In addition, groups are essential for the conduct of discussions which elicit new ideas, challenge and temper old ideas, and establish skills of group problem solving.

For presenting the stimulus situation, eliciting the response, guiding the learning, and providing feedback, individual methods and materials are likely to yield superior results. For problem-solving tasks, as well as for learning verbal information and acquiring motor skills, the success of the learning can be enhanced by materials and exercises designed for individual rather than group learning. While there is a place for inspiring lectures, interesting films, TV presentations, and other "mass media," school learning would be much less successful than it is were private study by the learner eliminated from the range of methods employed. Imagine, for example, earning an advanced degree in a research field without doing independent study and supervised research! While there is probably no research evidence as to whether college students learn more in class or outside of class, undoubtedly the best students spend more time in study than in class.

The best applications of individualized instruction require attention to

(1) the development of appropriate learning materials; (2) a method for assigning tasks and monitoring pupil progress, and (3) training of the teacher in the methods to be used. These important matters are next to be discussed in turn.

MATERIALS FOR INSTRUCTION

In designing the instructional materials to be used in modules for individualized instruction, it is just as important to observe the three "anchor points" (Chapter 8) as it is when designing a lesson for group instruction. One might even say it is more important to do so in the case of modules because they are "predesigned," then set into print or other presentation forms, whereas in teacher-led group instruction, the teacher can spontaneously "redesign on the spot." While this is an important advantage of teacher-led instruction in some situations, it probably does not outweigh the advantages of individualized instruction in a general sense.

Since most of the instruction is in print or other media, and not in the teacher's voice, the modules of a course should be designed with at least the care that is given to planning a lesson. From the point of view of formative evaluation and revision of the course, the messages in the modules have the advantage of being unchanging and hence replicable in another group, whereas a live lecture "disappears" and is not open to inspection, revision, or repetition. Responses of students to modules are also usually in permanent written form, since all students answer all questions, not just some of them, as is the case with informal oral quizzing in a group.

Modules deserve great care in their design to achieve the standards suggested by the "three anchor points." The designed modules should, as a minimum: (1) contain a clearly stated performance objective in terms that the students can understand; (2) be followed by an appropriate assessment of student performance, to be sure that the capability identified in the objective has been achieved; and (3) contain necessary materials for presenting the instructional events needed, and for stimulating recall of needed prerequisite competencies or information when relevant. That is to say, the materials in the modules, or the materials that the modules direct the student to use, should *accomplish the instruction.*

Note that the three anchor points are needed for any form or degree of individualized instruction. They are needed whether or not all students study for the same objectives; whether or not more than one set of materials is provided for the same objective; whether the student merely paces himself within a total unit of time allowed for the objectives or whether he has no time limit; and whether the student is allowed to abandon an objective in which he loses interest, as opposed to being encouraged to continue his study until learning is completed.

Sometimes the module will contain all the instructional materials needed to pass a test over the objective. It usually also contains "practice tests" which the student can use to judge his own readiness for taking the actual test. In the event that materials and resources physically independent of the module itself are to be used, directions for how to locate and use them are included in the module. Thus the module itself, and its directions for using related materials, allow the learner to go about his learning task without directions from another person, except when he experiences difficulties.

Up to this point, our description of materials for individualized instruction assumes that modules will be used in a highly organized, carefully preplanned way to help the learner reach the objectives of a course. There are, however, alternative and less highly organized ways to individualize instruction. With greater maturity and practice in learning, the learner may make more of his own decisions about the events of instruction. Accordingly, we need to give further consideration to the nature of materials for a broader range of individualized procedures, applicable to both young learners and adults.

Components for Young Learners

A typical individualized program of instruction for children may be expected to have somewhat different components than a program for adults. The procedures for using the materials will also be different. The following is an outline of typical components of modules designed for children of about the sixth grade, who are assumed to have some reading ability.

A List of Enabling Objectives　Often the learner may benefit from seeing both the target objective for the module and the prerequisite capabilities he needs to acquire. These may be shown simply as a list, or they may be in the form of a learning hierarchy, as described in Chapter 6.

A Suggested Sequence of Activities　In part, the sequence of activities may be derived from the sequence of enabling objectives, and in some instances alternative sequences may be chosen. The sequence as a whole needs to make suitable provision for the enhancement of retention and transfer. Sometimes alternative materials, resources, or exercises may be offered as options. The student may be encouraged to find out for himself which materials seem suitable for him. One student may prefer or profit most from a programmed text; another may find a slide-tape presentation more effective for his learning.

A Menu of Modules　Some programs contain only required modules. The total menu, however, should be designed to meet the needs of fast learners, not solely those of slow learners. Alternatively, programs may offer both "core" (required) and "excursion" (enrichment) modules, while still others may consist entirely of student-chosen modules. The student-selected modules may be designed to provide only self-evaluations of student performance, since the objectives represent what the student wants to learn.

Programs may be designed to make use of the principles of contingency management—using a preferred (high reward) activity as an inducement to undertake a less favored activity. Often such programs include procedures which give the student opportunities to make "contracts," with some required minimum number of modules to be completed by each student. The student may receive a number of "points" at the outset, which he can "spend" to negotiate time to complete a module; and he may, in turn, earn points for successful completion within the contract period. The earned points, within limits, may then be spent to earn free time for preferred new learning, or for other kinds of preferred activity.

A more extreme curriculum philosophy holds that there should be no "modules" and no objectives. According to this view, the learner would simply be put into a learning environment which includes learning resources, laboratory materials, supplies, etc., perhaps attractively arranged to induce interest, but with no requirements, "points," or other rewards, other than the intrinsic reward of enjoyment of learning.

Opinions differ greatly on whether the student should be required to learn or required even to try to learn anything he does not voluntarily undertake. Opinions also differ on how specific objectives for individual learning should be. Those who dislike specific objectives usually shun the use of modules, preferring an "open environment" which permits choice by the student of what is to be learned. It would seem, however, that society must take responsibility for teaching children how to live in our culture as productive, happy, responsible, adult citizens. Since it is difficult to determine the exact nature of human capabilities a given child will need to achieve his goals and to solve problems not yet foreseen by present adults, emphasis needs to be placed on intellectual skills and problem-solving strategies, rather than simply upon presently known "facts" (cf. Rohwer, 1971). A program in elementary science such as *Science—A Process Approach* (AAAS Commission on Science Education, 1967), for example, stresses the methods of science rather than the content of science. A number of other programs in science and social studies similarly emphasize the attainment of "process" objectives.

Alternate Materials for Single Objectives   It is evident to most teachers that some children master a given learning objective better by using one book, medium, or exercise, than by using another which may have equally good theoretical merit. In some cases the reason may be obvious; a poor reader will understand a tape-slide series better than a book. In less obvious cases, "individual learning styles" are cited, although the specific meaning of this phrase is not entirely clear. Research studies, however, have identified few intellectual and personality characteristics which are related to success with specific forms or media of instruction (Briggs, 1968). This finding may result either from the existence of differing entering capabilities which match the specific content of various materials, or on the fact that more appropriate instructional events for the individual learner are found in certain materials. It is often unclear, too, whether it is the sensory mode being stimulated (eye or ear), or whether it is how the ideas are conveyed that accounts for the differential effectiveness of materials designed for the same objective. It may be features of the "style" of the instructional materials—small versus large steps; inductive versus deductive; concrete versus abstract; or other characteristics of this sort. At any rate, providing several versions of a module is often worthwhile. One version might have a simpler vocabulary; one might employ a shorter sentence length; and another might combine an outline or "advance organizer" (Ausubel, 1968) with a terse presentation.

The alternate module concept clearly raises an economic question. Research is needed to assess the extent of advantages of alternate materials so that these can be considered in light of costs. Similar data are needed relevant to the instance in which one form of materials is superior for most learners to other materials which cost less.

A Feedback Mechanism   For young learners and lengthy modules, it may not be wise to wait until a test is given to provide feedback. Feedback after small increments of study is usually desirable. Feedback at frequent intervals is a built-in feature of programmed instruction, and can also be designed for media that normally present uninterrupted messages, such as TV or films. The effectiveness of many media can be improved by building in explicit responding and feedback. In addition to enhancing learning, such responding and feedback serve an alerting function, suggesting the need for diagnostic testing and remedial instruction, or for restudy of the module when performance is poor. One reason for identifying prerequisite capabilities, as is done in a learning hierarchy, is to permit the development of a diagnostic test to show which part of the module is not working well for a particular student, that is, which subordinate capabilities have not been learned or are not recalled when needed.

Several physical means have been developed for providing feedback before a test over the module is taken. One technique, originated by Pressey (1950), is called adjunct autoinstruction. Sample test questions are provided for the student to refer to before, during, or after reading a chapter in a book or using some other form of materials. Such questions have been found to increase learning, both of the content covered by the sample questions and of material for which no questions were made for self-study. Thus they provide a general "reading to learn" set for the entire chapter, and they enhance retention of the specific materials covered by the questions.

TV teachers can pose questions after a brief lecture segment, pausing for the viewer to write his answer or just to think the answer; after the pause, feedback can be given. Questions used with live lectures have also been found of benefit to learning and usually to retention. When immediate automatic recording of answers (for multiple-choice questions) is available to the view of the teacher, he can "reprogram" his lecture on the spot.

When a module is brief, or when the learner typically succeeds readily, a parallel form of the formal test on the objective can be used after learning is completed. In using the test, the student is alerted to a need for any further study, thus avoiding taking the time of the teacher to score the formal test only to discover that further learning is required. An answer key, perhaps including additional explanation, may be sufficient to correct misconceptions; at other times restudy or changing to an alternate module is needed. The learner can consult the teacher when he is uncertain of the most appropriate action.

Some form of self-testing or responding-with-feedback can usually be devised as part of each module. This enhances learning and saves time for the teacher, who can then do individual remedial teaching when all other means fail—a valuable activity for which teachers have too little time when employing conventional group instruction. Such a procedure provides an added bonus—the teacher has time to guide thinking and provide added feedback on an individual basis when most needed. There is a sharp contrast with techniques of group instruction, in which only one child may be asked to respond to each question. In that setting, one does not know how many questions a given student can answer, and any response may be a misleading indicator of the learning accomplished by the entire group.

Components for Adult Learners

The nature of both the materials and the procedures may properly be less highly structured for the college student or other experienced adult learners.

Objectives   Course objectives for adults may sometimes be quite precise and specific, but may still assume that evaluation of learner performance can safely be made at less frequent intervals than would be the case for children. Whether one broad objective or many more specific ones are employed in modules, the adult learner may not have his progress checked until after a rather long period of study.

Directions   Directions for pursuing study may also be greatly abbreviated for the adult learner. He may be provided with a list of resources, or he may simply be told to "use the library and the laboratory." The objective itself may be the main source of directions.

Learning Materials   Materials for learning may be highly structured, as in a programmed text; semistructured, as in an outline or laboratory guide; or unstructured, as would be the case when the student does library research on a topic.

Evaluation of Performance   The student may have an entire semester to complete the unit, or he may receive a grade of "progress" for each semester until finally the product is accepted. While working on the unit, the student usually receives feedback from his teacher or advisor, and from conferences providing reactions to draft plans and preliminary reports. He may also receive direct instruction on a variety of subordinate capabilities, such as writing skills, techniques for finding sources, and others. Usually the evaluation is based on the appropriateness of procedures employed, competence in reporting and interpreting data, and ability to defend a rationale for the product or study which has been completed.

Functions of Modules

Modules may specify activities for groups, small or large. In such instances, a class chart shows the progress of each pupil, and is used to form groups which are at the same point of progress. For such group activities within modules, test items sorted by completed subordinate capabilities can be used to discover when a group should be formed, that is, when several learners have reached a defined stage of progress toward the total module objective.

Modules can also be designed as directions for laboratory or field exercises, or for independent learning not based on instructional materials. In one industrial course for adults, the learners were given the entire set of course objectives, and shown where they could go to take tests. They were then free to visit employees in appropriate departments to observe, ask questions, or seek other ways to learn.

It should be noted that modules need not be restricted to cognitive objectives. Objectives in the affective or motor domain can as well be devised. In shop courses, where machine time must be carefully planned, it can be arranged that all needed cognitive learning has taken place before a skill is practiced with the equipment. This saves not only money for duplicate machines, but also avoids injury to persons and damage to equipment by insuring that the trainee knows safety precautions and correct procedures before he has access to the machine. In many cases, a simulator of the actual machine also brings benefits in cost, safety, and efficiency. Simple simulators can be used for parts of the total task, reserving the more expensive complex simulator for consolidation of skills and practice of emergency procedures in a safe environment.

USE OF MATERIALS IN INDIVIDUALIZED INSTRUCTION

A particular set of instructional materials has been developed for use with an individualized system called PLAN (described in Weisgerber, 1971). This particular system will be described in order to provide a concrete illustration of how such materials are employed in individualizing instruction. PLAN is used by a number of schools throughout the United States.

The instructional objectives of PLAN form the basis of a curriculum in language arts, social studies, science, and mathematics for grades 1–12. Within each grade and subject, these objectives are organized into modules of study for use by students. Usually, five or six objectives constitute a module. A program of studies is developed by the student and teacher, and this program guides the student in selecting modules appropriate to his needs and interests.

A central feature of the PLAN system involves the use of a computer, a terminal for which is usually located in each school. PLAN is a "computer-supported" system. The computer receives and stores records about each student's previous study, his progress, and his performance record. On a daily basis, information is printed out for the teacher indicating (1) which lesson objectives have been completed by which students, and (2) what activities have been begun or completed by each student. In addition, the computer furnishes periodic reports of progress on each student. In general, the information stored in the computer constitutes a base of essential information for planning individual student programs and guiding student learning activities.

Modules and TLU's

The module is a unit of study lasting approximately two weeks, on the average. Sometimes modules deal with single topics, sometimes not. They may be collections of activities representing closely related objectives, such as those in writing, speaking, and spelling. In any case, modules are composed of several *teaching-learning units* (TLU's), each of which has a single objective.

The TLU begins with the learning objective which tells the student what he is going to learn. Following this is a list of a number of learning activities. A typical TLU pertaining to a social studies module for the seventh grade is shown in Figure 8.

As will be seen, the TLU describes the learning activities to be undertaken by the student, and the references to be studied. Self-test questions and discussion questions are also included. In the early grades, pictorial techniques are used to communicate the objective and the learning activities to pupils. An accompanying sheet, called the Activity Sheet, describes additional activities for the student to do in learning about the topic of the TLU. Once the student has completed the activities given in the TLU and the Activity Sheet, he should be able to do what is called for in the objective. Then he is ready to take a performance test. If his performance is satisfactory, he is ready to move forward to a new TLU; if not, he undertakes additional work as suggested by the teacher.

Teacher Directions   The Teacher Directions which accompany each TLU are designed to communicate the objective, the plan for student activities, materials needed, and test directions. Using this sheet, the teacher is able to see at a glance what kinds of activities must be planned—whether discussions, game playing, field trips, or self study by the student. The Teacher Directions make evident what modes of instruction may be needed, such as small group work, partners working together, tutoring, or other modes. Thus it is possible for the teacher to advise the student about options for learning activities.

Instructional Guides   Another kind of material which sometimes accompanies TLU's is Instructional Guides. Such guides may provide direct instruction to the student when it is unavailable in published sources. They often make it possible for the student to develop an intellectual skill necessary for his further progress in a TLU. Figure 9 is an example of an Instructional Guide in fourth-grade language arts, related to the objective, "given a root word, change its form-class by adding suffixes."

Performance Measures   When the student has completed a TLU, he takes a test, designed to assess his performance on the stated objectives. In some instances, the test has a multiple-choice format which can be scored by the computer. In others, his performance is observed and evaluated by the teacher in accordance with definite standards. The teacher then transmits this evaluation to the computer for record-keeping purposes. Computer printouts of performance records for all students are ready for the teacher's use on the next day.

THE MANAGEMENT OF INDIVIDUALIZED INSTRUCTION

Just as specially designed materials are needed for the modules of an individualized program of instruction, so also are management procedures required to keep track of these materials, to keep the system going and to monitor the progress of students in their learning efforts.

Patriots and Politicians

4712-1

OBJECTIVE

Identify reasons for the development of political parties in the United States.

1   When the founders of our country were writing the Constitution, there were many different opinions about what should be done. Read *The Promise of America*, pp. 140-143, and *Promise of America: The Starting Line*, pp. 129-134. Make a list of at least four issues on which the authors of the Constitution disagreed. Were these the first differences of opinion among Americans?

2   When George Washington became President, there were no political parties. Read *The Promise of America*, pp. 153-155. With a partner, look at the filmstrip, **The Beginning of Political Parties.** If you were in George Washington's place, what problems would you have had to deal with? Discuss this question with your partner.

3   Raising money was a big problem for President Washington and his Secretary of the Treasury, Alexander Hamilton. Read *The Promise of America*, pp. 157-162. Which groups in the colonies supported Hamilton's policies? Why? Which groups opposed them? Why?

4   Americans also differed on how to treat foreign countries. Read about these differences in *The Promise of America*, pp. 164-167, and *History of Our United States*, pp. 206-208. Why did some Americans favor France and some favor England?

5   Not long after Washington became President it became apparent that there were two major groups with different solutions to our problems. One of these groups was called the Federalists; the other was called the Anti-Federalists, or the Republicans. These two groups became the first two political parties. Political parties are organizations of men with similar views who work together for the same goals. Read about the beginnings of political parties in *History of Our United States*, pp. 205-206, and *The Promise of America*, pp. 162-164. Now do the Activity Sheet.

6   Have a debate with a partner. Pretend that you are a farmer and a supporter of Jefferson. Your partner is a merchant and a supporter of Hamilton. Try to convince your partner that your party's programs are best for the United States.

7   George Washington was very disappointed by the development of political parties. He believed that everyone should be able to agree on policies that were good for everyone in the country. Discuss the following questions with a partner.

   a. Were Hamilton's programs "better" for everyone in the country than Jefferson's programs?

   b. Can we say that there really is one program that is best for the *whole* country?

   c. Why do some people favor one program rather than another?

   d. Today's political leaders also say their programs will be good for everyone in the country. Is it possible that these programs might be good for some people and bad for others?

   Look through the newspaper. Can you find examples of politicians who disagree about what is good for the whole country?

8   In the filmstrip there is a statement that "the formation of our first political parties was an important development in the democratic process of government." Would Washington have agreed with this statement? Do you agree? Do you think that it is possible to have a democratic government without competing parties? Can you think of any alternatives to the two party system?

OBJECTIVE

Identify reasons for the development of political parties in the United States.

FIGURE 8   An example of a TLU from PLAN, with an objective in seventh-grade social studies. (By permission of the copyright owner, Westinghouse Learning Corporation.)

Food for Thought   1413-1

INSTRUCTIONAL GUIDE

Every pet needs pet food, **EVEN** pet words like the little feller you see here.

The best pet food for pet words happens to be Suffix Leaves like those on the bush here.

A suffix is a group of letters which when attached can change the meaning and the form-class of the word.

Let's feed our hungry word and see what happens!

Now let's find out if our pet word has changed form-class. Remember the test sentences:

Noun: I have one **noise**. I have many **noises**.

                        noiseless   **noiseless**.
Adjective: The **noisy** boy seemed very **noisy**.

                               noisily.   **Noisily**
Adverb: The boy ate the cake **noiselessly**. **Noiselessly** he ate the cake.

Can the pet word **noise** change form-class to become a verb? Try the verb test to find out! Write your answer below. Discuss your answer with a partner.

FIGURE 9   An example of an Instructional Guide from PLAN. (By permission of the copyright owner, Westinghouse Learning Corporation.)

Materials Handling

One distinctive feature of materials in modular form is that they tend to be arranged in smaller "chunks" than is the case with traditional instruction. The materials for a single objective must be either physically separate from the materials for other objectives, or they must be clearly identified and indexed to match the objective and the test for the module.

Whether the materials for a module represent one chapter in a book, several chapters from different books, or a specially designed programmed instruction sequence, there must be a system by which the student, the teacher, and any teaching aides can locate the materials quickly. This requires either an indexing system or the separate physical packaging of all materials for each module. The materials may be collected into a folder which is properly stored for easy retrieval. Some kind of numbering system is convenient to use, both for planning and record keeping for each pupil, and for locating and storing materials. It is handy, for example, to have "Module No. 1, converting fractions to decimals," listed on planning sheets, record sheets, and on the materials themselves, when filed on shelves or in cabinets.

A planning sheet of some kind is needed for each student, particularly where some freedom in choosing objectives is given to the student. In this case, the student may confer with the teacher at intervals to plan in advance for taking one or more modules. If, on the other hand, all students begin with module no. 1, and complete as many modules as time permits, a single sheet for the entire class may be used for planning, monitoring, and record keeping.

It is no small task, even after the modules themselves have been designed and developed, to be sure there is a sufficient supply of each module, and that the supply is stored for ready access, selection of material, and return of material. If some of the materials are expendable, someone (perhaps an aide) must be sure that after each use, the expendable portion is restocked and made ready for use again.

TEACHER TRAINING
FOR INDIVIDUALIZED INSTRUCTION

At first glance, the task of storing, arranging, and using modules for instruction may lead one to believe it is all more trouble than it is worth. Indeed, teachers need training in how to manage individualized instruction. At first, such training may lead the teacher to feel that his most cherished functions are being usurped by the system, and that the teacher is being asked to perform only the tasks of a librarian or clerk. This is because some of the teacher's tasks *are* new and strange as compared to those required under a conventional method of teaching. All teachers need special training for conducting and managing individualized instruction, and they cannot be expected to function adequately, let alone enthusiastically, without such training. As such training in the future becomes more frequently a regular part of preservice teacher training programs, the problem will likely be handled at that point in the teacher's education rather than later on.

Even with appropriate training, not all teachers will like the individualized approach. Experienced teachers are accustomed to holding the center of the stage as platform performers; and many will not wish to relinquish that role. Others, who are tired of saying approximately the same thing year after year in class, will welcome the change in role. Theoretically, a dedicated teacher should welcome the use of whatever method helps the students the most. However, this implies that results with students should take precedence over the teacher's role preference—admittedly a difficult choice to face for many. Once teachers are trained and experienced in the new role, most come to prefer it.

Monitoring Student Progress

Monitoring the progress made by students consists of two related functions—knowing what each student is undertaking to learn, and knowing how fast and how well he is progressing. A glance at the class chart can show which modules a student has finished, and which one he is currently attempting. For a module to be recorded as "finished," the student must have met some minimum standard of performance on a test or other evaluation of his achievement of the objective. Sometimes this standard is stated in the objective, as "by solving correctly 8 of 10 linear equations." At other times a product is to be evaluated: a laboratory report, a work of art, or an analysis of an editorial with respect to evidence of bias. To make such evaluations as objective and reliable as possible, a "grading sheet" or "criterion sheet" may be used; this sheet lists the features to be looked for in the student product, and some system for deciding whether it meets the standard. For example, points may be assigned on each separate feature to be evaluated; or the number of features present and satisfactory may be counted. Either of these techniques is preferable to the making of a single overall judgment, not only because it improves the evaluation, but also because it can serve a diagnostic function—it can show the student where he needs to improve. This same "criterion sheet" can be given to the student at the outset of instruction, and thereby serve the function of informing him what is expected, suggesting how it may be done, and stating how the product will be evaluated.

Some evaluations can be done orally. By discussing the module and the work done on it by the learner, the teacher can often test in a more probing fashion than can be done in written form, and the assessment can also involve the planning of the next work to be undertaken or the remedial work needed. While oral tests may be less standardized than written ones, they are often convenient and effective when conducted with an individual student.

Regardless of how progress is monitored, the teacher usually knows more about the progress of each student in a well-designed individual plan than when group instruction is used. One reason is that in individualized instruction every student responds to every question. Even if all students work on the same objectives, this is a desirable feature. Of course, when students work on unique objectives or unique clusters of them, evaluation must be done individually.

Assessment of Student Performance

The performance of students is assessed throughout the conduct of an individualized instruction program to achieve a number of purposes: (1) initial placement of students in an approximate "level" with respect to first assignments in each subject; (2) assessment of mastery of each module, and of the completion of instructional objectives on enrichment tasks; (3) diagnosing learning difficulties in order to identify needed assignments; and (4) measuring student progress in areas of the curriculum over a yearly period.

Placement Testing   At the beginning of each school year, pupils may be given placement tests in various areas. Testing is done on an individual basis when necessary (as, for example, in oral reading for young children). On the basis of performance in these areas, a general plan is made for each student covering a six-week period, and initial assignments are made accordingly. In the case of subjects the objectives of which are to be chosen by students, performance scores and records of activities performed in the previous year are used to complete the six-week plan, forecasting desirable activities in these subjects from which choices can be made.

Assessment of Mastery   The assessment of student performance is of particular importance to an individualized system, particularly in the area of intellectual skills where new assignments are made on the basis of mastery of prerequisite skills. Such day-to-day assessment should not be considered a matter of formal "testing," but instead likened to the informal "probing" typically done by every teacher in the classroom. It differs from the latter not in its formality of administration, but in its provision of pre-established standards ("criteria") used by the teacher or by the student, to judge when mastery has been achieved. Criteria for mastery are specified in programs designed for individualized instruction, along with procedures and items used for the observation of individual student performance.

Diagnostic Testing   When a student encounters a difficulty with an assignment, a brief diagnostic test is administered by the teacher or aide. Diagnostic procedures provide an indication of prerequisite skills and information which have been inadequately learned or forgotten by the student. They therefore provide an indication to the teacher of a desirable next assignment or review assignment which will re-establish the necessary competence in the individual student.

Attitude Assessment   The assessment of student attitudes in areas such as cooperation, helping, control of aggressive acts, displaying kindness, and others, will be done by the teacher by means of checklists completed on each child at periodic intervals. Other socially desirable attitudes, such as those attitudes of citizenship which may be prominent objectives in social studies instruction, can be assessed in other ways, as by means of questionnaires. Records of student attitudes often form the basis for reports by teachers to parents, or serve as items to be discussed in parent-teacher conferences.

Yearly Testing   Tests of student achievement are also administered to students near the end of each school year, or more frequently. Scores from these tests are used to compare the performance of pupils with the performance of other groups, as provided by age-level norms. Norm-referenced tests (see Chapter 9) are often employed for this purpose.

Typical Daily Activities

The various activities of managing an individualized system suggest typical daily activities of students, teachers, teacher aides, and (when applicable) student tutors. As all these participants gain experience with individualized methods, things go more smoothly. At first there may be quite a bit of "slack time" while a pupil is waiting for help or to be told what to do next, and while the teacher attempts to keep everything going. Gradually the pupil becomes more skilled as an independent learner, and he "finds his way about" within the system and with the resources. From a rather harrassed feeling at first, to a calm, easy pacing, the teacher also becomes both more skilled and more at ease. Initially it may seem that there are too many things to keep track of, but this changes with time.

Student activities are often quite varied over a relatively short time period. Especially when an entire school, rather than just one course or one classroom, is engaged in an individualized system, the concept of "flexible scheduling" is combined with individualized instruction. Then a student may spend most of one day on one subject, but the next day may find him engaged in brief activities ranging over many subjects. This freedom to concentrate heavily at one point but to diversify at other points relieves schooling of much of the boredom resulting from the same schedule every day. If school architecture has been designed to enhance such a flexible mode of scheduling of pupil activities, often more teachers and other resources are literally in sight of the pupil at any given moment. Team teaching arrangements are also compatible with these concepts of space usage and flexible scheduling.

A student may thus move from a study carrel, to a slide-tape area, to a small group activity, to a conference with one or more teachers, to a test station, and on to band practice or basketball, all in less than one complete school day. At other times, a three-hour laboratory and writing session may complete the work in chemistry for a week.

Teachers usually spend some time each day for advance planning sessions with one to six students; they may review progress and test results and give next assignments to other students. On still other occasions, the teacher may do individual diagnosis and remedial instruction, or confer about a change in a planned schedule. Usually the teacher arranges and conducts small group sessions for groups of students who are at approximately the same point in their learning progress.

To a great extent, students and aides keep the materials files straight, once they are taught the filing system. Teacher aides often administer and score tests, help keep records, and help students find materials they need. They may also serve as tutors, and generally provide back-up assistance when the teacher is especially busy. In general, their role is to help implement the plans agreed upon between teacher and student.

Classroom Control

While in general the principles of classroom control and discipline are the same for individualized as for group instruction, several factors usually tend to minimize discipline problems in the individualized method. First, the personal attention and consideration given to the student and to his wishes, plans, ambitions, and interests, all tend to motivate him positively toward achievement of success. Second, the method itself is designed to promote success in learning, and this becomes rewarding in itself and motivating for continued effort. Third, the teacher spends less time "teaching" the class by a group procedure; this makes fewer opportunities for a student to engage the attention of the entire class to his attention-seeking behavior. The teacher's dealing with a disturbance or a lack of attention to work on the part of a student is less likely to be noticed by the entire group, thus removing some of the fun of "baiting" the teacher. All these factors help lessen the traditional adversary relationship that tends to grow between teachers and students.

Since a system of individualized instruction is clearly designed to help each pupil succeed, fair-minded youngsters usually respond favorably. Just as the system discourages "baiting" of the teacher, it also discourages public confrontations in which neither side wishes to "back down." Finally, it removes temptation for a teacher to employ sarcasm or ridicule of poor work. It quietly reminds the teacher that the goal is learning, not platform performance or crowd psychology. Most important of all, an individualized system emphasizes learning and achievement, privately attained and privately evaluated, by a student who has accepted major responsibility for his learning.

Contingency Management   Techniques of contingency management are of enormous usefulness in the administration of a system of individualized instruction. In simply stated form, these are techniques the teacher uses to arrange successions of student activities in such a way that an initially non-preferred activity will be followed by a preferred activity, thus providing reinforcement for the former. The concept of reinforcement contingencies has been developed and elaborated by Skinner (1968). Application of the techniques of contingency management to school situations has been described by a number of writers (Homme, et al., 1969; Buckley & Walker, 1970; Madsen & Madsen, 1970).

When used properly, contingency management aids in the accomplishment of three objectives which form a part of successful instruction:

1. Establishing and maintaining orderly student behavior, freeing the classroom from disruption and distraction, and aiming students toward productive learning activities.
2. Managing learning so as to instill in students a positive liking for learning and for the accomplishments to which it leads.
3. Capturing the interest of students in desirable problem-solving activities as sources of satisfaction for mastery of the intellectual skills involved in them.

In general, the teacher needs to learn to identify differences in the interests, likes, and dislikes of individual students, and to employ these in selecting specific contingencies to achieve a task-oriented learning environment.

SUMMARY

Individualized instruction is designed by the same processes of planning that apply to design of individual lessons for conventional group instruction. Our previous descriptions of performance objectives, learning hierarchies, sequencing, and employment of appropriate instructional events and conditions of learning, apply to the design of "modules" for individualized instruction.

It is the "delivery system" that primarily distinguishes the design of modules from the design of lessons. The characteristics of materials for individualized instruction include the following:

1. Modules are usually more distinctly self-instructional than are conventional lessons. More of the needed instructional events and conditions of learning are designed into the materials making up the module than is the case for conventional materials.

2. The materials incorporated into modules do more of the direct teaching, while in conventional methods the teacher presents more of the necessary information. Thus the role of the teacher changes somewhat. Individualized instruction depends to a lesser degree on the teacher's function as provider of information; more stress is placed on counseling, evaluating, monitoring, and diagnosing.

3. Some systems provide alternate materials and media for each objective, thus letting the selection vary according to the learner's preferences as to style of learning.

Modules for individualized instruction sometimes contain all the materials, exercises, and tests needed. In other instances, they refer the learner to external materials and activities at appropriate times. A single module usually includes as a minimum:

1. A performance objective
2. A set of materials and learning activities either self-contained in the module, or external to the module itself
3. A method for self-evaluation of mastery of the objective
4. A provision for verification of the learning outcome by the teacher.

As a consequence of its nature, individualized instruction typically provides more frequent feedback and more frequent progress checks than is the case for conventional instruction. It may permit more freedom of choice on the part of the learner, depending on the extent to which objectives are "optional" or "required." Usually, as a minimum, the learner sets his own pace in learning activities.

Management of individualized instruction requires a way to index and store modules, a way to schedule modules to be used by each learner, a way to monitor pupil progress, and a way to assess performance. Sometimes "contracts" are arranged to provide for required work, for enrichment work, and for earned free time for activities the learner prefers.

Classroom control problems are usually less in individualized instruction than in conventional instruction. Teachers usually need special training in the management of such systems. Once they master the necessary routines, they often prefer individualized to conventional methods.

REFERENCES

Ausubel, D. P. *Educational Psychology. A Cognitive View.* New York: Holt, Rinehart and Winston, 1968.

Briggs, L. J. Learner variables and educational media. *Review of Educational Research*, 1968, *38*, 160–176.

Buckley, N. K. & Walker, H. M. *Modifying Classroom Behavior: A Manual of Procedures for Classroom Teachers.* Champaign, Ill.: Research Press, 1970.

Edling, J. V. *Individualized Instruction: A Manual for Administrators.* Corvallis, Oregon: DCE Publications, 1970.

Homme, L., Czanyi, A. P., Gonzales, M. A., & Rechs, J. R. *How To Use Contingency Contracting in the Classroom.* Champaign, Ill.: Research Press, 1969.

Madsen, C. H., Jr. & Madsen, C. K. *Teaching/Discipline: Behavioral Principles Toward a Positive Approach.* Boston: Allyn and Bacon, 1970.

Pressey, S. L. Development and appraisal of devices providing immediate automatic scoring of objective tests and concomitant self-instruction. *Journal of Psychology*, 1950, *29*, 417–447.

Rohwer, W. D., Jr. Prime time for education: early childhood or adolescence? *Harvard Educational Review*, 1971, *41*, 316–341.

Skinner, B. F. *The Technology of Teaching.* New York: Appleton-Century-Crofts, 1968.

Weisgerber, R. A. *Developmental Efforts in Individualized Instruction.* Itasca, Ill.: Peacock, 1971.

11

DESIGNING INSTRUCTIONAL SYSTEMS

A system is usually considered to be a human enterprise of a complex nature which serves a purpose valued by society. One could use the term American Educational System to include the operations of all the schools and other institutions having educational purposes in the nation as a whole. More frequently, "Educational System" refers to all the schools in a city or district which operate under a single superintendent and school board. Within such a local school system, the term "instructional system" is often used to distinguish those operations dealing with the instruction of students from those that pertain to transportation, financial management, or administration.

The scope encompassed by a system has no fixed boundaries. In a narrow sense, a single course or instructional method could be considered an instructional system. At the other end of the scale, the entire American society may be called a social system, containing within it a business system, a government system, a school system, and several others. It is evident, then, that the use of the word system is a relative one, meaning any organized way of accomplishing certain goals, whether these pertain to a whole society, a portion of a society, or even to a single teacher. As the title of this chapter implies, we intend to deal with instruction more or less independently from school administration, budgeting, and other aspects of school management.

Instruction is the means employed by teachers, designers of materials, curriculum specialists, or other persons concerned in developing an organized plan to promote learning. The system of instruction which is designed may be intended for use in public or private schools, in industry, or in military training installations. No particular distinction is here drawn between education and training, since systems of both types are designed to promote learning leading to outcomes of the categories described in previous chapters.

The Systems Approach and Educational Technology

In recent years, systematic efforts to design instruction have come to be identified as exemplifying "the systems approach." This mode of planning has become familiar to managers of business concerns, industrial and military operations, and school systems. While not enough time has elapsed for emergence of a widely accepted standardized meaning for this phrase, generally it may be said that the contents of the present volume are compatible with a systems approach to instructional design. This is particularly evident in its emphasis upon learning outcomes as the goals of an instructional system, and in its attempts to bring to bear systematic knowledge of the learning process on the design of instruction.

Designing an instructional system utilizes a kind of knowledge called *educational technology*. This term has sometimes been associated with computers and other media hardware used for instruction. However, there is a growing tendency to relate educational technology in meaning to the *process of planning* by means of which an instructional system is developed, implemented, controlled, and evaluated. The procedures to be described in this chapter for planning instructional systems are consistent with this latter meaning of educational technology (cf. Davies & Hartley, 1972).

In providing a historical framework for educational technology, Davies (1971) points out that it is an outgrowth of a number of converging influences upon present concepts and practices in instructional design. According to Lumsdaine (1964), these earlier "inputs" include the following developments: (a) *interest in individual differences* in learning, as seen in educational and military research and development programs; in self-instructional devices such as those of Pressey (1950) and Briggs (1960), and Crowder's (1959) branching programs; in computer applications to instruction; and in product-testing concepts for hardware; (b) *behavioral* science and learning theory, as seen in Skinner's emphasis upon contingencies of reinforcement and in his teaching machines (1968); and in Guthrie's contiguity theory (1935); and (c) *physical science technology*, as represented in motion-picture, television, and video-tape instruction; and in audio-visual devices to supplement printed media. All of these streams of development, along with the emphasis in this volume upon categories of learning outcomes and their associated instructional events, can be harmoniously utilized in the design of instructional systems which give primary attention to the individual learner's activities and to the testing of their outcomes.

Another historical event related to these earlier developments was the recognition by the military services that the development of a weapons system requires the concurrent systematic development of a "personnel system," including plans for the training of personnel. A parallel development within industry and business further disseminated the idea of the need for a systems approach to the management of any organization.

Since the specific objectives for military and industrial training are more specialized, narrow, and concrete than are many statements of educational objectives, some critics of educational technology have been led to question the relevance of a systems approach to education. Many of the first examples of instructional systems design seen by educators focused upon relatively simple forms of learning, or upon objectives considered trivial. These unfortunate circumstances have made it difficult to persuade some educators to consider the genuine merits of instructional systems technology, and have probably led a few educators to take a more extreme position against any form of systematic instructional planning than they otherwise might have adopted. This negative view appears to be related to a phenomenon noted in an earlier chapter, namely, the opposition to statements of educational objectives because education often results in the achievement of unforeseen objectives. Apparently it will be some time before demonstrations of the effectiveness of the systems approach to instructional design occur in sufficient numbers to overcome the skepticism entirely.

The Systems Approach and Humanistic Goals

A designed instructional system is not of necessity highly "mechanistic" or "prescriptive," nor should it neglect goals of a humanistic nature. Previous chapters of this book, while they are intended as contributions to a systematic technology, have nevertheless encompassed planning for such areas of school activity as the development of personal values and socially desirable attitudes, the acquisition of broad knowledge of history and literature, and the cultivation of strategies of productive thinking. So far as goals are concerned, these varieties of learning outcome, often considered as reflecting a humanistic intent, are seen as having a high value in educational planning.

As Chapter 10 has indicated, systems of instruction may be designed to depend upon a greater or lesser degree of "learner control." Thus, a system may be planned so that students choose a schedule for devoting time to various objectives of learning, or the sequence of subjects to be studied, or the kinds of problem-solving and creative activities to be undertaken. The practical limitations of such choices may be determined by availability of instructional materials and settings; but there is nothing in the systems approach itself which sets limits to these varieties of educational planning. If learners are to control one or more aspects of the external situations surrounding their learning activities, design in the systems sense must seek ingenious ways of making available the materials, media, and other environmental supports which make such choices practically feasible. The requirements for systematic planning of instruction may be altered by differing kinds and amounts of learner control, but they are not reduced, and may in fact be increased.

Accordingly, it should be recognized that designing instructional systems is not an enterprise in which goals of instruction, humanistic and others, are predetermined in their emphasis. A community or school district may choose whatever goal priorities it wishes, and still face the problem of system design. What is important is that goals be chosen and communicated so as to be clearly understood by system designers, in order that expected outcomes can then be identified.

STEPS IN INSTRUCTIONAL SYSTEM DEVELOPMENT

As implied by its name, the development of an instructional system involves a series of procedures. Often, these procedures and their relations to each other are depicted in flow charts and diagrams. We prefer here to list the steps involved in instructional system development, and to describe the ways in which they are related as procedures. As given here, the steps in development derive from a variety of sources (cf. Gagné, 1962). Table 7 lists these steps as they are typically described.

In general, these twelve steps take place in the order shown, but in practice there are both feedback and "feed-forward" relationships among them. Decisions made in early stages influence those made in later stages,

TABLE 7   *Steps in Instructional System Development*

1. Analysis and identification of needs
2. Definition of goals and objectives
3. Identification of alternative ways to meet needs
4. Design of system components
5. Analysis of (a) resources required, (b) resources available, (c) constraints
6. Action to remove or modify constraints
7. Selection or development of instructional materials
8. Design of student assessment procedures
9. Field testing; formative evaluation and teacher training
10. Adjustments, revisions, and further evaluation
11. Summative evaluation
12. Operational installation

and insights gained in later stages lead to revision of plans made earlier. Of course, the latter events lead to still other adjustments in later stages. This cyclical, or iterative, characteristic of instructional system design, while costing time and effort, is actually one of the strengths of the method. New information, new conceptions, and "second thoughts" are often better than earlier plans which are tentatively made. The exact timing and frequency of such recycling cannot be fully respresented in any general form, because the situation is different for each system designed.

Of particular significance is the recycling that follows Step 9, formative evaluation. This is a *planned* recycling. Instructional theory is in such a relatively immature stage that even the most experienced designer expects imperfections in his first instructional effort. In fact, there is not usually just one formative evaluation and recycling, but a whole series of such modifications to the system. It is this empirically based recycling which is the "acid test" of all the work done before. Early recyclings or iterations are based on logical insight, review of consistency among all planning stages, and continued thinking about the system. But even these revisions must be put to empirical test. Although logic is the basis for some recycling, hard data, in the form of how well the learners perform as a result of the instruction, must be brought to bear in making later changes in the system.

It is apparent, then, that the "systems approach" to the design of instruction is based on one hand in logical, systematic thinking and planning, making use of all theory and research evidence available, and on the other hand upon empirical test and fact-finding. The combination of systematic thinking, use of theory, use of facts from evaluation studies, and recycling, represents an improvement over earlier ways of planning for instruction. The entire procedure, while lacking the elegant precision and predictive power of physical science, is closer to a science of education than are other approaches to the design of instruction. It is not contended that a highly intuitive approach is always inferior to a systems approach, since planners vary in both their intuitive powers and in their systematic planning efforts. However, what the systems approach does make possible is a verification of whether or not the system has achieved its design objective—that is, whether student performance shows that the need was met. This provides the basis for an accountability system by means of which educators can report to the public the extent to which design objectives have been attained.

Who Designs Instructional Systems?

Designing a system of instruction is an enterprise that is likely to involve a variety of specialized people and agencies. The size of such an effort will of course depend upon whether the design is for a single lesson or module, for an entire new school system, or for a new curriculum to be installed in an existing school system.

Most current instruction has not been designed as an instructional system, following the steps of Table 7. Instead, different agencies, acting almost entirely independently from each other, have each provided some of the resources used in conventional instruction. Universities have trained teachers; publishers have provided textbooks; and local communities have constructed the school buildings and employed the people to operate the schools. Teachers perhaps deserve more credit than they customarily receive for trying to adapt components of instruction which do not fit well together because there has not been sufficient coordination to make the components compatible with each other. It is not an easy task to use available instructional materials aimed at objectives for which the materials were not designed, or to try to effect individualization of instruction with materials not designed for such systems.

It seems evident that a joint effort of schools, industry, universities, and other agencies and organizations, working in consortia, and applying a systems approach, represents the ideal model of instructional systems design in the future. Other sorts of efforts to bring about improvements in instruction also have merit and will be attempted. For example, closer joint sharing of teacher-training responsibilities between schools and universities seems a likely development. However, production of instructional materials also needs to become integrated with other aspects of the total educational endeavor, in order that optimal systems development can be undertaken.

When efforts to design entire school curricula by a systems approach are attempted by piecemeal methods, problems are usually encountered. Separate curricula for different school subjects, designed by independent groups, while appealing from the point of view of a single discipline, are less appealing in meeting system goals. Efforts by a single teacher or department within a school to install a new partial curriculum may flounder by being out of step with the rest of the school. Even the school building itself may not be appropriately designed to accommodate a new system.

In an ideal situation, a group of people, possibly representing a number of organizations, would be given the responsibility for designing an entire school system. For example, in the model cities program, a portion of a city might literally be torn down and rebuilt to suit the needs of the community. No plans for school buildings would be made except as an integral part of the design of the entire section of the city. No assumption would even be made that school buildings are necessary, until the educational and other needs of the people in the community were analyzed. Then all buildings would be designed to accommodate the needs of the people for activities and a style of life which they had chosen.

Designing systems of instruction in this complete sense seems likely to be the most promising course of action to follow if highly satisfactory results are to be achieved. Most cities or communities would undoubtedly prefer to seek gradual improvement of their schools and their curricula rather than literally building entirely new systems of instruction. This may mean that the changes undertaken are not as satisfactory in the long run. Nevertheless, it is possible to design and install new systems of instruction within existing conventions. Such programs are more likely to be intended for a single classroom, school, or subject area, than for entire schools or curricula. Even relatively small efforts may be capable of meeting some new needs, or more satisfactorily meeting long-recognized needs.

For example, the school system of the city of Duluth, Minnesota, by its own efforts, introduced individualized instruction into several elementary schools (Esbensen, 1968). The American Telephone and Telegraph Company replaced numerous locally developed courses in first aid (accomplished by the member Bell Companies) by a uniform, contractor-developed new first aid course (Markle, 1967). Training time was reduced with concomitant large gains in trainee performance. The new course, developed by a systems approach, was more economical than the former courses. The first example (Duluth) involved the instruction in entire schools; the second example (AT&T) involved 7.5 clock hours of instruction. Thus, the systems approach can involve any amount of instruction one wishes to undertake in a single coordinated planning and development effort.

DESIGN STAGES

The various steps in the design of an instructional system have been listed in Table 7. In this section, these steps are further described, along with some suggestions for alternate ways for their accomplishment.

Needs Analysis

The design of an instructional system results from some perceived need. In terms of school curricula, the perceived need usually falls into one of the following classes: (1) a need to conduct instruction more effectively and efficiently for some course which is already a part of the curriculum; (2) a need to revitalize both the content and the method for some existing course; or (3) a need to develop a new course.

Thus a course in chemistry which has long been accepted as a part of a high school or college curriculum may need to be redesigned in order to change the methods, the content, or both. Or, the traditional content may remain valid and up-to-date, but the need may be to de-emphasize large lecture classes in favor of an individualized mode of instruction for both the lecture and laboratory portions of the course. Alternatively, the primary need may be to update the course content, but since this requires a new development, methods of instruction may also be reconsidered. And perhaps of increasing frequency in future years, the need may be for an entirely new course, oriented around contemporary problems rather than around a traditional discipline. Thus a new course in "preserving natural resources" may draw upon several disciplines, with the emphasis upon problem solution, rather than on the structure of any single discipline.

In the elementary science curriculum discussed in an earlier chapter (*Science—A Process Approach*, AAAS Commission on Science Education, 1967), the perceived need was to focus upon the intellectual skills employed in science. Alternatively, one could perceive the need in this field as one of providing instruction in the solution of a particular class of problems such as pollution, or fostering development of classes of skills useful in solving problems, or teaching the "content" of a discipline. In any event, when the nature of the need has been clarified, the next step is to develop goals and objectives which are used to bring proper focus to the remainder of the steps in the design of the instructional system.

As the tempo of change in society increases, the frequency of reviewing educational needs should also increase, or else the lag between actual curricula and needed curricula will widen rather than close. It is this discrepancy between what is and what is needed that generates the need for a new instructional system, or at least a redesigned system. Sometimes there is a need to update a system in content to improve its effectiveness, to change the methods to reach a greater number of learners, or to improve the learning accomplished by each learner. In other cases, entirely new systems must be created to meet new needs.

The federal government and private foundations sponsor research designed to predict the kinds of changes in society which will appear in the future. Using special methods to utilize consensus among experts, the effort is made to depict the future status of society in order to identify new curriculum needs. Realizing that even the best prediction techniques for such an undertaking are likely to be faulty, educators emphasize trying to teach children to become problem-solvers. They also recognize the need to provide lifelong learning opportunities which will help people change the focus of their problem-solving abilities when the locus of the greatest need changes.

While such efforts as these are aimed at preparing learners for the future of society, there is no need to overlook the kind of needs analysis which focuses upon the individual rather than upon society. These two kinds of needs are surely to be viewed together in order that relevant instruction be systematically developed for the students who will be tomorrow's adults.

Analysis of Goals and Objectives

Beginning with the results of the needs analysis, the next step to be undertaken is to describe goals and objectives for the instructional system. In doing this, one needs to work from the general to the specific. The "size" of the system to be designed determines how many "levels" of goals and objectives need to be defined.

There are two reasons for working from general to specific. One reason relates to communicating with others. The goals of an entire school or of a single course need to be communicated in quite general terms to the public and to the school board. The curriculum supervisor needs to communicate to the principal at one level, and to the teacher at perhaps a more detailed or specific level. The teacher and the designer of the system (in case they are different persons) need to communicate at a very specific level. And the system designer who supervises the work of a design team must communicate even more explicitly.

Some terms which describe the levels at which goals and objectives may be communicated are as follows: The K–12 curriculum; the K–12 science curriculum; the sixth grade science course; topic objectives within the sixth grade course; specific objectives within the lesson; subordinate capabilities for a specific objective; a particular communication in a lesson for one subordinate capability.

The second reason for working from general to specific is for the designer's own use—detailed objectives can be justified only in terms of some broader objective or goal. The reason for requiring a student to memorize something which could be just "looked up" in a reference book is that he frequently needs it to solve a given kind of problem. The kind of problem (specific objective), in turn, is needed to reach a topic objective; and mastery of the topic objective is needed to reach the course objective, which, in turn, is part of the K–12 science curriculum.

Just as the objective for a single intellectual skill may be broken down into a learning hierarchy (see Chapter 6), so one large, pyramid-like chart may be developed to show all the levels in a K–12 curriculum. Charts having this purpose were developed in planning the program, *Science—A Process Approach* (AAAS Commission on Science Education, 1967).

To make the idea of working from general to specific more manageable, one might first think of a diagram for a one-year course. This might consist of an end-of-course objective, three unit objectives, and 20 or 30 specific objectives under the three units. By doing the diagramming first in simple words and phrases and in diagram form, one arrives at the total organization of the course. After that, he can describe a "box" in the diagram in more detail, and in behavioral terms. (See Briggs, 1972b, for examples.)

Should each "box" in such a diagram be described in behavioral terms? If the entire set of such descriptions is not needed to communicate to others, then the rule is to convert the phrases to behavioral terms for those levels at which assessment of student performance is to be undertaken. These behavioral statements are needed to form the basis upon which such measurement will take place. Otherwise, some of the levels of analysis are done only to aid in arriving at the next lower level which would be stated in behavioral form. This procedure is used to justify the relevance of the simpler types of learning outcomes in terms of the more general levels of goals and objectives.

There is no fixed number of levels of such goals and objectives. For a one-year course, only four levels are needed to go from the course objective to subordinate capabilities of specific objectives. These subordinate capabilities represent the most detailed level of objective needed in order to design instruction. Below that, one speaks of the sets of instructional events needed to attain the subordinate capability.

Efforts to reverse the direction of planning can have undesirable results. One may be tempted to start at the lowest level, because this is closest to the "content" one wishes to teach (or has taught in the past). One must resolutely resist such impulses; otherwise he will end up teaching the old course instead of designing the new one; or he will create foolish general goals to justify the familiar subordinate ones. One can deceive himself quite easily by failing to work from general to specific. The only occasion for doing otherwise is when one "gets stuck"—when he can, for example, state a higher level "A," but cannot, for some reason, define the next lower level. In this case, it is permissible to "jump over" one level to get to a third that is defensible, and later to see what the middle one really should be. The search for the "middle one" is not done to slavishly "fill in the outline"; it may be needed as an organizing and connecting link. Examples of learning hierarchies in this book (Chapter 6) illustrate the principle. Leaving out a level may result in incomplete analysis, and a reduction in effectiveness of the system.

Analysis of Alternate Ways To Meet Needs

Up to this point, it has simply been assumed that the way to meet a need is to provide instruction, so that the development of an instructional system is the mechanism for meeting the need. This seems, in general, a reasonable assumption, since our context is education. The next questions are concerned with what to teach and how to teach it. This becomes an "educational needs analysis."

Studies of military and industrial training suggest that problems that are initially thought to represent training needs often actually represent other kinds of needs. Frequently, when a given function of an organization is not operating at the desired level of effectiveness, the immediate conclusion may be that the personnel performing the function need more or better training. In some such cases, a careful needs analysis has shown that the problem could be solved by means other than training, such as the restructuring of jobs; reassignment of personnel; changing company policy; issuing new directives or operating procedures; or by providing a "job aid," a kind of reference sheet for job procedures.

One caution in education, as a parallel to the industrial situations just mentioned, is implied by the question: "If a mismatch exists between education and society, which needs to be changed?" Perhaps there is currently too great a tendency to assume that education is to blame for the ills of society. While education should constantly seek to improve itself, even without pressure to do so from the society of which it is a part, there are many present ills of society which are more clearly attributable to government and private business than they are to education. In a long-term sense, education may have contributed to present problems; also, some present problems may be due to faulty support of education or to unrealistic expectations as to its effect upon the behavior of its students years later. In addition, it must be borne in mind that many basic attitudes are formed as a result of home and community influences, rather than by those of the school.

This somewhat general discussion helps to make a balanced transition between two apparently opposing points: (1) that instructional systems for educational curricula should be designed to help bring about future solutions to problems of the society, and (2) that society should not look exclusively to the schools as a way to correct present problems. If our present need is to build a "better society" (however defined), it is clear that education must play a major role; but it is equally clear that we need to work for the improvement of many other societal institutions and practices.

Returning, then, to the major strand of thought of the present chapter, once a major educational need or curriculum reform has been identified in the form of broad curriculum goals, it is desirable next to consider major alternative means or strategies before going into more detailed planning.

Alternate Strategies There are usually several viable strategies for attaining a major goal in order to fulfill a need. Often these choices involve a determination of who will design (or select) the instructional system. In the past, the choices have been public schools, private schools, or tutors. Currently, alternatives to the usual public school chain of command are made possible by the "voucher system" and by "performance contracting" arrangements. Decisions on "which school to attend" are often tied in with "who is responsible for designing the instructional system." Once such decisions are made, it is then possible to consider the alternate learning environments that are available under each major strategy for allocating responsibility for education.

Alternate Learning Environments Assume that planning is to occur with the strategy of public school responsibility for education. This assumption usually rules out "correspondence courses" as the learning environment, except perhaps for public college-level institutions. But it leaves the alternatives of classroom versus laboratory, large group versus small group, lecture versus individualized study, and choices among "problem centered," "process centered," or "content centered" curricula. It is worthwhile to go to the trouble of making explicit the alternatives available, within the general constraints of the public school strategy for education, before making decisions about the preferred learning environment. When this latter decision has been made, one is ready to decide the nature of the components of instruction.

Designing Instructional Components

Following the determination of the assumed learning environment, certain other general decisions need to be made concerning the nature of instruction to be designed. Decisions of this general sort must be made for the following aspects of the instructional system:

1. Planning the nature of materials for study
2. Specifying the method of studying the materials

3. Deciding between self-pacing and group-pacing of materials for presentation
4. Identifying the nature of the activities the learner is to engage in with respect to the materials, or with respect to the objectives
5. Planning how to keep track of student progress and how to direct such progress
6. Making explicit the role of the teacher in respect to materials and pupil progress
7. Scheduling group activities and the teaching methods to be employed
8. Deciding upon time limits for self-paced learning, or "open scheduling," if mastery rather than time is the scheduling constraint
9. Assessment of student performance
10. Devising "guidance" procedures, where options in objectives are offered, or where different "routes to the goal" are provided.

The specific characteristics of instruction may be expected to vary among objectives representing different domains or types of learning outcomes, with the nature of the students and their entering capabilities, and with the assumed learning environment.

The general constraints upon planning are set by the strategy selected and by the assumed learning environment. Alternates or options in planning the components of instruction should be noted, so that final decisions about the nature of the components can be made at the end of the next step.

Analysis of Resources and Constraints

At the conclusion of the preceding step in which the components of instruction are designed, one has arrived at a "middle-grained" definition of how he would *like* to operate the instructional system. Before it is worthwhile to go on to "fine-grained" plans, the feasibility of the plan as developed to this point needs to be checked.

Each component is reviewed in terms of available resources and constraints. If particular types of materials desired are not on the market, a decision must be made as to whether resources are available to develop them, either "in-house" or by contract. If the answer is no, and if there is no likelihood of obtaining increased resources, then a modification in the plan is in order. If the plan calls for using earned "free time" as an incentive for students, and if the free time is to be designed so that the student can go anywhere he wishes within the school or elsewhere, legal or administrative constraints may be encountered. If efforts to remove the constraints fail, other plans must be made. If groupings of various sizes are planned, but if this conflicts with space and schedules, other space must be found and approved or schedules changed; if again no way out is available, the grouping plan must be modified.

Constraint Removal Actions

Regardless of who the designer of the instructional system may be (teacher, curriculum specialist, contractor, or a consortium of organizations), constraints of some kind are the rule. There are limits to resources, and limits to the speed with which the laws and customs relating to education can be changed. Granting this practical fact of life, if the system designer is charged with bringing about radical change and great improvements in effectiveness, it may simply be wishful thinking to ask at the same time that the new system be more "cost effective" than the old.

Constraints centering on the issue of cost effectiveness may be particularly difficult to remove. The following observations are relevant to these issues:

1. The cost of "failure" (in terms of dropouts, delinquency, and incompetent graduates) ought to be considered in any genuine cost-effectiveness analysis of an educational system. A few hardened criminals or a few dozen individuals on relief might well cost more tax money (to say nothing of human misery) than would the removal of some constraints in resources for a new instructional system.

2. Hidden costs of present educational programs may easily be overlooked. One objection to the design of systems is the "development cost"; yet one may fail to compare the retail price of current materials with the cost of new materials. One needs to assume a large enough user population so that he can determine whether the amortized costs of new materials exceed present costs over the same time period.

3. Industrial instructional systems have been designed which are cost effective because they reduce training time while increasing amount of learning. Again, when development costs are amortized, the new system is preferred to the old by the cost-conscious consumer industry. Education may also need to reconsider the value of "time" as against dollars, rather than keeping time constant for all learners.

The system designer usually has little political influence, hence he is in a poor position to achieve removal of constraints pertaining to law and budgets. But if the public is to demand "accountability" (as appears likely), the measures which are the indexes of this accountability must include both cost and effectiveness and incorporate the hidden costs of failure.

Selecting or Developing Materials

Once the consideration of resources and constraints has led to decisions about what *can* be done that fits the plan for the components of instruction, the designer is ready to make decisions about the instructional materials needed.

If the course, unit, or curriculum which represents the instructional system to be designed is an entirely new one, it is likely that most or all the instructional materials must be developed rather than simply purchased. If, on the other hand, an existing course is being redesigned to change the content or the methods or both, some "on-the-shelf" materials may be usable. A third possibility is that some existing materials may be modified to meet the needs reflected in the new plan.

Suppose, for example, one is designing a course on "How to prevent future shock." A book on this topic could be examined to see if its contents could help the learners achieve all or some of the specific objectives for the course. Search could be made to locate other relevant materials. One might need to design components of instruction in such a way that the teacher and the learners are shown how to use available materials to meet the objectives. Performance tests or other assessment measures would be designed to show when the objectives have been met. In this case, the objectives would have a reference to the future behavior of the learners—behavior which cannot be measured directly at the end of the course. One might then attempt to predict which end-of-course behaviors provide indications that the long-term objectives would be reached. Alternatively, simulated situations for performance tests may be designed, or measures of attainment of the subordinate capabilities needed now to enhance future attainment of the objectives. However, most courses will not face such extreme difficulties; usually the end-of-course objectives can be assessed directly (see Chapter 9).

A systematic procedure for developing instructional materials for a new course is described in Chapter 8. Related models of design are described by Briggs (1970) and by Tosti & Ball (1969). The development or selection of appropriate instructional materials is an extremely important step in the design of a total instructional system. It is not an overemphasis to say that materials can make or break the system as a whole.

The media by means of which the materials are delivered can also be a crucial factor. Appropriate materials, as described in Chapter 8, constitute the stimuli needed to implement instructional events. Once the correct form of stimulation has been determined, several different media may be equally capable of "carrying" these stimuli to the student. But media vary greatly as to frequency with which they stimulate explicit responses from the learner, and in their capability for providing feedback. When these events are crucial to learning of the objective or competency, they must be provided either by means of some instructional medium or by the teacher. When courses are to be managed by individualized instruction, the communications, the stimulation of student responding, and the provision for feedback should all be built into the materials and media insofar as possible. Then the remaining instructional events need to be handled either by the teacher or by the learner himself.

Most teachers today have not been taught how to design instructional materials by means such as described in this volume. Nor do teachers have the time to do this under today's typical job conditions. Materials must either be designed by other people, or by teachers who are trained and given released time to do it. While there is some trend in this direction, it appears that unless major changes are made in the staffing of schools, private industry must learn to produce materials by the systems approach. A number of private firms are developing increased capability in this direction. Some experience relevant to this effort springs from curriculum development projects in which educators design the materials, and industry markets them. However, not all curriculum projects have employed the systems approach to the design of the materials. As mentioned earlier, a consortium of organizations, including schools, universities, business firms, and other agencies might be a promising way to develop materials for new instructional systems and for insuring in advance that the new materials would be used.

Designing Student Performance Assessment

This step in system design deserves particular prominence, and is described more completely in Chapter 9. In practice, many designers prefer to place this design step earlier in the sequence of activities, making it follow immediately after constraint removal actions, and before the selection or development of instructional materials. Designing performance measures before materials are developed helps focus the tests on the objectives and the instructional components assumed as a part of the learning environment. Such a procedure also helps avoid measuring "content of the instructional materials" rather than performance of the learner, as is the intent in a systems approach. When one is concerned with the training of a systems designer, it may be well to require him to make the tests just after the objectives are defined, even if he has to revise them as a result of the analysis of resources and constraints. In contrast, the experienced designer has learned to avoid the "content trap," so that when he comes to the point of designing tests, he considers all the plans made up to that point.

The development and use of measures of student performance has many values. Such tests make it possible for:

(1) the teacher to discover when a learner has mastered an objective, and is therefore ready to go on to the next one;

(2) the teacher to detect failure on a small unit of study and to prescribe diagnostic testing (of subordinate capabilities) and remedial instruction;

(3) the designer to detect objectives on which many students fail, thus signifying a need to revise the course materials or procedures for that objective; and

(4) the designer eventually to evaluate the system as a whole, when used as one portion of a system evaluation (see Chapter 12).

Field Testing and Formative Evaluation

In actual practice, often small portions of the new system are tried out with a few individual learners in a "one-to-one" situation. The designer observes the student at work, records the questions he asks or the comments he makes, and analyzes test responses in order to spot weaknesses in the program. These data are used to revise the materials or procedures, or both.

Following the individual tryouts, small group tryouts of the system are held and further revisions made. Then "field tests" of parts or all of the system are made in the environment for which the system is intended; that is, these tryouts are made with normal-sized groups under "actual" conditions.

Studies conducted while the instructional system (including the materials) is in a formative stage are called formative evaluations. The purpose of these evaluations is to improve the system. When a series of such evaluations and revisions results in a successful field test under normal (operational) conditions, the system may then be installed for regular or widespread use. A summative evaluation can then be undertaken to assess the effectiveness of the new system when operating under normal conditions.

During the conduct of formative and summative evaluations, there is usually a need for giving the teachers special training in the use of the new system. This is usually done by conducting workshops, or by arranging for the teachers to see demonstrations of the course conducted by a selected teacher who has been given special training in advance. Often the demonstration teacher is a member of the team which designed the system.

Further Adjustments and Revisions

A standard number of tryouts of the new system with individuals, small groups, and large groups, cannot be specified. The size of the budget, the time schedule, and the results of early tryouts determine how much revision needs to be done and how much can be done. In some cases, increasingly large numbers of schools use the new system or curriculum each year, with gradual changes up to the point of publication of the materials in final form. Even after that, feedback from teachers may be encouraged, resulting in the publication of newsletters or supplementary materials and suggestions for teachers for several years after the operational installation of the new system. This systematic series of evaluations and revisions is a major feature which distinguishes the systems approach to design from the methods conventionally used in developing materials and planning a course.

An outstanding feature of the systems approach is that "design objectives" can be set in advance, and revisions made until these objectives are reached. This is a highly useful form of course evaluation, supplementing the familiar practice of comparing results of a new system with results from a previously used system of instruction. Design objectives can be expressed in many ways. One form of expression is: "The new system will be considered satisfactory when 90 percent of students pass the minimum standard set for 90 percent of the objectives of the course, when the course is taught by regular teachers under normal conditions." The knowledge that such a design objective has been attained makes it possible to interpret additional findings concerning student performance on standardized tests which may be given when instruction has been completed.

Summative Evaluation of Systems

Studies of the effectiveness of the system of instruction as a whole are called *summative evaluations*, and are described more fully in Chapter 12. As the term implies, a summative evaluation is normally conducted after the system has passed through its formative stage—when it is no longer undergoing point-by-point revision. Such a stage may occur at the time of the first field test, or as much as five years later when large numbers of students have been taught by the new system. If there is expectation that the system will be widely used in schools throughout the country, summative evaluations need to be conducted under an equally varied range of schools and conditions.

Operational Installation

This stage of instructional system development has been anticipated in some of the preceding discussion. After an acceptable degree of merit has been reflected by one or more summative evaluations, the new system (course, or curriculum) is ready for widespread adoption and regular use.

In the course of "operational installation," a number of practical matters receive final attention or adjustment. For example, storage of materials may have to be handled differently in some schools than in others, owing to differences in building design and space situations. Time schedules planned for the new system may require adjustment to fit the scheduling pattern for a particular school. While these are necessary practical requirements, most of them need not interfere with the success of the system as a whole. Cooperative efforts of school administrators can usually be counted upon to arrange satisfactory local adjustments to the basic system.

A problem frequently arising in large-scale instructional system revisions is the matter of securing adoption of a new system by enough schools to make the costs of system development worthwhile and economical. It is beyond the scope of this book to describe methods for bringing about such adoptions. Techniques relevant to the dissemination and diffusion of educational theory, research findings, and products have been the subject of considerable research. Two useful sources pertaining to methods for securing acceptance of new systems and new practices are: Havelock, Guskin, et al. (1969) and Briggs (1972).

SUMMARY

The term "systems approach" often is used to refer to a systematic process for designing any sized "chunk" of instruction, ranging from a lesson or module to an entire course or even to a curriculum. In this sense of the term, our treatment of the design of lessons and modules is as system-oriented as is the present chapter on design of instructional systems. Many identical elements and similarities can be noted between the process described earlier for designing a lesson, and the process described in this chapter for designing an instructional system.

Systems analysis and design procedures are not limited to instructional systems. There are general parallels between designing an instructional system and designing an administrative, transportation, or any other kind of system. For example, needs analysis, consideration of alternate solutions, and evaluation, should be part of all systems designs. However, some of the design components are different for an instructional system from those applicable to other systems. Such components include "development of instructional materials" and "teacher training."

This chapter discusses a number of values related to the systems approach to instruction. It is pointed out that such an approach makes no prejudgments about the nature of educational goals, or about the objectives derived from them. Thus it encounters no difficulty in encompassing broad varieties of outcomes of learning. The various domains of learning outcomes previously described, including the development of cognitive strategies and attitudes, are as highly valued and as feasible for systems planning as is the learning of information or simple varieties of intellectual skills. Instruction designed by a systems approach also reflects a high value on honesty and openness between the learner and the teacher or instructional designer. Emphasis can be given to the dignity of the learner as a person, and to his right to fair and considerate treatment.

Ways of organizing a system design and development effort are discussed. One of the main problems to be faced is avoiding discontinuities among the contributions to education made by industry, by universities, and by the schools themselves. A consortium-like manner of operation is described as a desirable mechanism for system design.

Since the design of an instructional system is usually a large undertaking, emphasis is again placed on the importance of the needs analysis. An additional critical feature is the necessity to consider alternate solutions in order to work within various kinds of constraints, including cost and the assumed learning environment.

The general steps in the design of an instructional system may be listed as follows:

1. Analysis and identification of needs
2. Definition of goals and objectives
3. Identification of alternative ways to meet needs
4. Design of system components
5. Analysis of (a) resources required, (b) resources available, (c) constraints
6. Action to remove or modify constraints
7. Selection or development of instructional materials
8. Design of student assessment procedures
9. Field testing; formative evaluation and teacher training
10. Adjustments, revisions, and further evaluation
11. Summative evaluation
12. Operational installation.

A major advantage of the systems approach is that it encourages the setting of a design objective, and it provides a way to know when that objective has been met. The thorough evaluation of a system can and probably should include formative and summative evaluations that are both "goal based" and "goal free." In other words, such evaluations should assess directly the specific outcomes of learning, and the broader effects of instruction which include unanticipated outcomes. The logic of evaluation is described in the next chapter.

REFERENCES

AAAS Commission on Science Education. *Science—A Process Approach. Hierarchy Chart*. New York: Xerox, 1967.

Briggs, L. J. Teaching Machines. In G. Finch (Ed.), *Educational and Training Media: A Symposium*. Washington, D.C.: National Academy of Sciences-National Research Council, 1960. (Publication 789). Pp. 150–195.

Briggs, L. J. *Handbook of Procedures for the Design of Instruction*. Pittsburgh, Pa.: American Institutes for Research, 1970. (Monograph No. 4.)

Briggs, L. J. Development and diffusion as mechanisms for educational improvement. In H. D. Schalock & G. R. Sell (Eds.) *Research, Development, Diffusion, Evaluation: Conceptual Frameworks*. Vol. III. Monmouth, Oregon: Oregon State Department of Higher Education, 1972. (a)

Briggs, L. J. *Student's Guide to Handbook of Procedures for the Design of Instruction*. Pittsburgh, Pa.: American Institutes for Research, 1972. (b)

Crowder, N. A. Automatic tutoring by means of intrinsic programming. In E. H. Galanter (Ed.), *Automatic Teaching: The State of the Art*. New York: Wiley, 1959, pp. 109–116.

Davies, I. K. *The Management of Learning*. London: McGraw-Hill, 1971.

Davies, I. K. & Hartley, J. *Contributions to an Educational Technology*. London: Butterworth, 1972.

Esbensen, T. *Working with Individualized Instruction*. Belmont, Calif.: Fearon, 1968.

Gagné, R. M. (Ed.) *Psychological Principles in System Development*. New York: Holt, Rinehart and Winston, 1962.

Guthrie, E. R. *The Psychology of Learning*. New York: Harper & Row, 1935.

Havelock, R. G., Guskin, A. L., *et al. Planning for Innovation Through Dissemination and Utilization of Knowledge*. Ann Arbor: Institute for Social Research, University of Michigan, 1969.

Lumsdaine, A. A. Educational Technology, Programmed Learning, and Instructional Science. In H. G. Richey (Ed.), *Theories of Learning and Instruction*, Chicago, Ill.: University of Chicago Press, 1964.

Markle, D. G. Final Report: *The Development of the Bell System First Aid and Personal Safety Course*. Palo Alto, Calif.: American Institutes for Research, 1967.

Pressey, S. L. Development and appraisal of devices providing immediate automatic scoring of objective tests and concomitant self-instruction. *Journal of Psychology*, 1950, *29*, 417–447.

Skinner, B. F. *The Technology of Teaching*. New York: Appleton-Century-Crofts, 1968.

Tosti, D. T., & Ball, J. R. A behavioral approach to instructional design and media selection. *AV Communication Review*, 1969, *17*, 5–25.

12
EVALUATING INSTRUCTION

Every designer of instruction wants to have assurance that his topic, or course, or total system of instruction is valuable for learning in the schools. This means that he wishes to know in a minimal sense whether his newly designed course or system "works" in the sense of achieving its objectives. More importantly, perhaps, he is interested in finding out whether his product "works better" than some other system it is designed to supplant.

Indications of how well an instructional product or system performs are best obtained from systematically gathered evidence. The means of gathering, analyzing, and interpreting such evidence are collectively called methods of *evaluation,* which is the subject of this final chapter. The placement of the chapter, by the way, should not be taken to indicate that the planning of

231

evaluation for instruction should be undertaken as a final step. Quite the contrary is the case; as will be seen, the design of evaluation calls upon principles of instructional planning that have been described in every chapter of this book.

Evidence sought in an enterprise whose purpose is the evaluation of instruction should be designed to answer at least the following specific questions concerning a lesson, topic, course, or instructional system:

Question 1. To what extent have the stated objectives of instruction been met?
Question 2. In what ways, and to what degree, is it better than the unit it will supplant?
Question 3. What additional, possibly unanticipated, effects has it had, and to what extent are these better or worse than the supplanted unit?

As will be seen in this chapter, these questions in turn give rise to others which must be answered in a prior sense. It is also true that these questions do not necessarily provide "ultimate" answers. For example, were it to be shown that all of the objectives of a designed unit of instruction were well met, one might still be left with the question, "What difference does that make in the life of the individual?" In still another vein, a school board may be interested in the question, "Is the instruction not only better, but more effective in terms of cost?" Such questions as these are surely important. However, they require a fuller treatment than can be given them in this book. Consequently, we shall confine our discussion of evaluation to the three listed questions, including a consideration of the kinds of prior evidence they require for their answers.

THE TWO MAJOR ROLES OF EVALUATION

The question that evaluation is designed to answer may be put to use in two different areas of decision-making. It has become customary, since the appearance of a definitive article by Scriven (1967), to refer to these two roles as *formative evaluation* and *summative evaluation*.

Formative Evaluation

One purpose for which evidence of an instructional program's worth is sought is for use in making decisions about how to revise the program while it is being developed. In other words, the evidence collected and interpreted during the phase of development is used to *form* the instructional program itself. If one discovers by means of an evaluation effort that a lesson is not feasible, or that the newly designed topic falls short of meeting its objectives, this information is used to revise the lesson, or to replace portions of the topic, in the attempt to overcome the defects which have been revealed.

The decisions made possible by formative evaluation may be illustrated in a number of ways. For example, suppose that a lesson in elementary science has called for the employment of a particular organism found in fresh-water ponds. But when the lesson is tried in a school, it is found that this particular organism cannot be kept alive for more than two hours when transplanted to a jar of ordinary water, without taking some elaborate precautions. Such an instance calls into question the practical *feasibility* of the lesson as designed. Since valuation has in this instance revealed the specific difficulty, it may be possible to revise the lesson by simply substituting another organism and changing the instructions for student activities appropriately. Alternatively, the lesson may have to be rewritten completely, or even abandoned.

Another type of example, illustrating *effectiveness*, may be provided by an instance in which a topic such as "use of the definite article with German nouns" is found to fail to meet its objective. Evidence from a formative evaluation study indicates that students use the definite article correctly in a large proportion of instances, but not in all. Further examination of the evidence reveals that the mistakes students are making center about the identification of gender of the nouns. The designer of instruction for the topic is consequently led to consider how the lesson, or lessons, on the gender of nouns can be improved. He finds, perhaps, that some necessary concept has been omitted, or inadequately presented. This discovery in turn leads him to revise the lesson, or possibly to introduce an additional lesson, designed to insure the attainment of this subordinate objective.

Conducting Formative Evaluation   The manner of conducting formative evaluations varies widely. Obviously, some observations, such as those pertaining to feasibility, may be made with only a few students or none at all. In contrast, the evaluation of an entire course is likely to require at the least a reasonably large number of students in several classrooms. Thus, no simple rule can be given for the extensiveness of student, teacher, or classroom involvement in a formative evaluation effort. It is always a matter of seeking evidence that is *convincing*. When a lesson's objective is successfully met by a single bright student, this is hardly convincing evidence that the lesson would work with students of the entire range of abilities typical of a total class. However, if the same lesson's objective is achieved by virtually all the students in a class which is representative of the population for whom the lesson is intended, this *is* a reasonably convincing piece of evidence.

Formative evaluations often are characterized by informality. The instructional entity—the lesson, topic, course, or system—is being tried out, and many kinds of observations are being made at the same time. Lessons and topics are carried through to their conclusions, and the collection of data is not permitted to interfere to any great extent with the progress of instruction.

Observations may be made of the students while they are at work on the lesson (by the teacher or other observer), and still other observations are left until the lesson has been completed. Some of the teacher's observations may be recorded from memory following the conduct of the lesson, rather than during it.

The informality of data collection procedures, however, need not be permitted to affect the precision of the data themselves. Quantitative data are definitely necessary for formative evaluation. The teacher's opinion, for example, that "students did well in this lesson" fails to meet the standard of convincing evidence. If one seeks evidence that the lesson's objectives have been met, no evidence is as convincing as an assessment of the performance of students on a properly designed test of these objectives.

Evidence Sought   In order to make good decisions about the further development of an instructional entity, a variety of kinds of evidence is needed. As an initial step, and one which is repeated on later occasions when other evidence becomes available, the essential accuracy of the content must be reviewed by a "subject-matter expert," usually a person who has much knowledge of the field in which the instruction lies. Knowledge of the field of genetics, for example, may be used to detect inconsistencies in a lesson on hybrid animals; similarly, a historian's knowledge may be brought to bear on the accuracy of events reported in a lesson on United States tariff policy.

Having satisfied himself that accurate communications will be made, the designer is interested in evaluating both the feasibility and the effectiveness of instruction. Usually, this means that data must be sought from both teachers and students, and preferably also from an "observer" who may be a member of the design team (or the designer). Typically, each formative evaluation study uses its own particular methods for collecting data, designed in part to meet local conditions; there are, therefore, no thoroughly standardized methods. The kinds of data sought may be listed as follows:

From the *observer*:
1. In what respects are (are not) the materials and media employed in the manner intended by the designer?
2. In what respects does (does not) the teacher carry out the procedures and make the decisions intended?
3. In what respects do (do not) the students follow the general procedures specified?

From the *teacher*:
1. What practical difficulties are encountered in conducting the lesson? (Examples: running overtime, setting up equipment, etc.)
2. Estimate the degree of interest or absorption of the students in the lesson.
3. What difficulties were encountered in carrying out the intended teacher procedures?

From the *student*:
1. How likely are you to choose to do the things you learned in this lesson?
2. How likely are you to recommend this lesson to your friends?
3. Results of a test of performance of the lesson's objectives.

It needs to be emphasized again that this list is intended to identify the *kinds of evidence* sought, and that it does not represent the content of the instruments used to collect this evidence. The student question, "How likely are you to choose to do the things you learned in this lesson?", for example, does not represent an actual question to be asked of students. Finding the answer to this question is likely to require a number of specific questions designed to reveal the students' attitudes. As given here, the question simply reflects what the evaluator wants to be able to conclude from the data collected.

For formative evaluation purposes, evidence relevant to these questions is normally collected on each lesson. The evidence may then be collated in some appropriate manner as applicable to topics or to an entire course. Needs for revision or expansion of these larger units of instruction is usually revealed by data on the lessons which comprise them.

Interpretation of the Evidence These various kinds of evidence, collected by means of observational records, questionnaires, and tests, are now employed to draw conclusions as to whether a lesson needs to be kept as is, revised, reformulated, or discarded.

The question of *feasibility* may be decided, for example, by considering reports of the difficulties experienced by teachers or students in the conduct of the lesson. The question of *effectiveness* is a somewhat more complex judgment. It may depend, in part, on the reports of the observer to the effect that the materials could not be used in the manner intended, or that the teacher did not carry out the intended procedures. It may also depend, in part, on the attitudes of students that are incidentally established by the lesson, as revealed by answers to questions to both teachers and students. And, of course, it may depend to the most important degree upon the extent to which the performance of students, as revealed by tests, is successful.

It will be evident that formative evaluation, in contrast to summative, is most cogently concerned with Question 1, to what extent have the stated objectives of instruction been met? This is one of the principal kinds of evidence which may be brought to bear on the revision and improvement of the designed instruction. On occasion, evidence may also become available which permits comparison with an alternative or supplanted instructional entity (Question 2), and such evidence may also be utilized for formative purposes. Similarly, observations which reveal unanticipated effects (Question 3), good or bad, may surely have an effect on decisions about revision or refinement of instruction. However useful these additional pieces of evidence may be, it remains true that Question 1 defines an essential kind of evidence leading to decisions about revising and improving the instructional unit which is being developed.

Summative Evaluation

Summative evaluation is usually undertaken when development of an instructional entity is in some sense completed, rather than on-going. Its purpose is to permit conclusions to be drawn about how well the instruction has worked. Such findings permit schools to make decisions about adopting and using the instructional entity.

In general, summative evaluation concerns itself with the effectiveness of an instructional system, course, or topic. Individual lessons may of course be evaluated as components of these larger units, but rarely as separate entities. The evaluation is called summative because it is intended to obtain evidence about the *summed* effects of a set of lessons making up a larger unit of instruction. Naturally, though, such evidence may include information pointing to defects or positive accomplishments of particular lessons, and this can be used in a formative sense for the *next* development or the *next* revision.

The main kind of decision for which the evidence of a summative evaluation is useful is whether a new course (or other unit) is better than one it has replaced, and therefore should be adopted for continued use. Conceivably, it may be no better, in which case considerations other than effectiveness *per se* (such as cost) will come to determine the choice. Also conceivably, it might be worse than what it has replaced, in which case the decision would likely be an easy one to reach.

Suppose that a newly designed course in American government has replaced one by the same title, and has been adopted by a school for the purpose of trying out the new course. A summative evaluation finds that student enthusiasm for the new course is little changed compared with that for the old; that 137 of the 150 defined objectives of the new course are adequately met by students (the previous course did not have defined objectives, nor means of assessing them); and that a test of American government given at the end of the semester yields an average score of 87 as opposed to 62 on the same test in the previous year. The new course is liked by teachers, for the specific reason that it permits them to take more time for individual student conferences. Provided, now, that the new course does not cost more than the old, this set of evidences would very likely lead to a decision to adopt and continue the new course, and to abandon the old.

In contrast to formative evaluation, summative evaluation usually has many formal features, some of which are indicated by this example. Measures of student attitudes, for example, are likely to be based upon carefully constructed questionnaires, so that they can be directly and validly compared with those of last year's students. The assessment of mastery of each objective is also systematically done, in order that there will be a quantitative indication of the accomplishments of the entire course. In addition, measures of achievement are taken from a test serving as a "semester examination." As is true of formative evaluation, each of these summative measures needs to be obtained with the use of methods that make possible the collection of convincing evidence of effectiveness.

Evidence Sought   Summative evaluation of a topic, course, or instructional system is primarily concerned with evidence of learning outcomes. As will be discussed in the next section of this chapter, obtaining such evidence requires the collection of data on "input measures" and "process measures," as well as on those measures which directly assess outcomes. Learning outcomes are assessed by means of observations or tests of human capabilities, as reflected in the objectives specified for the instruction. Accordingly, the measures of outcomes might consist of any or all of the following types:

1. Measures indicating the mastery of *intellectual skills*, assessing whether or not particular skills have been acquired. Example: A test requiring solutions for designated variables in linear algebraic equations.
2. Measures of *problem-solving ability*, assessing the quality or efficiency of the student's thinking. Example: Exercises requiring the design of a scientific experiment to test the effect of a particular factor on some natural phenomenon, in a situation novel to the student.
3. Tests of *information*, assessing whether or not a specified set of facts or generalizations has been learned. Example: A test requiring the student to state the names and roles of the principal characters in a work of literature. Alternatively, tests assessing the breadth of knowledge attained by the student. Example: A test which asks the student to describe the major antecedents of a historical event.
4. Observations or other measures of the adequacy of *motor skills*, usually with reference to a specified "standard" of performance. Example: An exercise in which the child is asked to print the alphabet in capital letters.
5. Self-report questionnaires assessing *attitude*. Example: A questionnaire asking the student to indicate "probability of choice" for actions concerned with the disposal of personal trash.

Interpretation of Summative Evidence   The various measures appropriate for the outcomes of learning are interpreted mainly in comparison to similar measures obtained on an instructional entity representing an alternative method of instruction. Thus, the primary emphasis of evidence obtained for summative purposes is on the answer to Question 2 (p. 232), "In what ways, and to what degree, is this entity better than some other?" Usually, the comparison to be made is with a topic or course which the newly designed unit is intended to replace. Sometimes, two different newly designed instructional entities may be compared one with the other. In either case, such comparisons require methods of data collection which are able to demonstrate that "all other things are equal," which is by no means an easy thing to do.

Answers to Question 1 and 3 are also desirable outcomes of a summative evaluation. One wants to determine, as a minimal condition, whether the objectives of the new instructional unit have been met (Question 1). Should it turn out that they have not, this result will obviously affect the possible conclusions to be drawn from comparison with an alternative unit. In addition, it is always of some importance to explore whether the newly designed instruction has had some unanticipated effects (Question 3). A topic designed to teach basic musical concepts, for example, might turn out to have some unexpected effects on attitudes toward listening to classical music.

CONDUCTING AN EVALUATION

The various measures of outcomes of instruction that have been mentioned obviously require a good deal of careful thought and effort. In some instances, the required measures, tests, observation schedules, or questionnaires can be purchased or adapted from instruments already available. In most cases, however, they must be *separately developed* to meet the needs of the instructional design effort. Methods for the development of outcome measures have been described in Chapter 9.

Besides the development of tests or other types of measures, the enterprise of evaluation, both formative and summative, requires careful scientifically based methods which serve to insure that the evidence obtained is truly convincing. To describe these methods in full detail would require at least a separate volume; in fact, a number of books are available that deal with the design of evaluation studies (for example, DuBois & Mayo, 1970; Isaac & Michael, 1971; Popham, 1972). In this chapter, we can deal only with the *logic* of evaluation studies, beginning with the logic of data collection and interpretation already introduced. Beyond this, however, is the rationale for identifying and controlling variables in evaluation efforts, in order that valid conclusions can be drawn about instructional outcomes.

The Variables of Evaluation Studies

The intention of studies to evaluate an instructional entity is to draw conclusions about the effects of the instruction on learning outcomes—on the human capabilities the instruction has been designed to establish or improve.

But these capabilities are affected by other factors in the educational setting, not only by the instruction itself. It is therefore necessary to *control or otherwise account for these other variables*, in order to draw valid conclusions about instructional effectiveness. Considered as a whole, the educational situation into which instruction is introduced contains the classes of variables described in the following paragraphs.

Outcome Variables We begin to list the variables of the educational situation with outcome variables, the dependent or measured variables which are the primary focus of interest. These have already been described as measures of the human capabilities intended to be affected by instruction. The classes of variables that influence educational outcomes, and their various sources, are shown in Figure 10.

Process Variables What factors in the school situation might influence the outcomes, given the existence of an instructional program? Obviously, there may be some effects of how the instructional entity (topic, course, system) is conducted. Outcomes may be influenced, in other words, by the *operations* carried out to put the instruction into effect, typically by the teacher (cf. Astin & Panos, 1971). For example, the instruction as designed may call for a particular type and frequency of teacher questioning. To what extent has this been done? Or, the designed course may call for a particular sequence of intellectual skills, some to be mastered before others are undertaken. To what extent has this operation been carried out? As still another example, the designed instruction may specify that a particular sort of feedback is to be incorporated in each lesson (see Chapter 7). Has this been systematically and consistently done?

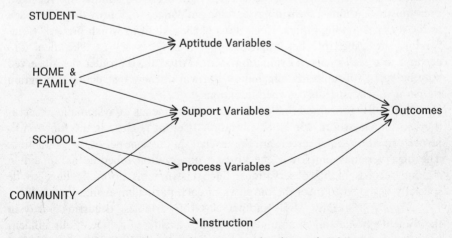

FIGURE 10 Variables influencing the outcomes of an instructional program.

One cannot simply assume that process variables of the sort specified by the designed instruction, or intended by the designer, will inevitably occur in the way they are expected to. Of course, well designed instruction provides for whatever action may be required to insure that operation of the program will go as planned; for example, provisions are often made to train teachers in these operations. Nevertheless, such efforts are not always fully successful —teachers are no more free of human inadequacies than are the members of any other professional group. Designers of new programs of individualized instruction, for example, have rather frequently found that the operations specified for these programs are not being executed in the manner originally intended. As a consequence, it is essential that assessments be made of process variables, and particularly is this so when the newly designed instructional entity is being tried out for the first time.

Process variables comprise any factors in the instructional situation which may directly affect student learning. Such factors, then, may concern matters of *sequence*, or matters of institution and arrangement of the *events of instruction*, both of which are described in Chapter 7. Another factor is the *amount of time* devoted by students to particular lessons or portions of a course. Of course, one of the major variations to be found in topics or courses of instruction is the degree to which these classes of process variables are specified. A textbook, for example, may imply a sequence for instruction in its ·organization of chapters, but may leave the arrangement of events of instruction entirely to the teacher, or to the learner himself (as does this book). In contrast, a topic designed for instruction in language skills for the sixth grade may not only specify a sequence of subordinate skills, but also particular events such as informing the learner of objectives, stimulating recall of prerequisite learnings, providing learning guidance, and providing feedback to the learner, among others. Regardless of the extent to which process variables are prescribed by the designed entity, it is necessary to take them into account in a well-planned evaluation study. After all, the outcomes observed may be being substantially affected by the ways a new instructional program is *operated*, whatever its designed intentions.

Typically, process variables are assessed by means of systematic observations in the classroom (or other educational setting). Here is the function to be performed by the observer, not the teacher, in the conduct of the evaluation. The observer may employ a checklist or observation schedule as an aid in making records of his observations. Such instruments normally have to be specially designed to meet the purposes of each particular evaluation study.

Support Variables   Still another class of variables, occurring partly in the student's home and community, has to be considered as potentially influential upon the outcomes of an instructional program. These include such factors as the presence of adequate materials (in the classroom and the school library), the availability of a quiet place for study, the "climate" of the classroom with reference to its encouragement of good achievement, the actions of parents in reinforcing favorable attitudes towards homework and other learning activities, and many others. The number of different variables in this class is quite large, and not enough is known about them to make possible a confident differentiation among them with regard to their relative importance.

The general nature of this class of variables is to be seen in their effects on the *opportunities for learning*. Materials in the classroom, for example, may present greater or fewer opportunities for learning, depending on their availability; parents may make opportunities for adequate attention to homework more or less available; and so on. In contrast to process variables, *support variables* do not directly influence the process of learning as the former set of factors is expected to do. Instead, they tend to determine the more general environmental conditions of those periods of time during which process variables may exert their effects. For example, the designed instruction may call for a period of independent study on the part of the student. In operation, the teacher may make suitable time provisions for this independent study, thus insuring that the process variable has been accounted for. But what will be the difference in the outcome, for (1) a student who has a relatively quiet place in which to pursue his learning uninterruptedly, and for (2) a student who must perform his independent study in an open corner of a noisy classroom? This contrast describes a difference in a *support* variable. The opportunities for learning are presumably less in the second case, although the actual effects of this variable on the outcome cannot be stated for this hypothetical example.

Support variables require various means for their assessment. What parents do in encouraging homework may be assessed by means of a questionnaire. The availability of materials relevant to a topic or course may be assessed by counting books, pamphlets, and other reference sources. The "climate" of a classroom may be found by the use of a systematic schedule of observations. Other measures of this class, such as number of students or the pupil-teacher ratio, may be readily available at the outset of the study. For any of the variety of support variables, it is likely to be necessary to select or develop the technique of assessment best suited to the particular situation.

Aptitude Variables   It is of great importance to note that, of all the variables likely to determine the outcomes of learning, the most influential is probably the student's *aptitude for learning*. Whatever may be accomplished by improved methods of instruction, by arrangements of process variables, and by insuring the best possible support for learning, it is well to keep in mind that this entire set of favorable circumstances cannot influence learning outcomes as much as can student aptitude.

The aptitude for learning that a student possesses at any given point in time is undoubtedly determined in part by his genetic inheritance. It is also determined in part by environmental influences, some of which (like nutrition) may exert their effects even before birth. An individual's aptitude is partly determined also by the kinds of prior learning he has done and by the opportunities he has had to learn. It should be clear, then, that aptitude is a variable that has its own multiple determinants. As it enters an evaluation study, however, aptitude is usually an *input* variable (Astin & Panos, 1971). As such, it is not subject to alteration by the evaluation; it can only be measured, not manipulated.

Traditionally, aptitude for learning is measured by instruments called *intelligence tests*. Many well-designed and carefully validated tests of this sort are available. Criticisms of "unfairness" are sometimes raised concerning intelligence tests, based in part upon the demonstrable fact that they contain items sampling information and skills that may be more readily available to one ethnic group than they are to another. We cannot devote space to a consideration of this criticism in these pages. For the purposes of conducting evaluation studies, however, it may be noted that the important characteristic sought in a test of learning aptitude is not "fairness," but *predictive power*. By this phrase is meant the power of an aptitude test score to predict variations in the achievements of different students, considered as learning outcomes. That intelligence tests do accomplish such prediction is a fact that has been shown in studies too numerous to cite. On the whole, these studies have shown that intelligence (aptitude for learning) may account for as much as fifty percent of the variations in learning outcome, measured as student achievement in capabilities falling in the categories of information, intellectual skills, and cognitive strategies.

Obviously, then, the aptitude for learning which a student brings to the instructional situation is likely to have a very great effect on his learning, when the latter is assessed in terms of its outcomes. This is true, so far as is known, quite independently of the student's ethnic or racial background. Thus, if effectiveness of an instructional program is to be assessed, the effect of the instruction itself must be demonstrated by instituting controls which make possible the separation of the influence of the student's "entering" aptitude for learning.

While measures of learning aptitude are often most conveniently identified by scores on intelligence tests, other measures are sometimes employed. A *combination* of several aptitude tests may be used to yield a combined score to assess learning aptitude. (Actually, most intelligence tests are themselves

collections of subtests sampling several different aptitudes). Another procedure involves the use of measures which are known to *correlate* with intelligence scores to a fairly high degree. Previous school grades exhibit such high
correlations, particularly in subjects such as reading comprehension and
mathematics. Still another correlated measure is family income, or family
socioeconomic status (SES). It seems reasonable, though, that while correlated
measures are sometimes useful, they are not to be preferred in evaluation
studies over measures which attempt to assess learning aptitude in the most
direct manner possible.

INTERPRETING EVALUATIVE EVIDENCE

We have pointed out that measures of the outcomes of an instructional
program—that is, measures of learned intellectual skills, cognitive strategies,
information, attitudes, motor skills—are influenced by a number of variables
in the educational situation, besides the program itself. Process variables in
the operation of the instructional program may directly affect learning, and
thus also affect its outcomes. Support variables in the school or in the home
determine the opportunities for learning, and thus influence the outcomes of
learning that are observed. And most prominently of all, the learning aptitude
of students strongly influences the outcomes measured in an evaluation study.

If the effectiveness of the designed instruction is to be evaluated, certain
controls must be instituted over process, support, and aptitude variables, in
order to insure that the "net effect" of the instruction itself is revealed. Procedures for accomplishing this control are described in this section. Again it
may be necessary to point out that only the basic logic of these procedures
can be accounted for here. However, such logic is of critical importance in
the design of evaluation studies.

Controlling for Aptitude Effects

The assessment of outcomes of instruction in terms of Question 1 (To
what extent have objectives been met?) needs to take account of the effects of
aptitude variables. In the context of this question, it is mainly desirable to
state what *is* the level of intelligence of the students being instructed. This
may be done most simply by giving the average score and some measure of
dispersion of the distribution of scores (such as the standard deviation) on a
standard test of intelligence. However, correlated measures such as SES are
frequently used for this purpose. Supposing that 117 out of 130 objectives of a
designed course are found to have been met; it is of some importance to know
whether the average IQ of the students is 115 (as might be true in a suburban
school) or 102 (as might occur in some sections of a city, or in a rural

area). It is possible that, in the former setting, the number of objectives achieved might be 117 out of 130, whereas in the latter, this might drop to 98 out of 130. The aims of evaluation may best be accomplished by trying out the instructional entity in several different schools, each having a somewhat different range of student learning aptitude.

When the purposes of Question 2 (To what degree is it better?) are being served in evaluation, one must go beyond simply reporting the nature and amount of the aptitude variable. In this case, the concern is to show whether any difference exists between the new instructional program and some other —in other words, to make a *comparison*. Simply stated, making a comparison requires the demonstration that the two groups of students were *equivalent* to begin with. Equivalence of students in aptitude is most likely to occur when successive classes of students in the same school, coming from the same neighborhood, are employed as comparison groups. This is the case when a newly designed course is introduced in a classroom or school, and is to be compared with a different course given the previous year.

Other methods of establishing equivalence of initial aptitudes are often employed. Sometimes, it is possible to assign students *randomly* to different classrooms within a single school, half of which receive the newly designed instruction and half of which do not. When such a design is used, definite administrative arrangements must be made to insure randomness—it cannot be assumed. Another procedure is to select a set of schools which are "matched" insofar as possible in the aptitudes of their students, and to try out the new instruction in half of these, making a comparison with the outcomes obtained in those schools not receiving the new instruction. All of these methods contain certain complexities of design which necessitate careful management if valid comparisons are to be made.

There are also statistical methods of control for aptitude variables— methods which "partial out" the effects of aptitude variables and thus reveal the net effect of the instruction itself. In general, these methods are following logic such as this: If the measured outcome is produced by A and I, where A is aptitude and I is instruction, what would be the effect of I alone, if A were assumed to have a constant value, rather than a variable one? Such methods are of considerable value in revealing instructional effectiveness, bearing in mind particularly the prominent influence the A variable is likely to have.

Whatever particular procedure is employed, it should be clear that any valid comparison of the effectiveness of instruction in two or more groups of students requires that equivalence of initial aptitudes be established. Measures of intelligence, or other correlated measures, may be employed in the comparison. Students may be randomly assigned to the different groups, or their aptitudes may be compared when assignment has been made on other grounds (such as school location). Statistical means may be employed to make possible the assumption of equivalence. Any or all of these means have the aim of making a convincing case for equivalence of learning aptitudes among groups of students whose capabilities following instruction are being compared. No study evaluating learning outcomes can provide valid evidence of instructional effectiveness without having a way of "controlling" this important variable.

Controlling for the Effects of Support Variables

For many purposes of evaluation, support variables may be treated as "input" variables, and thus controlled in ways similar to those used for learning aptitude. Thus, when interest is centered upon the attainment of objectives (Question 1), the measures made of support variables can be reported along with outcome measures in order that they can be considered in interpreting the outcomes. Here again, a useful procedure is to try out the instruction in a variety of schools displaying different characteristics (or different amounts) of "support."

Similarly, the comparisons implied by Question 2 and part of Question 3 require the demonstration of *equivalence* among the classes or schools whose learning outcomes are being compared. Suppose that outcome measures are obtained from two different aptitude-equivalent groups of students in a school, one of which has been trying out a newly designed course in English composition, while the other continues with a different course. Assume that, despite differences in the instruction, the objectives of the two courses are largely the same, and that assessment of outcomes is based on these common objectives. Class M is found to show significantly better performance, on the average, than does Class N. Before the evidence that the new instruction is "better" can be truly convincing, it must be shown that no differences exist in support variables. Since the school is the same, many variables of this sort can be shown to be equivalent, such as the library, the kinds of materials available, and others of this nature. Where might differences in support variables be found? One possibility is the "climate" of the two classrooms—one may be more encouraging to achievement than is the other. Two different teachers are involved—one may be disliked, the other liked. Student attitudes may be different—more students in one class may seek new opportunities for learning than do students in the other. Variables of this sort which affect opportunities for learning may accordingly affect outcomes. Therefore, it is quite essential that equivalence of groups with respect to these variables be demonstrated, or taken into account by statistical means.

Controlling for the Effects of
Process Variables

The assessment and control of process variables is of particular concern in seeking evidence bearing on the attainment of stated objectives (Question 1). Quite evidently, an instructional entity may "work" either better or worse depending upon how the operations it specifies are carried out. Suppose, for example, that a new course in elementary science presumes that teachers will treat the directing of students' activities as something left almost entirely to the students themselves (guided by an exercise booklet). Teachers find that under these circumstances, the students tend to get into situations raising questions to which they (the teachers) don't always "know the answers." One teacher may deal with this circumstance by encouraging students to see if they can invent a way of finding the answer. Another teacher may require that students do only what their exercise book describes. Thus the same instructional program may lead to quite different operations. The process variable differs markedly in these two instances, and equally marked effects may show up in measures of outcome. If the evaluation is of the formative type, the designer may interpret such evidence as showing the need for additional teacher instructions or training. If summative evaluation is being conducted, results from the two groups of students must be treated separately to disclose the effects of the process variable.

In comparison studies (Question 2), process variables are equally important. As in the case of aptitude or support variables, they must be "controlled" in one way or another in order for valid evidence of the effectiveness of instruction to be obtained. Equivalence of groups in terms of process variables must be shown, either by exercising direct control over them, by a randomizing approach, or by statistical means. It may be noted that process variables are more amenable to direct control than are either support or aptitude variables. If a school or class is conducted in a noisy environment (a support variable), the means of changing the noise level may not be readily at hand. If, however, a formative evaluation study shows that some teachers have failed to use the operations specified by the new instructional program (a process variable), instruction of these teachers can be undertaken, so that the next trial starts off with a desirable set of process variables.

Unanticipated outcomes (Question 3) are equally likely to be influenced by process variables, and accordingly require similar control procedures. A set of positive attitudes on the part of students of a newly designed program *could* result from the human modelling of a particular teacher, and thus contrast with less favorable attitudes in another group of students who have otherwise had the same instruction. It is necessary in this case also, to demonstrate equivalence of process variables before drawing conclusions about effects of the instructional entity itself.

Controlling Variables by Randomization

It is generally agreed that the best possible way to control variables in an evaluation study is to insure that their effects occur in a random fashion. This is the case when students can be assigned to "control" and "experimental" groups in a truly random manner, or when an entire set of classes or schools can be divided into such groups randomly. In the simplest case, if the outcomes of Group A (the new instructional entity) are compared with those of Group B (the previously employed instruction), and students drawn from a given population have been assigned to these groups in equal numbers at random, the comparison of the outcomes may be assumed to be equally influenced by aptitude variables. Similar reasoning applies to the effects of randomizing the assignment of classrooms, teachers, and schools to experimental and control groups, in order to equalize process and support variables.

Randomization has the effect of controlling not only the specific variables which have been identified, but also other variables which may not have been singled out for measurement because their potential influence is unknown. Although ideal for purposes of control, in practice randomizing procedures are usually difficult to arrange. Schools do not customarily draw their students randomly from a community, nor assign them randomly to classes or teachers. Accordingly, the identification and measurement of aptitude, support, and process variables must usually be undertaken as described in the preceding sections. When random assignment of students, teachers, or classes is possible, evaluation studies achieve a degree of elegance which they do not otherwise possess.

EXAMPLES OF EVALUATION STUDIES

The four kinds of variables in evaluation studies—aptitude, support, process, and outcome—are typically given careful consideration and measurement in any evaluation study, whether formative or summative. Interpretation of these measures differs for the two evaluation roles, as will be seen in the following examples.

Evaluation of a Program in
Reading for Beginners

A varied set of lessons in reading readiness and beginning reading was developed and evaluated over a two-year period by the Educational Development Laboratories of McGraw-Hill, Inc., and by the L. W. Singer Company, of Random House, Inc. This system of instruction is called *Listen Look Learn*. In brief, the instructional materials include: (1) a set of filmstrips accompanied by sound, designed to develop listening comprehension and oral recounting; (2) an eye-hand coordination workbook dealing with the identification and printing of letters and numerals; (3) a set of filmstrips providing letter-writing tasks, accompanying the workbook; (4) letter charts for kinesthetic letter-identification; (5) picture sequence cards, and other cards for "hear and read" practice; (6) a set of colored filmstrips for the analysis of word sounds and the presentation of words in story contexts.

As reported by Heflin and Scheier (1968), a systematic formative evaluation of this instructional system was undertaken, which at the same time obtained some initial data for summative purposes. Table 8 summarizes some of the main points of the study, abstracted from this report. The purpose of the table is to illustrate how the major classes of variables were treated and interpreted; naturally, many details of the study covered in the report cannot be reported in the brief space of such a table.

Classes of first-grade pupils from schools located in eleven states were included in the evaluation study. A group of forty classes comprising 917 pupils were given instruction provided by the *Listen Look Learn* system, and a group of 1000 pupils in forty-two classes was constituted as a control group. Control group classes used the "basal reading" instructional system. Each school district was asked to provide classes for the experimental and control groups which were as equivalent as possible in terms of characteristics of teachers and pupils.

Aptitude Variables Owing to differences in the availability of aptitude scores in the various schools, no initial measures of aptitude were employed. Instead, information was obtained concerning the socioeconomic status of the pupils' families, as indicated in Table 8. When aptitude measures were administered during the second year of the study (Metropolitan Readiness, Pintner Primary IQ), verification was obtained of a broad range of aptitude, as well as of equivalence of the experimental and control groups.

For purposes of formative evaluation, one wishes to know that the classes selected for instruction have included a range of student aptitudes which is representative of schools in the country as a whole, since that is the intended usage for the system being evaluated. From the report (Heflin and Scheier, 1968), it would appear that the schools taking part in the study represented a great majority of United States elementary schools, although by no means all of them. For example, inner-city schools were apparently not included. Nevertheless, the study offers reasonably good evidence that a broad range of pupil aptitudes was represented. In addition, it is clear from the reported data that the two groups of pupils were reasonably equivalent in aptitude.

TABLE 8   *Variables Measured and Their Interpretation for Formative and Summative Evaluation in a Study of a System of Instruction for Beginning Reading* (Listen Look Learn) *

Type of Variable	How Measured	Interpretation
Aptitude	Initially, by means of socio-economic status (SES), a correlated measure	*Formative*: A variety of classes providing a range of SES from high to low
	During second year, standardized test scores for IQ and Reading Readiness	*Summative*: Equivalence of SES, and later of aptitude, shown for experimental and control groups
Support	(1) Level of formal education of teachers (2) Amount of teacher education in reading methods (3) Years of teaching experience	*Formative*: Range of these variables typical of most elementary schools *Summative*: Reasonable equivalence of experimental and control groups on these variables
Process	(1) Appropriateness of lessons as judged by teachers (2) Success of program components as judged by teachers (3) Strength and weaknesses of individual lessons judged by teachers	*Formative*: Judgments of appropriateness used to test feasibility Indirect indications of effectiveness of pupil learning, based on teachers' estimates
Outcome	Metropolitan Primary I Achievement Word Knowledge Means: LLL Group–25.5 Control Group–24.1 Word Discrimination Means: LLL Group–25.9 Control Group–24.7 Reading Means: LLL Group–27.3 Control Group–25.2	*Summative*: Achievement scores on standardized test indicate scores on component reading skills significantly higher than those of an equivalent control group

* Information and results abstracted from Heflin and Scheier, *The Formative Period of Listen Look Learn, a Multi-Media Communication Skills System.* Huntington, N.Y.: Educational Development Laboratories, Inc., 1968.

Support Variables   The range of SES of pupils' families provides the additional indication that support for learning, insofar as it may be assumed to originate in the home environment, exhibited a suitable range of variation for the study. Other evidences of learning support are inferred from measures of the characteristics of teachers, as indicated in Table 8. The inference is that teachers having typical range of educational backgrounds will conduct themselves in ways that provide a range of differential opportunities for learning. A reasonable degree of equivalence is also demonstrated on these variables between experimental and control groups.

Other measures of support for learning, not systematically obtained in this study, are perhaps of greater relevance to summative evaluation. Such variables as "availability of reading materials," "encouragement of independent reading," and others of this general nature would be examples. In the *Listen Look Learn* study, incomplete evidence was obtained of the number of books read by individual children, and this number was found to vary from zero to 132 (Heflin and Scheier, 1968, p. 45).

Process Variables   As Table 8 indicates, a measure of the feasibility of the various parts of the program was obtained by asking teachers to judge the appropriateness of the materials for groups of fast, medium, and slow learners. Various features of the individual lessons might have contributed to appropriateness, such as the familiarity of the subject of a story or the difficulty of words employed. Teacher's judgments led to conclusions about feasibility which resulted in elimination or revision of a number of elements of the program.

Teachers' estimates also formed the bases for evidence of the "success" of the various activities comprising the *Listen Look Learn* program. Such measures are of course indirect evidence bearing on process variables, as contrasted with such indicators as how many exercises were attempted by each student, how long a time was spent on each, what feedback was provided for correct or incorrect responses, and other factors of this nature. The materials of this program do not make immediately evident what the desired process variables may have been. Consequently, teachers' reports about "how effective the lesson was" were probably as good indicators of these variables as could be obtained in this instance.

Outcome Variables   Learning outcomes for this program were assessed by means of standardized tests of word knowledge, word discrimination, and reading (portions of the Metropolitan Primary I Achievement Test). As can be seen from Table 9, mean scores on these three kinds of activities were higher for the experimental group than for the control group, which had been shown to be reasonably equivalent so far as the operation of aptitude and support variables were concerned. Statistical tests of the differences between the various pairs of means indicated that these differences were significant at an acceptable level of probability.

It should be pointed out that the evidences of learning outcome obtained in this study were considered by its authors as no more than initial indications of the success of the *Listen Look Learn* program. Further studies were subsequently conducted to evaluate learning outcomes in a summative sense (Brickner and Scheier, 1968, 1970; Kennard and Scheier, 1971). In general, these studies have yielded data and conclusions which show improvements in early reading achievement considerably greater than are produced by other instructional programs they are designed to supplant (usually basal reading approaches).

Evaluation of an Individualized Arithmetic Program

A second example of an evaluation study, summative in character, is provided by an investigation of an individualized instruction system developed by the Learning Research and Development Center, University of Pittsburgh (Cooley, 1971). In this study, a program of individualized instruction in arithmetic for the second grade of the Frick School was compared with the previously used program. The new program had undergone several years of formative evaluation and development. It provided for individual progress of pupils in attaining arithmetic skills, based upon mastery of prerequisite skills.

Table 9 summarizes the treatment of variables in this evaluation study, and presents the major outcome findings.

Aptitude Variables   First, it will be seen from the table that aptitude variables were measured from year to year at the time the children first entered the school. Over a period of several years, the aptitudes of entering classes was found to be essentially the same. In addition, the correlated variable of socioeconomic status (SES) was found to remain stable. Accordingly, it was considered a reasonable assumption in this study that successive classes of pupils would have the same initial aptitudes. An experimental group (individualized instruction) in the second grade in 1971 could be compared with a control group (regular instruction) who were in the second grade in 1970.

Support Variables   So far as support variables were concerned, these were not specifically singled out and measured individually. Instead, there was a demonstrated equivalence of classrooms and teachers. Under these circumstances, particular support variables were assumed to be equivalent for both groups. Similarly, those support variables originating in the home could be assumed equivalent, in view of the demonstrated absence of differences in SES variables for the two classes.

TABLE 9 *Variables and Their Interpretation in an Evaluation of an Individualized Program in Arithmetic for the Second Grade, Frick School**

Variable	How Controlled or Measured	Interpretation
Aptitude	Classes of pupils used in Control and Experimental Groups equivalent in aptitude when they entered school	Aptitude of classes of pupils remains unchanged in this school from year to year
	SES of pupils in both groups shown to be equivalent	
Support	Same school facilities present for both groups, and same teachers involved.	Specific support variables of the school and the home are equivalent
	SES of pupils equivalent	
Process	Contrasting process in individualized and regular instruction	Effects of process variables in individualized instruction to be examined; other specific process variables equivalent in both groups
	Same teachers involved in both groups	
Outcome	Wide Range Achievement Test —Arithmetic	Significant differences obtained in outcome scores for equivalent groups
	Mean Scores in Second Grade: Experimental Group (1971)–25.22 Control Group (1970)–23.40	

* Information and results abstracted from Cooley, W. W. *Methods of Evaluating School Innovations.* Pittsburgh, Pa.: Learning Research and Development Center, University of Pittsburgh, 1971 (26).

Process variables The most important process variables, those associated with the specific technique of individualized instruction, were deliberately contrasted in the two groups, and this variation was verified by classroom observations. Other process variables (such as the encouragement provided by teachers to pupils) could be assumed to be equivalent because the same teachers were involved for both experimental and control groups.

Outcome As a consequence of this study design, certain influencing variables in the categories of aptitude, support, and process are either shown to be, or reasonably assumed to be, equivalent in their effects on both groups of pupils. Outcome variables are therefore expected to reflect the effects of the changes in instruction in an unbiased manner. Measures of arithmetic achievement, as shown in the final row of the table, indicate a significant improvement when the new (individualized) instruction is compared with the previously used instruction.

A Generalized Example

Every evaluation study presents the evaluator with a different set of circumstances to which he must apply the logic we have described. In practice, compromise must sometimes be made, because of the existence of inadequate measures of learning outcomes, the difficulties of achieving equivalence in groups to be compared, the occurrence of particular events affecting one school or class without affecting others, and many other possibilities too numerous to mention. Part of the evaluator's job, of course, is to judge the severity of these occurrences, and the ways in which they must be taken into account to arrive at convincing evidence.

A reference set of representative evaluation situations is shown in Table 10, together with their most likely interpretations. These situations serve as one kind of summary of our previous discussion of the types of variables affecting learning outcomes.

The hypothetical comparisons of Table 10 suppose that School A has been trying out a newly developed course (also labeled "A"), and that its outcomes are being compared with those from School B, which has been using a different course ("B"). In all cases, it is further supposed, the measures of outcome have been found superior in School A to what they are in School B.

Situation 1 is that in which support variables and process variables have

TABLE 10   *Comparisons of Learning Outcomes in School A (Using Course A) and School B (Using Course B), and Their Interpretation*

Situation		Outcome Comparison	Most Likely Interpretation
1. Aptitude variable:	A > B	A > B	Most of the outcome difference, if not all, attributable to aptitude differences
Support variables:	A = B		
Process variables:	A = B		
2. Aptitude variable:	A = B	A > B	Differences may be caused by instruction, by support, or both
Support variables:	A > B		
Process variables:	A = B		
3. Aptitude variable:	A = B	A > B	Differences may be caused by instruction, by process differences, or both
Support variables:	A = B		
Process variables:	A > B		
4. Aptitude variable:	A = B	A > B	Difference is attributable to effects of instruction
Support variables:	A = B		
Process variables:	A = B		

been controlled, that is, shown to be equivalent. Aptitude variables indicate higher intelligence, on the average, in School A than in School B. Since this variable is such a powerful one, the effects of instruction cannot be expected to show up, and the likely interpretation is as shown in the final column. Situation 2 is one in which all influencing variables have been shown equivalent except for the support variables. Differences in outcomes may be caused by these variables, by the instruction, or by both in some unknown proportion. Similarly, Situation 3, in which process variables differ, can lead only to the conclusion that either process or instruction, or both, have produced the observed differences in outcome.

Situation 4 is what is aimed for in studies of summative evaluation. Here all the influencing variables have been shown to be equivalent, by one method or another. This situation is one that makes possible the interpretation that outcome differences are attributable to the instruction itself.

SUMMARY

Evaluation of courses, programs, and instructional programs usually has at least the following questions in view: (1) have the objectives of instruction been met; (2) is the new program better than one it is expected to supplant; and (3) what additional effects does the new program produce?

Formative evaluation is undertaken while the new unit is being developed. Its purpose is to provide evidence on feasibility and effectiveness, so that revisions and improvements can be made. It seeks evidence from observers, teachers, and students.

Summative evaluation is concerned with the effectiveness of the course or program, once it has been developed. Mainly, the evidence sought is in terms of student performance. Measures are taken of the kinds of student capabilities the program is intended to establish.

When summative evaluations are undertaken to compare a new instructional unit with an "old" one, other variables besides the unit itself must be taken into account. The outcomes of instruction are influenced by variables whose effects must be "controlled," in order to test the effects of instruction. These variables include the following:

1. Aptitude variables, reflecting the students' aptitude for learning
2. Process variables, arising from the manner of operation of instruction in the school
3. Support variables—conditions in the home, school, and community which affect opportunities for learning.

Evaluation studies use various means to control these influencing variables, in order to demonstrate the effects of the newly designed instruction. Sometimes, the operation of these variables can be made equivalent by assigning students, schools, or communities in a "randomized" way to different groups to be instructed. More frequently, statistical means must be employed to establish the equivalence of groups to be compared. If two courses or systems of instruction are to be evaluated to determine which is better, evaluation logic requires that control be exercised over these other variables. Ideally, everything should be equivalent except the two instructional programs themselves.

REFERENCES

Astin, A. W. & Panos, R. J. The evaluation of educational programs. In R. L. Thorndike (Ed.), *Educational Measurement*. 2d Ed. Washington, D.C.: American Council on Education, 1971. Pp. 733–751.

Brickner, A., & Scheier, E. *Summative Evaluation of Listen Look Learn Cycles R–40, 1967–68*. Huntington, N.Y.: Educational Development Laboratories, Inc., 1968.

Brickner, A., & Scheier, E. *Summative Evaluation of Listen Look Learn 2nd Year Students, Cycles R–70, 1968–69*. Huntington, N.Y.: Educational Development Laboratories, Inc., 1970.

Cooley, W. W. *Methods of Evaluating School Innovations*. Pittsburgh, Pa.: Learning Research and Development Center, University of Pittsburgh, 1971 (26).

DuBois, P. H. & Mayo, G. D. (Eds.). *Research Strategies for Evaluating Training*. AERA Monograph Series on Curriculum Education, No. 4. Chicago: Rand McNally, 1970.

Heflin, V. B., & Scheier, E. *The Formative Period of Listen Look Learn, a Multi-Media Communication Skills System*. Huntington, N.Y.: Educational Development Laboratories, Inc., 1968.

Isaac, S. & Michael, W. B. *Handbook in Research and Evaluation*. San Diego, Calif.: Knapp, 1971.

Kennard, A. D., & Scheier, E. *An Investigation to Compare the Effect of Three Different Reading Programs on First-Grade Students in Elk Grove Village, Illinois, 1969–1970*. Huntington, N.Y.: Educational Development Laboratories, Inc., 1971.

Popham, W. J. *An Evaluation Guidebook*. Los Angeles: Instructional Objectives Exchange, 1972.

Scriven, M. The methodology of evaluation. In R. Tyler, R. M. Gagné, & M. Scriven, *Perspectives of Curriculum Evaluation*. AERA Monograph Series on Curriculum Evaluation, No. 1. Chicago: Rand McNally, 1967.

AUTHOR INDEX

A

AAAS Commission on Science Education, 101, 119, 133, 136, 192, 216, 218, 228
Aronson, E., 71
Astin, A. W., 239, 242, 255
Ausubel, D. P., 8, 18, 48, 52, 60, 70, 106, 119, 144, 145, 157, 193, 208
Austin, G. A., 24, 33

B

Baker, E. L., 22, 34, 78, 79, 83, 97
Ball, J. R., 223, 229
Bandura, A., 64, 65, 70
Bilodeau, E. A., 106, 119
Bloom, B. S., 22, 33, 34, 61, 70, 88, 95, 97, 165, 180
Bretz, R., 57, 70
Brickner, A., 251, 255
Briggs, G. E., 67, 71
Briggs, L. J., 18, 79, 97, 115, 118, 119, 139, 150, 153, 155, 156, 157, 162, 180, 193, 208, 211, 218, 223, 227, 228, 229

Bruner

Bruner, J. S., 12, 18, 24, 33, 45, 47, 52, 87, 97, 101, 119
Buckley, N. K., 206, 208

C

Coleman, L. T., 115, 118, 119
Commission on the Reorganization of Secondary Education, 33
Cooley, W. W., 251, 252, 255
Cronbach, L. J., 179, 180
Crovitz, H. E., 144, 157
Crowder, N. A., 211, 229
Czanyi, A. P., 208

D

Dale, E., 151, 157
Davies, I. K., 210, 229
Deese, J., 7, 18, 57, 70
DuBois, P. H., 238, 255

E–F

Edling, J. V., 188, 208
Esbensen, T., 215, 229

SUBJECT INDEX

L

Learning
  conditions for instructional events, 147–149
  external and internal factors, 10–11
  guidance, as instructional event, 128–129
  information, attitudes, motor skills, 53–71
  intellectual skills and strategies, 34–52
  principles, 6–11
    contiguity, 7
    internal processes, 9–11
    reinforcement, 8
    repetition, 8
Learning hierarchies
  basic reading skills, 116
  cautions in deriving, 112–113
  elementary mathematics, 109
  examples, 113–118
  for intellectual skills, 108–113
  prerequisite skills, 110–111
  relation to types of learning, 111–112
  social studies problem, 118
  science problem, 117
  subtracting, 114
Learning outcomes
  five categories, 23–25
  from goal statements, 103–104
  and sequence characteristics, 105
Lesson
  designing, 137–157
    example, 153–155
  learning outcomes, 146–149
  planning, 138–140
  selecting media, 150–152
  selecting or developing materials, 152
  sequence of events in, 108
  steps in planning, 139–140, 156
  within topics, 104
Listen, Look, Learn, 247–249

M

Mastery
  assessment, in individualized instruction, 203
  concept in assessment, 164–167
  criteria in assessment, 165–167
  and performance objectives, 88
Media
  choosing for lessons, 150–152
  Dale's Cone of Experience, 151
  and learning environment, 152
  options related to types of stimuli, 150–151
Motor skills
  characteristics, 66–68
  criteria for assessment, 174–175
  description, 24
  executive sub-routine, 67
  integrating part-skills, 67
  learning conditions, 68
    in lesson planning, 149
  and performance, 29
  sequence in lesson planning, 144–145
  verb, in statements of objectives, 87

N–O

Needs analysis, 216–217
Objectives (*see also* Performance objectives)
  course, 22–23

P–Q

Performance
  assessing, as instructional event, 131
  eliciting, as instructional event, 130
Performance objectives, 75–97
  achieving precision in, 77–89
  analysis for systems design, 217–219
  choosing action words, 82–84
  describing human capabilities, 84–89
  descriptions, components of, 79–82
  examples analyzed, 79–82